T.Tamil
Tigress

Niromi de Soyza

Tamil Tigress

ALLEN&UNWIN
SYDNEY · MELBOURNE · AUCKLAND · LONDON

This edition published in 2012
First published in 2011

Allen & Unwin
Sydney, Melbourne, Auckland, London

83 Alexander Street
Crows Nest NSW 2065
Australia
Phone: (61 2) 8425 0100
Fax: (61 2) 9906 2218
Email: info@allenandunwin.com
Web: www.allenandunwin.com

Cataloguing-in-Publication details are available
from the National Library of Australia
www.trove.nla.gov.au

ISBN 978 1 74331 070 0

Set in Bembo by Post Pre-press Group, Australia
Printed and bound in Australia by the SOS Print + Media Group

10 9 8 7 6

To the ones I loved and lost

CONTENTS

1	The Ambush	1
2	The House of My Grandmother	6
3	Anger and Frustration	25
4	Dead and Buried	46
5	For the Greater Good	60
6	An Act of Betrayal	74
7	A Tiger Named Roshan	94
8	A Military-Style Training Base	112
9	There's Still Time to Change Your Mind	133
10	I Knew It Wouldn't Last Forever	156
11	Experience of the Battlefield	183
12	A Break in the Hostilities	201
13	Trying to Ignore My Reality	212
14	The Last Few Moments of Life	227
15	Where It All Ends	237
16	The Dream Beyond Reach	248
17	The Jungle Hide-out	263
18	Extraordinary Days	274
19	Where Do I Go From Here?	283
20	Afterwards	298

List of Acronyms	305
Tamil and Sinhala Words	306
Acknowledgements	308

1

THE AMBUSH

Concealed by the shadow of a large water tank, I sat on the heel of my right foot. The air was sweetly pungent with the smell of ripening bananas and palmyra fruit. Cicadas buzzed relentlessly as a blazing sun rose to evaporate the condensed dew in the fields we had just scurried through. The small, sparsely-populated village was luscious with its manioc and banana plantations, palm trees, and water birds in flight. But all this was lost on our small platoon of twenty-two; over half of us young women. Appreciation of beauty is a luxury of the untroubled mind.

It was two days before Christmas 1987 and I was seventeen years old. The only sound I could hear was that of my thumping heart; all I could see was the fear in the faces of the others. Sweat trickled down my back. We were silent. Our ears were finetuned to any sound of stealthy footsteps and our eyes to any sighting of strangers. Our fingers were primed on the triggers of our rifles. It seemed like a typical morning for us as Tigers, but that was about to change dramatically. By the time the sun would set on us this day, nothing would be the same again.

At first light, our sentry had reported seeing soldiers. 'Hundreds of them have just stepped out of the cover of the banana plantation,' a panic-stricken Vadhana had panted as she stood at the doorstep of the abandoned house we were occupying. There had been fear in her large brown eyes. We had barely put our weapons down after the usual dawn stake-out.

The house we were in was unfinished—floors had not been laid and, without doors and windows, the frames let the outside in. We had arrived the previous night in darkness and slept on the dirt floor. The night before that we had been elsewhere—in another abandoned house, in another village.

I had been on 2am sentry duty and there had been nothing unusual to indicate what was to come. I had stood under a mango tree with my AK-47 in hand, scanning the darkness and growing more tired as I watched the night sky. When a star shot past, I had wondered if Roshan too stood somewhere at sentry and was witnessing it. That thought sent a smile across my lips—I had seen him only two months before but already felt that I had lost him to another time, to another life. If we survived this war, no doubt we'd see each other again. Roshan had always known where to find me.

When Vadhana issued her warning we quickly gathered up our meagre belongings and scrambled out of the door in the opposite direction to the approaching soldiers. Over the past couple of months we had lost all our belongings. I now had only the shirt and jeans I was wearing (which stank of sweat and grime), my sarong (which doubled as a blanket and towel), an empty hessian sack (which functioned as a sleeping bag), my chest holster and rifle. We had lost our footwear in previous skirmishes; but we still had our *kuppies*, the cyanide capsules we wore around our necks. We were better prepared for death than for life.

We hurried through a banana plantation and entered a field of ploughed earth, where loose soil fell away under our feet. Wiry sunburnt men and women stopped work and gawked at us, shading their eyes with the palms of their hands.

'Everyone, move forward!' Muralie, one of our men-in-command, ordered. 'It's the only way out!'

That meant we would have to negotiate the main road we had

traversed the night before, which was heavily patrolled by armoured vehicles and jeeps. We would have to find a few seconds of opportunity to make it across alive.

We moved stealthily along a single dirt track leading to the road, flanked by palmyra trees, shrubs and overgrown vines. When we came up by the side of a water tank, Muralie positioned me there: 'I want you to cover the right side, so those ahead of you can cross the road one by one.'

And so I sat on my heel, cocked my AK-47 and held it in position. Those at the front of the line poised to charge across the road.

And then we heard it. Machine-gun fire. Three bullets fired in automatic. It came from our far right, beyond the fields and houses.

We froze. A flock of parrots took flight in pandemonium. Silence followed.

I looked at Muralie as I realised that the soldiers were closing in on us from the right. I had rarely seen panic in those almond eyes. He urged us to move forward.

'Hurry! Cross the road, one by one! Be very careful!'

I was behind Ajanthi and there were a few girls ahead of her. Cautiously we moved forward along the track towards the road. My heart was pumping rapidly. Occasional gunfire sounded a safe distance away. I tried to look ahead over Ajanthi's shoulder. The barbed-wire fence on either side of the lane, covered with runners, mostly obstructed my view of the main road. Then I saw Nira step forward.

Bang!

'*Amma!*' Nira screamed for his mother. His right hand went to his chest. Then he collapsed.

Suddenly heavy gunfire and hand grenades began to spray at us from the sides of the road.

'Get down to the ground!' Muralie screamed. 'Keep moving towards the road. We have to break through.'

We crashed to the ground.

The automatic gunfire sounded like festive firecrackers, interrupted by exploding grenades and mortars. Bullets whistled past my ears. Acrid smoke from the explosions was thickening the air and beginning to irritate my eyes and lungs. I shuffled forward on my elbows and knees behind Ajanthi. My heart felt as if it would explode out of my chest.

Then I heard more gunfire from behind us, a couple of hundred metres away. The enemy was now closing in on us from all directions and this time I knew that we wouldn't be able to escape. There was a metre-high water tank on my right and the few palmyra and banana trees that dotted the landscape on my left. There was no place to hide. Now the remaining twenty-one of us, with our few AKs and M16s, were going to have to face an enemy who was well prepared and equipped, and had been lying in wait for us since the early hours of the morning.

I saw Muralie grab his assistant Rajan's AK and run forward. Muralie usually carried a pistol. 'Idiots at the front-line, fire and break through! Break through!' he shouted, seeing us hesitate.

At the back of the line the bearded Sudharshan was yelling obscenities at us: 'Get going, you mother-fuckers! If not, I'll blow your brains out myself!'

I aimed my AK-47 at the road while keeping an eye on my comrades in front of me. One of the girls, Sadha, made a dash across, followed by Jenny. I saw Sadha fall.

The noise of exploding grenades and gunfire was deafening. There was a lot of screaming. More and more jeeps and tanks arrived on the road, bringing reinforcements. A helicopter gunship hovered low above us, strafing.

I crawled forward on my elbows, still holding my AK in position, my forefinger stroking the trigger.

One of the girls, Saaradha, screamed, 'My leg! My leg! Someone help me . . . !'

Then I saw a hand grenade flying over from the left side of the road in my direction. As I scrambled on my hands and knees to get away, I realised that Gandhi was in its path, behind the palmyra tree, firing with his AK.

'Gandhi anna, duck!'

4

The grenade hit Gandhi and exploded. The young man's head blew into smithereens and its contents of flesh and blood splattered, drenching me. His headless torso fell to the ground like a tree trunk. I wanted to scream but no sound came from my throat. Everything felt strange—as if I wasn't physically there any more. I saw a smoke-screen around me, but I couldn't tell if it was real.

By now, all those in front of Ajanthi had attempted to cross the road. Holding her AK in position, Ajanthi got off the ground and on to her knees. Briefly she turned around to look at me, just like she had at school, where I had sat behind her in the third row. Whenever she turned around to talk to me, a chalk duster would come flying at her.

'I'll see you on the other side,' she muttered hurriedly.

I nodded, completely unsure.

2

THE HOUSE OF MY GRANDMOTHER

S chools in Jaffna have the highest standard of education in the country,' Appa, my father, had reasoned when the decision was made to send me, at eight years old, to Jaffna, 300 kilometres north of our home in Norton Bridge, a small town up in the central mountains of Sri Lanka, outside Kandy. 'My mother has been kind enough to accept you into her home there, so you can become a doctor like your aunts and uncles.'

It was true: all of Appa's seven siblings were highly educated and successful, seemingly in control of their lives. I had often heard Appa openly admire his sisters as beautiful, elegant and intelligent women. I knew he had similar aspirations for my little sister Shirani and me. I was glad of the opportunity, even if it meant that I would leave behind my hometown.

Kandy and the capital, Colombo, also had good schools, but I knew my parents had chosen Jaffna because it was a Tamil stronghold. They were feeling vulnerable living among Sinhalese in the south of the country.

Only a few months before, in July 1977, there had been violence against Tamils all over the country, and a few hundred Tamils were killed by Sinhala mobs. The riots had begun because, for the first time ever, a Tamil political party had been elected in opposition, giving them relative power. During this time, my parents had instructed us to speak only in whispers after dusk, when the mobs mobilised, while they drew all the curtains and kept the lights off. We were sent to bed early.

I had also overheard my parents speaking of their luck that their requests for job transfers to the ancient city of Anuradhapura hadn't come through, because in this city all the Tamils on board a train had been massacred. My parents had chosen Anuradhapura because it was halfway between my father's city of Jaffna and my mother's city of Kandy, which also meant that it separated the Tamil and Sinhala strongholds of Sri Lanka. Because the adults did not discuss such matters with us, I listened in quietly. There had been a real threat to all the Tamil homes in the Up Country where we lived—groups of rampaging Sinhala thugs had already looted and burnt down a few Tamil businesses. These groups had also tried to enter the Tamil settlements within the tea estates but were deterred by the large number of Indian Tamil estate labourers guarding their commune with machetes and batons. As a result, all the Tamils living in the Up Country were spared, workers or not.

'We've been lucky this time. The Sinhala thugs weren't able to take on the Tamils in this area,' said my father to my mother. 'But next time, who knows, the Sinhalese could bring in reinforcements.'

This was the first time I became aware that my family was one of only a handful of Tamils in the area that did not live and work in the tea estates, and it worried me. Nearly all of our neighbours, my parents' friends, colleagues and some of my mother's extended family were either Sinhalese or Burghers. When in public, we spoke either English or Sinhala although I had never once wondered why. I began to notice that we were different to each other although we looked much the same on the outside.

'Appa, why don't the Sinhalese like the Tamils?' I had asked my father one day when he was fixing the chicken-wire around a newly built coop. When he wasn't at work, Appa was always doing something in the garden or around the house.

'The Sinhalese and the Tamils have no problems, it is the political parties that stir things for their own gain,' replied my father, still focused on the task at hand.

'But why?'

'So you could ask why, that's why.'

That was how my father replied when he did not want me to ask any more questions, so I did not persist for fear of being scolded. In Sri Lanka curiosity was not a trait encouraged among children, particularly in girls, because those in power—often males, but anyone older, or of higher caste, education or influence—were always right and their reasons needn't be explained or understood to the subordinate. Questioning was seen as defiance or challenging authority, for which we were often ignored, scolded or smacked, so we quickly learned to never challenge authority. I was lucky; my father never hit us and rarely scolded us, but he knew how to stop me from asking questions he didn't want to answer.

He had replied the same way when I asked him about the distressing scenes I had witnessed at the town's British-built railway station two years earlier, on my way to pre-school. It resembled a funeral but I couldn't figure out who had died. Day after day scores of Indian Tamil estate-labourers and their families were boarding the train while others stayed behind on the platform. Everyone was wailing—it seemed to me that these people didn't want to go wherever they were going and those on the platform didn't want them to go. I saw children being pulled this way and that and elderly people being dragged along the platform against their will. There was always someone running after the moving train and someone jumping out of it. Also at the same railway station were mass loads of Sinhala Buddhist pilgrims on their way to the holy mountain, Adam's Peak, all dressed in white, carrying waterlilies and incense, muttering chants, completely indifferent to their fellow passengers' plight. This upset me greatly—something was terribly wrong.

Having realised the only way to know the truth was to eavesdrop into adult conversations, I had perfected the art of making myself invisible right in the room where the conversations took place by pretending to be reading, drawing or catnapping. This way I learnt that Prime Minister Bandaranaike was deporting the descendants of over half of the Tamil plantation workers brought over by the British nearly a century before back to India. Many of them did not want to go because Sri Lanka was now their home, and they were being separated from their families, perhaps forever. I was relieved to know that my family was not going to be deported because we were Ceylon Tamils, not Indian Tamils, but still we were Tamils living in a Sinhala neighbourhood with the threat that the townspeople could turn on us at any time. While our Sinhala family and friends would want to protect us, this could put them in harm's way too.

So the decision was made to send me to the Tamil stronghold of Jaffna so I could begin school in the first term of 1978, and my parents and little sister would follow once my parents' requests for transfers to Jaffna were approved. If my parents felt apprehensive sending me so far away, to a place where communication was possible only by letters, they did not show it.

Soon after Christmas of 1977, Appa and I boarded the first-class observation car of the express train, Udarata Menike, in the mid morning. It was a comfortable air-conditioned journey but, except for the steam train's rhythmic chugs and shrilling whistles, it was silent. In Sri Lanka it is considered disrespectful to speak to one's elders unless absolutely necessary, so while Appa read the newspapers or sat lost in thought, I looked out at the rapidly receding cloud-topped hills, that rolling carpet of green, packed with tea bushes and speckled by white-roofed tea factories and cascading waterfalls. The tea-leaf pickers snaked their way up the hills, swiftly pinching off the tender shoots and throwing them over their shoulders into the wicker basket on their backs. I knew that as they plucked the shoots they'd be chatting away rapid-fire in the distinctive Indian Tamil accents that I would no longer hear in Jaffna, where only native Tamil was spoken. When the train wound its way out of long dark tunnels, there were children at the water spouts gushing down from the hills, smiling and waving as the train passed.

The steam train slowed down and came to a stop at Gampola, leaving the tea estates behind. As I followed Appa out of the train for the brief stop, I was hit by the smells and sounds of the platform. There were vendors of all kinds walking up and down, selling everything from handmade toys, *thambili* (tender coconut drink) and food. I was trying to decide between wood-apples, jambus, mangosteens and rambutans.

'*Podi nangi* [Little girl], please ask your older brother to buy you a *malu banis*,' pleaded a vendor in Sinhala. My father was often mistaken as my older brother or a young uncle. I looked at the young boy's wicker basket—it was full of freshly baked triangular fish buns.

I resumed my position by the window, enjoying the delicious bun. The railway line wound its way besides Mahaweli Ganga, the longest river in our country, flanked by luscious green vegetation. On the river bed, a lean sunburnt man was scrubbing an elephant with a coconut husk. The afternoon sun shone on the distant mountains.

'Both your grandfathers were station masters,' Appa said suddenly as the train approached Peradeniya station. 'It used to be a prestigious position in the British railways.'

I looked at the man standing on the platform in his smart white uniform and hat, resembling a pilot. I remembered the large black-and-white photos that hung in my maternal grandparents' house in Hatton, a town outside Kandy—one of my Thaatha in his grand office, behind his desk in full uniform, and another one of him exchanging the baton with the guard. I had often asked Thaatha to elaborate on those photos, although I had heard all the stories many times before. I loved to see the look of pride on his face when he recounted those years as we walked through the garden down to the river—Thaatha in his tweed jacket, boots and hat, smoking his pipe. Grandmother, whom I called Aatchi, never allowed him to smoke indoors.

As an only son of wealthy Indian immigrants, Thaatha had been educated at the exclusive St John Boys' College, a boarding School in Jaffna, then had his marriage arranged at eighteen and was allocated a government job in British-ruled Ceylon. Aatchi, his equal in wealth and caste, was only fourteen when she married him. She was the granddaughter of a merchant landowner who had also made the move from India to Ceylon, seeking new opportunities. As a young mother, Aatchi had managed a household of twelve children and an equal number of staff, ensuring the children and the house were always impeccable. Even now, their elegant house was always filled with flowers, its walls and antique furniture adorned with her tapestries and crocheted pieces, and a magnificent garden surrounded the house.

Whenever I visited my grandparents, I could look forward to Aatchi making all my favourite foods. 'Go out to the garden and ask Nadesu to help you choose the vegetables you would like for lunch,' Aatchi would say, handing me a wicker basket and pointing outside to the gardener, her cluster-diamond jewellery dazzling in the sunlight. Her numerous diamond-covered piercings and stretched earlobes, and the traditional Indian tattoos that decorated her arms, were a constant source of wonder to me and Shirani. Although Thaatha had a few of those tattoos himself, they were more visible on Aatchi's fair skin.

I did not have the same familiarity with my paternal grandparents. Appappa had died of a heart attack, leaving behind a young wife and eight children. Despite our annual Christmas holiday visits to the ancestral home in Tellipalai, a village in Jaffna's countryside, I hardly understood my father's family or their ways as Jaffna Tamils. They spoke a pure and ancient form of Tamil, different to that spoken by my mother's family and in the Indian movies I had seen. It sounded more like a mix of two south Indian languages, Malayalam and Tamil. My father said it was because his ancestors had arrived from south India in the second century BCE and the contemporary language reflected the Dravidian language and culture of that ancient time. These people had settled predominantly in the north and on the north-east coast of Sri Lanka and now made up 13 per cent of the country's population.

The Sinhalese (74 per cent of the population) spoke a derivative of Indo-Aryan languages and had also arrived from India but from the north some three centuries earlier. Both ethnic groups were originally Hindu, but with the introduction of Buddhism from India in the second century BCE a vast majority of the Sinhalese had converted. My father's family were among the small population of Tamils and Sinhalese who embraced Christianity during the sixteenth century when Sri Lanka was colonised by the Portuguese, the Dutch and later the British. These Christian converts were favoured by their colonial masters, who provided them with Christian private school education, scholarships in British universities and government jobs, creating an elite class and adding yet another layer of complexity to the traditions, language, religion and caste system that existed in both Tamil and Sinhala cultures. Over time, educated Christians felt they were better than the Hindus and the Buddhists. And the Buddhists thought the country solely belonged to them.

My mother's grandparents belonged to the Indian merchant and landowner class of Hill Country Tamil Hindus, who migrated to Sri Lanka during the British era. The British also brought Indian labourers from South India to work in their tea and rubber plantations because the locals refused to. These recent Indian migrants and the Ceylon Tamils of the north did not mingle due to geographical isolation. My parents met when my father came to work in the south. They fell in love and married. Their families opposed their union because the northern Tamils (my father's people) thought the Tamils of the east coast and Hill Country (my mother's people) inferior. I, of course, had no idea of the tension that lay beneath the superficial politeness that existed between my family and my father's.

Now, in the train on my way to Jaffna, I felt as though I was going to a new town to live amongst strangers, comforted only by the knowledge that my family would join me soon.

I expected that my life in Jaffna would be vastly different to that in Kandy because, like the two sides of my family, the two cities were different from each other in so many ways. Although Jaffna had beautiful beaches to visit, there would be no lush green lawns lined with orchids to run around in, no walks up the hills of tea estates, no collecting pebbles by the streams with my cousins. I would not hear Sinhala being spoken or see many foreigners. I would miss the celebrations of the Buddhist and Hindu thanksgiving festivals, Esala Perahera and Thai Pongal.

In Jaffna at my Appamma's house, I knew that the only festivities I could expect would be muted celebrations at Christmas. Appa had described the elaborate month-long Christmas celebrations in their ancestral home when he was a young boy, but since my paternal grandfather died, my grandmother had moved to their house in the city of Jaffna and no longer celebrated Christmas in such an extravagant way.

Dramatic hills now gave way to lowland plains as night fell. I must have dozed off as our train approached Polgahawela interchange because my father had to tap me on the shoulder. As we stepped onto the platform with our luggage, I felt the warmth envelop me. True to its name, the small town was resplendent with coconut trees. We went into the waiting room and ate our packed dinner of stringhoppers (rice vermicelli noodles curled into spirals and steamed) with beef and potato curry.

After waiting a couple of hours in the darkness, we boarded the northbound Yarl Devi express from Colombo. I was passing my favourite part of the country, the hinterland, but it was too dark to look out of the window of our sleeping compartment. The best part of our annual trip to Tellipalai had always been this—paddy fields, water buffaloes, white cranes and ponds full of Nil Mahanel, the water lilies. I had never cared much for Jaffna itself—dry and arid, with its uninteresting flat lands dotted with extremely tall palmyra and coconut trees.

On our arrival at Jaffna railway station, after an 18-hour-long journey, the first thing I noticed was the heat. It was now the early hours of the morning, before sunrise, and yet it was humid. The warm breeze carried the scent of jasmine. The taxi drove a short distance through quiet, densely-populated city streets and pulled up in front of an old Portuguese-period house.

As my father unloaded my little suitcase from the taxi, I stood outside the house. I had never seen anything like it. The houses here were built right onto the street. Their front verandahs were enclosed by wooden lattice atop a short brick wall. There was no front yard. All the space I had enjoyed running around in the Hill Country had all but vanished here in Jaffna.

My father knocked on the door a few times before he yelled out '*Amma! Amma!*'

The door was flung open at last and a dark-skinned young woman, in a knee-length skirt and a white cotton sleeveless blouse, stood bleary-eyed.

'Go inside!' A voice came from behind her.

When the young woman stepped aside, I recognised the old woman in a white blouse and sarong—Appamma, my grandmother. The woman who had opened the door must have been her maid. Even at such an early hour of the morning, Appamma's hair was in a neat knot at the nape.

'*Vaango Thambi.*'

I thought the way Appamma welcomed her eldest son so formally—addressing him as her younger brother—was odd. And as was typical there was no exchange of warm embraces or pats on the back with us. In Sri Lanka, displays of affection in the presence of others were frowned upon, no matter the relationship between people; it was considered rude and disrespectful to those present. Even married couples in their own homes showed no signs of physical or verbal intimacy in front of their family. Children were treated the same way, and often the only physical contact made was for holding hands to help cross the road, or for smacking. So unsurprisingly Appamma now ignored me. We followed her with our luggage into a large, damp, dark house.

It was only when Appa left the following day, to return home to Norton Bridge, that I came to realise I would not see him or Amma or Shirani for a while. Suddenly, I felt lonely in the unfamiliar surroundings. No one here shared my past. I would no longer see my parents playing tennis together; or Appa dancing about the house to the Bee Gees, Tom Jones or the La Bambas; or Amma instructing the gardener or the cook. I would no longer witness parties where glasses clinked with Arrack while everyone spoke a mix of English, Tamil and Sinhala, their mouths filled with hot fish cutlets or beef and potato patties. Such parties always ended with everyone joining in on the Portuguese-inspired *baila*, dancing and singing along. I knew I'd miss all of it. But, above everything, I would miss my little sister Shirani, who was nearly three years younger than me.

Shirani and I had been fairly isolated from the other children in our neighbourhood because the split-level bungalow we lived in was set in a large estate. It was the latest housing provided to my father. The British-built house was fitted with all modern comforts, and with its many rooms and an established garden, it was enough to keep two imaginative young children largely occupied.

Despite this, Shirani was often down the hill at the corner shop smoking *beedi* (tobacco wrapped in coromandel leaf), freely handed to her by the shop owner. We had often watched with curiosity the strange ritual of the tea-estate labourers pulling out a *beedi* from the bundle and lighting them on the embers of a rope that hung on the side of the shop, and soon Shirani was doing the same. It did not matter to her, or to the shop owner, that she was the only girl at the shop, and a three-year-old at that. Every time, I would wave my finger at her in warning as I hung over the fence; but I would also feel envious—I simply did not have the courage to defy my parents' instructions, which were that we should not take one step past the cypress tree down the hill.

Shirani, of course, would dismiss my warnings with a wave of her hand as she puffed away. She knew that I did not have the courage to tell on her either. She was equally cavalier with the home-made *thambili* wine that Amma made for Christmas. It took me months to work out the inverse correlation between Shirani's extended day naps and the level of the wine left in the bottle.

In Jaffna my life soon became much more regimented. My days mostly began the same way: I woke up to the sound of bicycle bells and the cawing of crows, and by this time the house would be a hive of activity and outside would be awash with sunlight and rising heat. Then my cousin Manel, who also lived in the same house with her parents, my aunt Imelda and her husband Ratnam, and I were sent off to school on a bicycle rickshaw. At our Catholic school run by nuns, every school assembly began with a bible reading, a recital of a section of the rosary and a moral lesson, and every school lesson began and ended with a prayer. The lessons were intense and I found the standard of learning expected of us was way higher than what I was used to in Kandy. In the evenings and on the weekends we were expected to spend much time doing our homework and revisions. It seemed to me that there was a lot of studying to be done in Jaffna.

In the afternoons, I would look forward to a kind-hearted Uncle Ratnam coming home from work as I did not much care to remain in the confines of the house, which had little or no outdoor space. Most evenings he took Manel and me somewhere on his bicycle—the Jaffna library, Subramaniam Park, Pannai beach and even to the famous cricket matches between Central and St John's Colleges. If we had spare time after homework, Aunt Imelda sat us on the front verandah and asked us to guess the birth number (based on numerology) of unsuspecting passers-by, with prompts such as: 'If a young person wears reading glasses, then they must be a studious number 4.'

One typical morning, as I headed to the bathroom at the back of the house, I heard Appamma giving orders to the maids preparing breakfast. Appamma was a good cook although by then, because of arthritis in her fingers, she only prepared some of her signature dishes: the fried squid-ink curry, purple yam pudding and *odiyal kool*—a kind of seafood chowder made with palmyra root flour, chilli and jackfruit. Now, the smell of steamed string-hoppers and creamy *sodhi* (coconut milk and tomato gravy) wafted from the kitchen.

'*Ayyo*, St Anthony! How on earth did these devils return?' Appamma cried out, her silvery grey hair unravelling from the tight knot she always wore it in. She was referring to the kittens prancing about in the backyard. She yelled out to my uncle, the only man in the house: 'Ratnam, take these kittens away today and this time take them across a body of water before abandoning them. Then they won't know their way back.' No one had a moral dilemma over abandoning the stray kittens. She went back into her kitchen tying her hair, muttering 'St Anthony, save us.'

St Anthony was indeed Appamma's favourite saint. Every Tuesday she took me along to recite a rosary and a novena for him at the local Catholic church, Our Lady of Refuge, and then we went off to see Michael, who owned an idol-making business in a tin shack at the back of the church and was considered a quasi-spiritual leader, to be blessed. Michael was a big burly man with curly hair who wore a white singlet and *vaetti*. His little shop was hot and crowded with religious statues so Michael appeared perpetually sweaty. He'd climb onto a wooden stool and take a blunt knife and a statue of St Anthony out from a glass box perched on a shelf; he'd then place the statue on our heads and sketch crosses on our foreheads with the knife. Michael muttered something in what he claimed to be Latin while he carried out this performance.

Appamma would then consult Michael on all her important matters—marriages, jobs, and the health of her adult married children. Sometimes Michael would give her a charm—an aluminium heart with a haphazardly drawn cross on it—to be placed under a pillow, a doorstep or wherever a miracle was needed. Like most in their community, neither of them saw any conflict in being Catholic and superstitious.

Appamma was otherwise a fiercely independent, self-assured woman. Sometimes my cousins and I would accompany her to her ancestral home in Tellipalai. On these expeditions, she'd often take a large bundle of papers—land title deeds—to ensure that those who leased her lands still remembered that she was in charge. As part of the educated Christian elite under the Dutch, and later British, rule of old Ceylon, her ancestors were fair-skinned, high-caste landed gentry. As we gathered up dried tamarind fruit from under the massive trees surrounding her Spanish-style villa, she would tell us how her family had owned vast farming lands both here and in Kilinochchi. We would shell and sample some of the fruit, making funny faces at its sweet-and-sourness. The villagers would later salt the mature fruit, spreading the flesh on grass mats and letting it dry out in the sun. On an adjacent mat, red chillies would be dried.

'Here's some toddy for the young ladies,' offered the toddy-tapper.

We had been watching the wiry, half-naked man do what he did for a living—collecting the fermenting liquid from the flowershoot high up in the palmyra trees. Wrapping his hands and legs around the trunk, he would come back down to earth with the white liquid secure in the clay pot tied to his waist.

'That's alcohol, and the three of us are just eight years old,' said Manel, righteously.

'You can have a taste,' approved Appamma. And so he poured half a tumbler, from which we all took a sip. The sweet effervescent liquid numbed my tongue and went down refreshingly.

'*Chee, chee!*' spat one of my other cousins who was visiting. 'It's sour.'

Manel too made a silly face, pretending to be disgusted at the taste. I understood that this was a game—as young girls, we were supposed to show disdain towards such things. So I did the same, despite enjoying the drink.

Appamma, as usual, having sorted out all her land-affairs, would haul us onto the bus, along with large bundles of the dried tamarind and chillies, for the trip back to Jaffna.

One evening about three months after I had arrived in Jaffna, when I returned home from school Appamma was in the front room weaving yet another basket, a hobby of hers, despite the pain in her crippling fingers. 'This came for you yesterday,' she said and handed me a piece of paper. She censored all my letters, as dictated by our culture, where children had no identity of their own and were a commodity of their carer.

My chest tightened as I held the piece of paper. My father's distinct tiny writing sprawled across the page. A lump came into my throat as I read his news. Appa, an engineer, was leaving Norton Bridge for Dubai, having received a lucrative work contract. Although this was not our original plan, it was an offer he could not refuse. Tamil professionals were beginning to look for work overseas because it was becoming increasingly difficult to progress in their profession in their own country. I had once overheard Appa and his superior at our house talk about how very angry and disappointed they were for being questioned and put on notice by the local Sinhalese minister for granting merit-based admission to four Tamil men alongside ninety-six Sinhalese for the following year. They were ordered to decline two of these Tamils with top marks and offer their places to Sinhalese with lesser grades instead. There were many such incidences and Appa was getting fed up with the unfairness of it all. There were also economic reasons—educating Shirani and me in good schools and university, then amassing dowries to buy us good husbands. So even though Appa did not mention any of this as his reason, I knew why taking an offer overseas, even in a country where he knew no one, was more appealing than remaining in Sri Lanka with his family.

When I had watched him leave Appamma's house in a taxi, chequered by the wooden lattice enclosing the verandah, I had desperately hoped that this vision would be soon replaced by a very different one—of him arriving. But I knew now that I wouldn't be seeing him for at least another year.

But there was also good news. Amma and Shirani were due to come and live in Jaffna by the end of the year. My heart leapt with joy. I ran to my bookshelf, fetched a notebook and rapidly wrote a reply and handed it to Appamma as I was expected to. I watched her eyebrows pull together in displeasure as she read my letter. Then she looked up at me and tore my letter into pieces and dropped it on the ground. 'Pick it up, you bastard child,' she growled.

I wondered what in my reply could have upset her so much. I had written that I looked forward to Shirani, Amma and I living in our own house as a family again. I had said that I had not enjoyed living here in this hot and boring place without them.

As I picked up the pieces of paper off the floor, Appamma continued to shout: 'You should be happy that I accepted you in my house. You are the daughter of that low-life Hindu Indian woman who stole my son. I can't expect class and grace from you.' She spat on the floor—in a symbolic sense.

It wasn't the first time I had felt such hatred from her. There were occasions when, in the name of my mother, whom I believed had class and grace, I had been disparaged and even slapped. Only the previous week, when one of the visitors to the house commented how much I looked like my father, Appamma had remarked: 'No, you are mistaken Mrs Amirthanayagam. She's dark like her mother, with a face that never wakes up.'

I had always been aware that my mother's and father's families were different—my mother's family seemed a jovial bunch, showing their emotions openly, while my father's family were always guarded and measured, and I'd hardly ever seen them laugh. I had no knowledge of the circumstances under which these two families came together in marriage, but having listened to Appamma's insults over time, I concluded that Appa had been expected to choose his bride from among the Jaffna Tamil community—Catholic, high-caste, tertiary-qualified, professional, refined, fair-skinned women of impeccable character, whose parents were capable of buying him at a dowry well beyond what might be expected or offered by any competitor. After all, she told me, there had been many such women ready in waiting. Instead Appa had fallen in love with Amma and married her without his family's approval.

Soon after I arrived in Jaffna, I began to realise that I was a constant reminder to Appamma of her son's failure to meet her standards. Before I had left Norton Bridge, Amma had advised me rather opaquely: 'For the sake of the future, the past has to be sacrificed and the present endured.' Although I had not fully understood what she meant, I had stayed out of Appamma's way and in her presence spoke very little.

Perhaps because of this I had enjoyed being at school, where I could be myself. Despite the sometimes competitive hostility of my cousin Manel and her mother, my aunt Imelda, a teacher at our school, I enjoyed learning and everything about school, apart from sport. I started to do well academically and in extracurricular activities such as the choir, band, singing and dancing. I had little difficulty in forming friendships and, in my spare time, I visited the grand old library with Manel and Uncle Ratnam and read for hours. Manel read educational books while I read adventures and mysteries. Tintin was a particular favourite. In these books, at least, it seemed that the underdog eventually won and justice was always served.

By the time Amma and Shirani arrived in Jaffna, Uncle Ratnam had already found us a room to rent from one of his relatives just a street away from Appamma's house outside the centre of town. This had to be arranged by my father's family because Amma may have unknowingly chosen the 'wrong' house, in a lower-caste or Hindu neighbourhood. In the four-bedroom house lived a young Catholic, high-caste family with three little boys, their aunt, a parrot with clipped wings (which nibbled holes in our rubber slippers) and Lucky, a flea-ridden dog. The tiny storeroom at the back of the house was converted into a kitchen for our use. The house had no air-conditioning or ceiling fans; it was a hot, cramped environment with no running water and an outdoor squatting toilet. Near the toilet was a well from which we had to draw buckets of water for indoor use. Other than a pawpaw tree, a coconut tree and some four o'clock plants, there was no other vegetation in the white sandy yard where we played cricket with the other children in the neighbourhood, chased by Lucky when we had to run between the wickets. Although Amma said very little about it to us, I knew she was terribly unhappy here in Jaffna. In addition to the house she disliked the heat and, unlike in the Up Country, here she had no hired help with household chores. My father's family had welcomed her civilly, but without a kind word or a smile. Shirani was better accepted, and Amma reasoned that it was because of her fair skin and playful nature. I possessed neither of these attributes.

By the end of the following year, Amma, Shirani and I moved into our newly built bungalow in a leafy part of town, a few kilometres away from Appamma. Although I continued to feel my father's family's influence, the sense of suffocation I had felt was no longer so intense. Amma, on the other hand, bore the direct brunt of their dislike towards her.

At weddings and birthdays I overheard their slighting remarks to my mother: 'While you've put on weight and look well, the kids are skinny and poorly dressed.' I was partly to blame for this. Amma had forced Shirani and me to wear so much gold jewellery to these parties believing that 'Other people will say you're a peasant's child if you have no jewellery.' I felt that nothing mattered to Amma more than what these 'other people' thought, and though Amma had tried reasoning with me, I'd remove the jewellery and put it in my pocket before we'd arrive at a celebration.

I would watch Amma closely to see her response to her in-laws' insults. She'd flinch but that was all. She never uttered a word in reply, instead, she'd burst into tears when she got home.

'But why do you stay silent?' I'd ask.

'Speaking up would not achieve anything other than a bad name,' she'd say.

On one occasion when I was about ten years old, Amma was subjected to what appeared to be an interrogation by a couple of my aunts and Appamma at their house. For the first time my mother broke into sobs in front of them, but still she said nothing to defend herself from whatever she was being accused of. She was enduring the present for the sake of the future, when one day her status as daughter-in-law of the eldest of sons would be accepted and welcomed.

'Come on, let's go!' I said to Shirani, no longer able to tolerate this confrontation—neither the tyranny nor the timidity.

'But, we can't leave Amma on her own.'

'She can stand up for herself if she wants to,' I muttered and walked out in disgust. Shirani followed me, slamming the front door behind her.

One evening, Amma returned home in tears yet again from Appamma's house. I had started to find excuses not to accompany her on such visits, which she felt were her duty as a daughter-in-law. I thought that Amma's enormous capacity to forgive and forget made her prone to making the same mistake over and over.

'What did they complain about this time?' I asked, not really interested in her reply.

This time, however, her answer was unexpected: 'It's about you. They're accusing you of having a boyfriend, and that it's a reflection on me.'

A boyfriend? Then I remembered I had mentioned in passing my crush on a boy called Harry to one of my cousins. I should've known better. It was at the YMCA summer youth camp that I had first noticed him. I was now nearly thirteen and this had been the first time I had been in the vicinity of 'unrelated' boys. On the second day of the camp, I had noticed this tall, slim handsome boy at the back of the hall smiling at me. I suddenly felt an irrational fascination for him. But it all came to nothing—by the end of the camp, Harry and I hadn't progressed past a few smiles. I never saw him again.

Jaffna Tamil culture did not tolerate romantic relationships, simply because it needed to maintain control on its social hierarchy of caste, education, wealth and religion which was only possible through suitably-arranged marriages. If one happened to fall in love with the 'wrong' person they were persuaded to abandon the relationship at all costs, because marrying someone of a lower status, caste or a different religion would bring disgrace to one's entire family. Society did everything to discourage friendships between boys and girls from a very young age, and the whole town kept a close eye on our everyday behaviour in public. Even a split-second sideways glance at a boy passing on a bicycle was enough to have us reported to our school or family. A report such as this could cause you to be named and shamed by the nuns at a school assembly or, worse, expelled from school.

The same social codes applied to boys as well, but it did little to stop them from pursuing the girls relentlessly. It was our responsibility as girls to uphold our virtues. We were told: 'If the sari falls on a thorn or if the thorn drops on a sari, you know which suffers the damage.' By the time we were teenagers, we knew what we had to do to discourage boys: avoid eye contact, refuse to speak when spoken to, not reply to love letters and decline gifts.

At twelve years of age being falsely accused of having a boyfriend by my relatives incensed me. Their dislike of me seemed to have grown since my family's arrival and my better grades at school had worsened things with cousin Manel and Aunt Imelda.

'Amma, it's not true. You believe me, don't you?'

'They say, "As the sari is of its thread, a daughter is of her mother",' replied Amma, wiping away her tears.

I had thought that with my mother's arrival I was no longer answerable to anyone other than her. But I now understood Amma's desire to please her in-laws and what it meant for me—I would have to toe their line for the rest of my life.

It had been a terrible day for me, not only because of this unfair accusation by my father's family, but also because of what had happened in the early hours of that morning: the government's loyal armed forces had burnt down the magnificent Jaffna library I had so adored. I knew things were changing for the worse. Anger and frustration were mounting inside me.

3

ANGER AND FRUSTRATION

'Don't step out of the front door!' shouted Amma from the kitchen. 'Have you forgotten that a twenty-four-hour curfew has been declared? They have orders to shoot at sight.'

I walked back into my room and sat at my desk and stared out of the open window. In the warm, humid heat of July everything was eerily still. In the yard, not a leaf moved on the *nelli* tree outside. Inside, the ceiling fan whizzed and stirred the hot air around me. For four days now we hadn't been able to leave the house. The streets were empty, except for the soldiers, crows and dogs.

Since the library had been burnt down nearly two years before Jaffna had acted like a battered wife, pretending all was well. As a naive twelve-year-old, I had almost believed the adults who told me that the library was unintentionally set on fire by a stealthy smoker, that the frequent skirmishes were nothing more than gang fights, and that the boycotts were just school holidays. I'd continued to enjoy school, my time spent with friends and the many activities I did outside school hours—elocution, singing, dancing, and playing the piano, veena and violin.

But all that changed on the morning of Saturday 23 July 1983. I was eating my breakfast of *pittu* (steamed rice flour balls with grated coconut) with sliced mango and jackfruit when Theeban arrived on his bicycle. The twenty-year-old lived down the road with his mother, two brothers and grandmother. Like half of Jaffna's high-caste Vaelaalar Catholics, Theeban was related to us through Appa's family, and yet he and his family possessed none of Appamma's snobbery—they were her less-educated, poorer relations. Coinciding with Theeban's arrival, our next-door neighbour's head appeared over the fence. Everyone called her Upstairs House Auntie because hers was a two-storey house.

'There has been an attack,' said Theeban excitedly, still sitting on his bicycle beside the verandah. 'I know you usually spend your weekends going to lessons of all sorts so I thought I'd better warn you to stay home today.'

Shirani and I looked at each other and grinned. We were glad to have an excuse to miss our early morning piano lesson. If having to chase stray dogs away with our umbrellas while riding our bicycles there wasn't difficult enough, we usually had to endure Sister Francis beating our knuckles with a ruler, then stopping the lesson to make us sing on amid our tears and telling us to go cry in the garden, which needed watering.

According to Theeban, some young men calling themselves 'Liberation Tigers' had ambushed an army patrol not far from Jaffna University, which was a few kilometres away. Thirteen soldiers were dead. I remembered hearing a faint sound, like a distant explosion, around midnight but never having heard such a noise before, I hadn't given it much thought.

'I'd better go warn my daughters too,' said Upstairs House Auntie as she disappeared.

By the following day, terrible news reached us. There was severe unrest throughout the country. In the capital, Colombo, organised Sinhala mobs with electoral rolls in their hands were attacking Tamil homes and businesses. Tamils were being hunted and massacred— thousands were already dead.

'I received a phone call from my sister in Colombo,' said one of our neighbours to Amma. 'She and her family are being sheltered by their Sinhala neighbours. Bless their kind souls.'

The adults spent much of their time talking over the fence or gathering at each other's houses to listen to the BBC, their voices and faces brimming with concern. I listened in, pretending to read but feeling terrified inside.

'The army is everywhere apparently. But they are letting these thugs do whatever they please—in some cases, assisting them.'

'Yes, the government has to be behind this.'

'I heard they're raping and killing even young children and the elderly. God knows where all this is leading.'

I imagined a violent mob armed with machetes bursting into my house. I felt my blood freeze. Why was the government behind all this violence against its own citizens? Who was going to protect us now? I struggled to understand the revenge taken out on the innocent Tamils who lived nearly 300 kilometres away from where the ambush took place. After all, the ambush had not killed innocent civilians—the dead men were soldiers on patrol. And those now being punished for it had nothing to do with it.

'There's no bread today, Telephone Auntie,' shouted Kumar, one of our neighbour's sons, from the gate to Amma. (He called her that because she worked in telecommunications.) 'The bakery is shut and the rumour is that the owners have left Jaffna.'

The baker was Sinhalese. Most of the Sinhalese families of Jaffna had fled south, making Jaffna now a Tamils-only province.

'The Sinhala government has been discriminating against us Tamils since the British left in 1948,' Uncle Ratnam had explained when I asked him about the unrest. I believed him to be the one person who'd tell me the truth. He said that since ancient times, the Sinhalese had been paranoid about the Tamils because successive northern Tamil kings threatened the rule of the Kandyan Kingdom in the south. Then, during the British era, the minority Tamils were favoured, which led them to be better educated and fluent in English and in turn hold a disproportionately high number of prominent positions in government. With the departure of the British, the Sinhala-Buddhist national movement ensured that the Tamils shared no power in the new Ceylon—it introduced a quota system for university entry to reduce university places for Tamils and passed the *Sinhala Only Act* in 1956, making Sinhala the only official language. In 1972, Ceylon was given a Sinhala name, 'Sri Lanka', meaning 'the good island'. At the same time, a form of fundamentalist Buddhism way growing as the Christian Sinhala ruling class began converting back to Buddhism to win over the Sinhala-Buddhist majority. The Christian Burghers were leaving the country, seeing no place for them there, and the British-brought Indian plantation Tamils were being disenfranchised. Although in 1977, for the first time, the Tamil political party Tamil United Liberation Front (TULF) had had been elected as the opposition, the country was well on its way to becoming a place only for the Sinhalese. As with the anti-Tamil violence in 1956 and 1977, which resulted in the deaths of hundreds of Tamils, in 1983 the Sinhala government did nothing to stop it.

This, said Uncle Ratnam, proved that the Sinhala government was behind the violence against its own country's citizens. 'That's why TULF began to demand autonomy for the Tamils in the north and east in 1978. All our peaceful means over three decades for equal rights have failed and now our disillusioned Tamil youth have resorted to an armed struggle. Now a group of them called Tamil Tigers have carried out their first successful ambush. Perhaps it is the only answer.'

It was a lot to take in but it now made sense to me why the Sinhala policeman had burnt down the Jaffna library and the troops kept setting fire to the Poobalasingham Bookstore every time it was rebuilt—they wanted to show the Tamils that they were hated for their knowledge. Jealousy over tertiary qualifications seemed a poor reason for such hatred and violence. I felt comforted and proud that the Tamils were standing up for themselves, because as far as I was concerned, the timid deserved no sympathy.

The weekend passed and everyone remained indoors in fear of the violence taking place out on the streets. Some Sinhala landmarks such as the school and the *Vihara* (the Buddhist temple) had been subjected to arson and looting. Shirani spent the days prancing about the house pretending to be a dancer from the American TV show

Solid Gold, or watching music videos of Wham!, while I occupied myself painting or reading thrillers.

On the afternoon of Monday the twenty-fifth, the heat had subsided sufficiently for Shirani and me to sit with our Pomeranian dogs on the parapet that flanked our large iron gates, pretending to be contestants in a singing contest. Our house was at the end of our private laneway and not visible from the street. Amma was watering the garden, her pride and joy. She had brought many plants from the Hill Country with her and the whole garden was an oasis of canna lilies, anthuriums, dahlias, tea roses, carnations and guava trees—an unusual collection in Jaffna's warm climate.

'How are you girls?' asked Theeban's mother as she opened our gate. She was wearing a lilac cotton sari and her usual white blouse, symbolic of her widowed status.

'They've killed our boys in Welikada,' I heard her say to Amma. The people of Jaffna referred to young Tamil men as 'our boys', a term that was becoming synonymous with the militants, and Welikada was a notorious prison outside Colombo that housed the country's worst criminals as well as Tamil political prisoners. 'Apparently they tortured all of the thirty-five political prisoners to death, beating them with bicycle chains and doing other unspeakable things. It is a maximum security prison, so someone tell me the authorities aren't behind this . . .'

A sickening sensation rose inside me. I could not tell if it was sadness, disgust or anger. The same evening, the government declared an indefinite state of emergency and curfew two days after the worst of the anti-Tamil violence had taken place. The troops were ordered to shoot at sight.

As I sat at my desk at home the next morning, staring at the *nelli* tree, I wondered how the situation was going to be resolved. Eighteen more Tamil detainees and three Tamil prison deputies had been murdered by their Sinhala inmates the day before. With the riots continuing even after the declaration of the curfew and state of emergency, it seemed to me that we, the innocent, were imprisoned in our own homes while the Sinhala thugs ran riot. Was the government running an anti-Tamil pogrom? How were a few armed Tamil youth going to fight the military? And what were the Tamil politicians doing?

Unable to come up with any answers to my questions, I took out my poetry notebook and began to write a poem. Then I thought of my friend, Ajanthi, and wondered what she was doing, stuck in her house like me. She lived only a five-minute bicycle ride away, and yet I could not step out of the house to visit her or call her on the telephone. Over the past five years, I had seen her nearly every day. And every day I had told her everything, from the mundane to the exciting. Ajanthi listened and, when she spoke, it was mainly because I had asked her a question.

'Why is it that I have so much to tell you and you have so little?' I asked her one afternoon as we walked home from science coaching class. It was beginning to drizzle.

'Don't know. Interesting things seem to happen to you more than me,' she had replied unperturbed, kicking the stone back to me. That was one of those things we did whenever we walked instead of riding our bicycles—we took turns to kick a stone back and forth between us, all the way to our destination.

By mid August, three weeks after the ambush, the curfew was relaxed for a few hours a day so people could go out to shop for essential items. There was little fish in the markets, because the fishermen could not go out to sea during the curfew and since Jaffna relied on fresh produce from the south, vegetables became a rarity too. Spending so much time at home, cut off from my friends and school, I read to keep my mind off reality and wrote poetry when I couldn't.

When eventually the schools reopened, I continued to write poetry in my spare time, much to the dismay of my friends. They complained that I was taking life much too seriously.

'Stop that nonsense, and come and share this packet of sweets one of the boys sent for you,' Ajanthi once said.

'Could you not write about anything nicer than war and violence?' asked Shereena. 'The situation is depressing as it is without your poetry adding to it.'

'You girls lack passion,' I scorned. 'How can you not be stirred by injustice?'

'Of course, we're not as intellectual as you are!' laughed Shereena, and promptly ducked to avoid the pen I aimed at her.

Ajanthi did not read any of my poems, even the ones that won awards at school and in state-based competitions. 'I don't read,' she reasoned. It was true; she just did not care to read anything, even textbooks, and relied on me studying out aloud. We spent much of our evenings studying at each other's houses while munching on her mother's delicious beef and potato patties, or my mother's crepes filled with freshly grated coconut and palm sugar, or chickpeas tossed with coconut shavings, mustard seeds, fried onions and dried red chillies. And when there was nothing on offer, we resorted to raw green mangoes and nellis, salted and chilli-powdered.

By the end of the year, Jaffna had experienced a change of personality. Having lost its innocence in Black July, it no longer had the ordinary hustle and bustle of a normal town. Against the backdrop of a dusk-to-dawn curfew, its streets were now inhabited by anxious citizens, frightened refugees, arrogant military and furtive militants. Thousands of Tamils had fled the country, mainly to the UK and Europe, claiming political asylum. The government, instead of assisting the victims of the anti-Tamil riots to resettle in their homes in Colombo, shipped them along with additional Sinhala military to Jaffna. The Tamil militants in turn illegally shipped young men— their hordes of new, volunteer recruits, most of them victims of the riots—to India or Lebanon, where they received military-style training. Instead of quelling the uprising, the anti-Tamil pogrom of July 1983 had only fuelled it.

While the Tamils were united in their grievances against the oppression, the Tamil refugees from Colombo received little sympathy from their fellow Tamils in Jaffna. They were fashionable, English-speaking, affluent city folk in all their 1980s glory—the bobs, the shoulder pads, the Michael Jackson impersonations. None of this resonated with the conservative, largely Hindu, little-travelled Tamils of the north.

'Oh, I wish I was back in Colombo,' moaned one of the 'posh' refugee students at school. 'It is so hot here, and no swimming pools, and nothing exciting to do. Life is so boring.'

'Go back home then!' shouted someone.

It was true that Jaffna had little in the way of entertainment in those days. The curfew between 6pm and 6am remained, and since the government troops were stationed at the old Portuguese fort by the Pannai beach and not far from the town centre, sporting grounds, cinemas and theatres, most of these venues had been burnt down by the troops in an attempt to flatten the area around their camp. But life on the streets of Jaffna was not as boring as the Colombo Tamils made it out to be. The soldiers often conducted random searches, interrogating and threatening passers-by. '*Podi nangi* is one of us,' they often said, smiling when I answered their questions in Sinhala. As most Jaffna Tamils could not speak it, I was happy to be considered their little sister, if only to save my life. Many students were being abducted by soldiers, never to be heard of again, or else their mutilated bodies were found at street corners.

Having been given the licence to kill by the government, the military lacked any kind of discipline, raiding Tamil houses without good reason, then taking away the men, raping the women, looting property and murdering families simply because they were Tamil. We heard stories of young children hidden by their parents during an army raid of their neighbourhood eventually coming out to find their whole family murdered. Such stories struck real fear in our hearts. We'd discuss these scenarios during lunch breaks at school and arrived at certain conclusions—if we were raped, we'd immediately commit suicide because it would be too shameful to have lost our virginity to the enemy and fall pregnant, and if we happened to be the sole survivor of our family then we'd join the insurgency.

The new Jaffna inspired the brave and frightened the weak. Yet hope remained in its various forms—some dreamt of a return to the good old days, while others dreamt of an independent homeland called Tamil Eelam. Either way, by the time I turned fifteen, nothing was ever the same again. Death, violence and terror had become part of life. And, for me, it all began with Theeban.

Theeban lay in a cheap wooden coffin in the middle of the front room of his family home, dressed in a short-sleeved white shirt and a pair of grey trousers. His long slender fingers lay across his chest, broken and distorted as they clasped a dark beaded rosary. His eyes were partially closed; his strong jaw, hanging loose, was held by a bandage, exposing his once beautiful white teeth. His face had darkened, making him look many years older than twenty-one. The room was filled with mourners and was pervaded by the strong smell of chrysanthemum and jasmine, from the garlands around Theeban's neck. A tall candle-stand stood lit near his head, intensifying the heat in the room.

'Like a young calf you played around yesterday, my *Rasa*,' wailed an old woman beating her bosom, calling Theeban her 'king'. 'Today you lie lifeless. What did your mother do in her past life that she has to witness your death before hers?'

I looked at Theeban's mother, seated by the foot of the coffin. She had been muttering to herself, broken only by fainting episodes, ever since Theeban's lifeless body had been unloaded from a white van in front of her house two days before. Now her red, swollen eyes were in a flood of tears; her curly greying hair and her pale sari were ruffled. Theeban's younger brother stood beside her, sweating profusely. Veins on his forehead bulged, as if they were about to burst. That morning, when the funeral photographer had arrived, the eighteen-year-old had lifted the corpse and sat it upright, putting his arm around it, and demanding photos be taken. The bandage that held Theeban's jaw had then unravelled and the room had fallen silent, forebodingly.

Theeban's death had been unexpected, not only because he was young but also because he was a shy fellow who seemed far removed from anything violent. Nearly a year before, soldiers had come to our lane in search of him. When the news spread that soldiers were heading our way, Theeban and most of the other young men in our neighbourhood had jumped the fences and fled. The soldiers had had information that a prominent Tiger called Pandithar and his men frequented Theeban's house. Everyone in the neighbourhood knew this to be true and that Theeban was merely a sympathiser and not a member of the group. When the soldiers interrogated Theeban's mother that day, she had denied it.

Now at his funeral, suddenly someone was shouting: 'Kittu anna is here!'

Kittu, a popular Tiger guerrilla, was said to have been involved in the 1983 ambush that triggered Black July nearly two years earlier. Everyone referred to him as Kittu anna (older brother) as a mark of respect. It was because of this shrewd mastermind that the Tigers were increasingly controlling parts of Jaffna since then, people said. My eyes searched through the crowd for Kittu and settled on a short, bespectacled, balding man with a handlebar moustache. He stood by the bougainvillea-covered gate, surrounded by his bodyguards, his silver watch reflecting the sunlight. I was disappointed, having expected him to look like Che Guevara.

The wailing suddenly grew louder as the group of young men, who had been standing alongside the wall behind the mourners, steadily moved forward through the crowd towards the coffin. I could not hold back the wail that broke from my own throat or the tears that streamed down my face. I would no longer see Theeban at my house, laughing at *Tom and Jerry* cartoons or hear him complementing Amma's cooking. Although we hardly spoke to each other, I had come to regard him as a brother.

It was only the second time I had experienced such a feeling of loss. The year before Thaatha had died suddenly after a stroke, and I was only then coming to terms with it.

Theeban's funeral lacked the fanfare of a typical Tiger funeral, such as we had become accustomed to over the past year. Because the militants, especially the Tigers, controlled most of Jaffna peninsula, they held elaborate funeral ceremonies for their fallen comrades, printing posters and erecting statues. Theeban's body, however, was not paraded through the streets decorated with palm leaves; there were no poignant sentiments or music blared from loudspeakers; and no posters of him adorned lampposts. His funeral would not be televised on the Tigers' channel. It seemed the Tigers only gave such prominence to the deaths of their heroes, and Theeban had not died a hero's death in battle; nor did he take his own life by ingesting potassium cyanide to avoid capture, as the Tigers did. They said he had accidentally shot himself, skylarking.

There were also rumours of foul play, but it no longer mattered how or why Theeban died—his death would not be investigated and his family would never know the truth. In a country where hatred and violence had taken root, this was now our way of life.

It was the afternoon of 26 June 1985, the fortieth day of the commemoration since Theeban's death. I was reading Enid Blyton's *Five Go Off in a Caravan*. Amma was at Theeban's house with most of the neighbours, assisting with the luncheon. It was tradition in those forty days of mourning for neighbours, friends and relatives to take turns to cook, clean and launder for Theeban's family. That day, however, would mark the end of it all. The parish priest would bestow blessings on the house so Theeban's soul could leave in peace and everyone could get on with their lives. Then a feast would be held in his honour where Theeban's favourite foods would be served. I knew I should have been studying for my exams, but I found myself thinking about Theeban. I admired him for having the courage to be part of the insurgency. I wished I had that courage.

But even if I had the courage, it wouldn't be so easy for me to support the freedom struggle because I was not a man. It seemed unfair that men in our society had all the advantages and far less accountability, especially if they were Hindu. In general, they did whatever they pleased; no one expected them to do housework or behave in a certain way that pleased everyone, they were free to go out any time of the day (curfew permitting), demand respect and dowry from women at marriage even if they were good for nothing.

And now they could simply run away from home and become militants, saviours of the Tamils. Many of my Hindu school friends had lost their brothers and uncles to militant groups such as the Tigers (LTTE—Liberation Tigers of Tamil Eelam), TELO (Tamil Eelam Liberation Organisation), PLOTE (People's Liberation Organisation of Tamil Eelam), EPRLF (Eelam People's Revolutionary Liberation Front), EROS (Eelam Revolutionary Organisation of Students) and several other splinter groups. Their distraught parents could only run up to their nearest militant base and beg their sons to return home, mostly to no avail.

Female university students were becoming part of the political movement, but they were not enlisted to be combatants. It didn't seem fair to me that, once again, women were denied equality when they were just as capable. The great Hindu Tamil poet Subramanya Bharathi had said so in the previous century and yet nothing had changed. The Hindu goddess Kali was the most valiant god of them all and yet women were expected to remain docile. I disliked this hypocrisy, but as a fifteen year old girl there was little I could do to change the society's attitude.

So I could only watch with envy the young men who had returned with military-style training from India and Lebanon now openly setting up camps in various neighbourhoods, driving motorbikes and pick-up trucks, and flaunting their weapons. I admired the Tigers the most. They were considered the most successful group in the battlefront. The black thread around their necks that carried the cyanide capsule or *kuppie* gave them added prestige. Some of them had even met their enigmatic thirty-year-old Tiger leader Prabhakaran, a Hindu man from a village north of Jaffna, now exiled in India. In 1975, at just twenty years of age, he had shot dead at point-blank range Alfred Duraiappah, the Mayor of Jaffna, whom he considered a traitor for affiliating with the ruling Sinhala government. In 1983 he'd masterminded the ambush that killed thirteen soldiers and triggered the anti-Tamil pogrom. As a wanted man, he and the other leaders of the Tamil movement had fled to India, where they were sheltered by the Indian government's intelligence service RAW (Research and Analysis Wing), which turned them into militants. Although he was the youngest of the militant leaders, the charismatic Prabhakaran and his Tamil Tigers were fast gaining popularity among Tamils in India and Sri Lanka because of their single-minded discipline, courage and battle success.

While I was lost in thought a voice interrupted.

'Can we play a board game?'

I turned around to find Shirani behind me. She smelt of ripe guava. The gentle breeze of the fan ruffled her short hair and the sleeves of her floral cotton dress. Despite having a wardrobe full of many fashionable clothes, Shirani preferred to tailor Amma's dresses to her pint-sized frame and wear them out and about. She always seemed to know what she wanted—starting at just three years old when she had chosen the design for her dress for my birthday party, and had known how and where to pose for the photos. I, on the other hand, had always been happy to let my parents decide for me.

'Not now.'

'I even memorised those poems for you, and now you won't come and play with me.' Shirani pursed her lips.

It was true that I had asked her to memorise a few lines of the poems we saw on posters and banners on the streets. They spoke of oppression and uprising, and were used as propaganda by the many militant organisations. I found these street poems, whether on leaflets or on posters, fascinating, and I began collecting them. I did not want to stop to write them down, to avoid being caught in the act by soldiers, teachers or relatives. So I memorised the first few lines each time we rode our bicycles past them, and I asked Shirani to memorise the rest. That way, when we reached our destination, I could write the entire poem down.

'I know—thanks. But I'll play with you when I finish this book.'

'You say that all the time,' complained Shirani, and she disappeared into the lounge room, and I went back to reading the Famous Five.

By now, Shirani and I were pretty well settled in what my southern relatives called the 'insular capital'. They teased my newly developed Jaffna accent and said I had become one of those 'palmyra-fruit-suckers'. Amma on the other hand—as a single, working mother of two for eleven months of the year—still felt alien in Jaffna, although she was well-liked by neighbours and her colleagues. My father only visited us once a year, for just three weeks at a time. When there was political unrest either in Colombo or Jaffna, he could not visit us. This way he became nearly a stranger in the house, to whom Shirani and I showed our best behaviour.

Despite seeing less of Appamma and my aunts these days, Amma felt their influence was ever-present in her life. I, however, had grown indifferent to their negative comments and to my mother's sadness and tears because I had come to understand that nothing was going to change about their relationship.

As the surviving elder of Appa's side of the family, Appamma commanded unquestioning respect from all of us. The conservative Tamil and Sinhala cultures demanded that the young respect and obey the old, even if the 'old' was older only by a year; older girls were called *Acca* (which is what Amma called her older sisters, sisters-in-law and senior female colleagues, and what Shirani and her friends called me) and older men Anna. Although I was at the bottom of the hierarchy as a teenager, I found it difficult to always unquestioningly obey the elders.

On my father's last visit he had refused to allow me to join the church choir, because it was 'made up of low-caste girls and Appamma wouldn't approve of you singing with them'.

'But the first lesson in my textbook is a poem by Subramanya Barathi, who said that there is no such thing as caste and it's a sin to speak of it,' I retorted.

'That's a textbook and this is real life,' came the reply. 'Haven't you heard that "a picture of a gourd is no good for a curry"?'

I was perplexed by the elders' hypocrisy, and I covertly joined the choir and sang at mass, except on Sundays when I knew my relatives would attend. Only Shirani knew of my secret.

Just as I was fantasising about eating ham rolls and drinking ginger beer with the Famous Five, I heard three loud bangs out in the laneway. I tossed down my book and ran after Shirani, out of the house and into the lane to meet Amma hurrying towards us, her red batik sarong fluttering in the wind. She was returning from Theeban's house.

'A man is lying shot in the laneway,' she said, looking frightened. 'I saw two young men on a bicycle shoot him and disappear. I don't know what to do.'

Despite our mother's protests, we ran towards the crime scene. The smell of gunfire still hung in the warm air. At the side of the lane lay a balding, middle-aged man in a pool of blood; he had fallen off his orange scooter and its engine was still running. His right hand was on his chest, where the bullet had hit.

By now a few heads had appeared over the fences. Someone suddenly wailed: 'Oh, God! That's Mr Anandarajan!'

Mr C.E. Anandarajan was the principal of the prestigious St John's Boys' College and a well-respected member of the community. The news spread like wildfire and within a few minutes our quiet lane was swarming with mourners, mainly students. There was a great outpouring of grief and anger, and talk of revenge; but no one touched him, assuming he was dead. He died much later, on his way to the hospital.

The day after the murder, I heard the neighbours speaking over the fence. Other than the BBC, they were our most reliable source of information. 'The Tigers must have thought Mr Anandarajan a traitor for organising a friendly soccer match between his school and the Sinhala military,' said Kumar Auntie (she was Kumar's mother). Everyone suspected it was the Tigers who had shot him, although no one had claimed responsibility.

'But it was during a ceasefire,' remarked Upstairs House Auntie. 'I see nothing wrong with that.'

'All I can say is democracy in this country is sabotaged by both sides.'

They all sighed.

'Anyway . . . I have to go to the markets. Do you want any fish?' asked Kumar Auntie, and everyone's thoughts immediately returned to more mundane matters.

Contemplating this recent murder unsettled me. Obviously the moderates had been warned, put on notice. The murderers, who were possibly Tigers, were saying, 'If you're not with us, then you're against us.' I knew this was wrong; and yet another part of me refused to denounce the Tigers because without them, the Tamils had no hope for freedom and dignity. Then I decided not to think about it further—my exams were imminent. In the meantime, Shirani and I frightened each other with tales of Mr Anandarajan's and Theeban's ghosts roaming our laneway at night; not realising something truly frightening was yet to come.

One Sunday morning, a couple of weeks after Mr Anandarajan's murder, when Shirani and I sat down for breakfast, we heard the loud roar of a low-flying plane. Amma was at church, having recently embraced Christianity. She was christened Catholic immediately after her father recovered from an earlier stroke. It wasn't uncommon for Buddhists and Hindus to embrace gods of other faiths while maintaining their own. Amma, like most Sri Lankans of all faiths, made deals with gods for favours, a practice called *Naetthi*. In exchange for a granted wish, many an act was promised—to visit a holy site nine times consecutively, walk on knees to a distant temple, walk on hot coals, be suspended on hooks threaded through the skin, pierce a long needle through the tongue or cheek, starve for days, commit their eldest child to the clergy, and in extreme cases conversion of faith. So when Thaatha suffered his first stroke, Amma promised to convert to Christianity in exchange for his recovery (I was glad that she didn't promise me to the nunnery). He did recover that first time, and Amma went from being a devout Hindu vegetarian who at the age of seventeen flew to India on her own to visit the six holy Hindu sites, to a meat-eating Christian, going to mass every morning. Now she was making Shirani and I go to regular confession (where we lied for lack of sins to confess) and recite the rosary every evening (which the two of us hurriedly mumbled through) and follow the Way of the Cross all through Lent at the local church (where the teenage altar boys tried passing love letters to me behind my mother's back, making me sick with worry about getting the blame). Now, on hearing the planes, Shirani and I looked at each other uncertainly. Next we heard a deafening noise, louder than any clap of thunder. The house shook. I realised we were being bombed.

Instinctively, I grabbed Shirani's arm and ran into my bedroom and we hid under the bed. We were shaking. I had never been so scared. Each time the plane dropped the deafening bombs, we huddled further under the bed, our bodies trembling and our hearts racing. We were almost too scared to breathe. We stayed silently under the bed even after the roaring sound of planes had completely died away, too frightened to come out.

After what felt like eternity, we heard the front door open. It was Amma. The feeling of relief swept over me as we ran to the door. 'The air force bombed a suspected Tiger camp a few kilometres from here and destroyed the entire neighbourhood,' she told us.

I was shocked and very sad, yet glad it was over. But it was only the beginning of things to come. Over the next months, as air raids and artillery shelling became frequent, I studied for my impending exams in the poor light of the bomb shelter in our backyard with Amma, Shirani and our two dogs by my side. Every public building and most private homes built bomb shelters. These shelters were more like massive holes in the ground, covered with coconut tree trunks, topped with sandbags and camouflaged with palm leaves. When the army plugged the artillery shells at their barracks or the air force bombers left their bases the militants would sound their sirens from their watchposts, which gave schools, households and businesses a minute or two to evacuate into the shelters before the artillery or the bomb pounded the town.

While state-of-emergency and night-time curfews continued, during the day life carried on as normal as possible at least for a few hours—enough time for Shirani and me to attend school and Amma to go to work and do the shopping or banking and attend mass.

Jaffna peninsula, due to its mostly arid coastal landscape, had always relied on the south for much of its food supply, so when word was out that lorries carrying provisions from the south of the country had arrived safely through army checkpoints and looting Sinhala thugs, Amma would hurry into town and bring home sacks of rice, lentils, sugar, flour and canned or dried fish. Amma otherwise improvised with what she found in our backyard—coconut (for curries and sambols), moringa (drumsticks curry and leaf *mallung*), banana (fruit, fritters and ash plantain curry) and eggs and meat from the chickens we raised. We snacked on fruits of mangoes, *nelli*, pawpaw and guava trees. Since gas supply diminished and electricity was sporadic everyone, including Amma, began cooking on an outdoor fire. The fridge and freezer couldn't be kept running either.

Amma was so efficient in the way she managed our daily lives that I hardly noticed the change except for a few things—seafood, cream biscuits, freshly-baked white bread, sausages, beef, vegemite, pearl-like samba rice, cow's milk and shampoo. Instead we had starchy red rice, stinky goat's milk bartered from one of the neighbours, and soapnuts that Amma ground herself and forcibly washed our hair with. She told me to stop complaining because there were many who'd like to trade places with me—because our father was working for a British company and sent us sterling pounds, the banks readily accepted her cheques and she was favoured by the merchants, who gave her their best stock and in bulk. There were many who couldn't afford anything more than very small rations of rice and lentils, and some of her colleagues were re-using one spoonful of loose tea leaves three times over.

Despite our more fortunate circumstances, overall living conditions were deteriorating rapidly. Due to random bombing and shelling at all times of the day, a good part of the city had become rubble and there were many no-go zones all around the army barracks and along the coast where naval ships patrolled. Pedestrians and cyclists took to wearing helmets, pots or pans on their heads to protect themselves from randomly strafing helicopter gunships.

The air force often dropped leaflets from helicopters, warning of an air raid and ordering civilians to flee to a public landmark. Like most of our neighbours, we took shelter in our bunkers instead, as invariably those landmarks were the next target. Hospitals, churches, schools and homes were not spared, often resulting in large civilian casualties. My neighbourhood was out of range of the two army barracks and clear of any militant camps, so it was spared. But the possibility of a random bombing raid, strafing helicopters or losing someone dear to us elsewhere always loomed. The Sinhala government was dropping bombs on its own citizens—it was hard for me not to sympathise with fellow Tamils and be stirred by the injustice they were facing.

While the anti-Sinhala sentiment was running high in Jaffna, I found myself explaining to my friends that it was the government that deserved our hatred and not the people. 'The Sinhalese are no different to us,' I told them. I knew this because I had lived among them, was bilingual and had Sinhala relatives and friends in the south. Unlike me, almost all of my classmates couldn't speak Sinhala and had not travelled to Sinhala areas of the country. I told them that I felt that successive governments were destroying this magnificent country by polarising its psyche for their political gain, pandering to the extreme elements of the majority Buddhist-Sinhalese. These Sinhala extremists didn't know any Tamils or speak the language, and that's why it was easy for them to hate the Tamils. But the government had no such excuse.

It was becoming clear to me that Tamils collectively were being targeted as the enemy—whether they were separatist or nationalist, militant or politician, young or old, man or woman. I felt helpless, vulnerable and also angry. I wished I could do something to show that I did not approve of the government's treatment of Tamils other than joining in the anti-government marches organised by school students. After so many marches, the government was taking no notice of us because we were only school kids.

My hope of becoming a political correspondent one day to tell the world about Sri Lanka's war was thwarted when my father, in no uncertain terms, said that it was 'no job for a woman'. He insisted that female journalists only wrote about fashion and cooking. So I began to hope of becoming a Tigress, although it too was 'no job for a woman'. But in a war-zone like Jaffna, I had better chance of becoming a militant than a reporter. The militants were also becoming more and more accepted by the community, despite rumours of kidnapping, in-fighting, murder and extortion, which I had dismissed as rumours and continued to hope that there was room for female militants in the not-so-distant future.

'I wish the Tigers would enlist female members, so I could become one,' I moaned to Ajanthi.

'Even if they did, we can't do anything,' she remarked, flicking her auburn hair away from her face. 'We are just girls having to sit for our all-important O-Level exams in December, just three months away.'

I had little choice other than to agree with her. Fighting was something men did, not girls—especially not middle-class teenage girls. Such actions would certainly ruin our reputations forever. No one in my family had any militant alignment, and in any case, I had to wait 'til the Tigers enlisted females. So I decided to cast aside those thoughts and made a supreme effort to focus on my exams. Was not the whole point of living in Jaffna to become a doctor, just like my aunts and uncles who lived in the United Kingdom or Australia?

One cloudy October evening, I heard loud voices outside our neighbour's house. Shirani and I followed Amma to Upstairs House Auntie's to find her screaming at the top of her lungs at a young man. The sun had nearly set, and in the twilight I could hardly see his face.

'Can you believe the audacity of the Tigers?' Upstairs House Auntie continued at high pitch, although she was speaking to my mother now. 'He wants us to move out to a house he's picked for us, so he can turn this into a Tiger base. No way!'

As he shifted from one foot to the other, the street light fell on the young man's face. I thought I recognised him but I could not be certain. I had seen him fleetingly on the streets, often driving a black pick-up truck at high speed through pot holes. I was certain that he was a Tiger—his well-built body being an obvious sign of military training. I wondered why he wanted the house.

He ignored our presence and continued: 'The house we've found for your family is bigger and more modern. Why don't you go have a look at it before you scream at me?'

'This is my family home, you moron. If the other house is better, as you say it is, then why don't you set up camp there yourselves?'

'It's not about the house, but the location,' the man replied solemnly, brushing his hand through his hair. 'And there is no need to shout.'

Shirani and I sniggered, knowing that the poor fellow was asking the wrong person. Upstairs Auntie was the type to 'peel hair off an egg shell'. After an hour into his unsuccessful attempt to convince her, he left, murmuring that her bark was louder than an Alsatian dog's.

'These uneducated, low-caste boys have picked up guns and now they expect us to listen to them,' complained one of the neighbours, having listened in on the conversation.

'Well said!' added another animated talking head from over the fence. 'They are not capable of solving the Tamil problem, only adding to it.'

I wondered then what these high-caste intellectuals were doing to solve the Tamil problem. If they had cared to know the truth, they would have discovered that most militants were intellectuals, turned combatants. Regardless, anyone who stood up against tyranny had my respect. 'Who was that man asking for your house?' I asked one of Upstairs House Auntie's daughters.

'He said he was a Tiger named Roshan,' answered the twelve-year-old.

4

DEAD AND BURIED

A janthi and I were heading to school on our bicycles, along the Old Park Road. It was a warm day in April 1986, the north-east monsoon rains had eased and the morning was already warm. Sunlight filtered through the canopies of the grand oak trees that lined the road, releasing their scent into the air.

Late in the previous year, our national O-Level exams had gone ahead on schedule after much uncertainty. We had studied in bunkers amid frequent air raids and random artillery shelling. In addition, we faced threats from some youths who claimed to be members of the militant group TELA (Tamil Eelam Liberation Army), to boycott the exams as a sign of protest. They said it was unfair that the students of Jaffna had to sit a national exam under duress while the Sinhala students in the south sitting the same exam faced no such hardship. They believed that this was part of the government's ploy to reduce the number of Tamil students eventually gaining university admission and attacked the van that delivered the exam papers from Colombo, and disrupted our science practical trials by bursting into the examination hall and turning the room upside down—we had frozen in shock.

Although everyone sympathised with their reason, none of us

wanted to risk our education and be left behind. Who knew, we may never have been allowed to sit the exams again or the war could worsen. I certainly didn't want to endure studying for the same exam another year. When the Tigers offered protection for our final exams Sister Joseph, our principal, was grateful. We sat for the exams while trying to ignore the young Tiger men who patrolled the examination hall, armed with automatic rifles. We were sixteen-year-old girls and we felt as if our resolve was being tested.

Nevertheless, both Ajanthi and I achieved good results—I was ranked in the top five—making us eligible for the science or maths stream at A-Levels and holding out the prospect of us qualifying for either medicine or engineering in two years' time. Despite my apathy towards medicine, I chose the science stream to please my parents. I told myself that if it was tougher for Tamils to gain university admission, as they said it was, then it did not matter what I did.

'We want Ajanthi to attend the private Anglican girls' college around the corner,' said Ajanthi's mother, Mala Auntie to me one day in January, while Ajanthi and I were awaiting our results. 'They're better at preparing for university admissions. Perhaps you should think about it too.'

I adored Mala Auntie. Ajanthi and her only sibling, her younger sister Nilanthi, had both inherited their mother's beauty and gentle nature. They were a happy, pet-loving family. I could not imagine not spending time with them, so I decided to sit the entrance exams for the Anglican college with Ajanthi. Our friend Shereena had migrated to Canada and others were fleeing Sri Lanka for Europe, North America or Australia. I had called Shereena a deserter, much to the annoyance of her mother, who had been very fond of me until then. But that is how I felt: no matter how bad the situation was, we should stay and fight.

The nuns then accused us of being deserters when Ajanthi and I requested that we be released from their school. 'We educated you 'til now, and you show your gratitude by joining that Anglican school. You are two of our best and brightest. Losing you would mean we'll have less students entering university from your year. The Anglican college will get all the glory instead.'

Despite the nuns' promise to me that I could be school captain, I joined Ajanthi at her new school. 'You girls will never prosper,' cursed Sister Joseph, the principal, rolling up her sleeves and shaking her index finger at us. Our siblings, Shirani and Nilanthi, stayed on at the school and bore the brunt of the nuns' anger, being locked outside the school gates during the first lesson each day.

Although I was now at a new school, my routine was still the same—every morning I would ride my bicycle to Ajanthi's house and from there we rode together to school. That morning in late April was no different as we rode along the Old Park Road. But we were only a few hundred metres from school when Ajanthi applied the brakes on her bicycle and exclaimed, 'Look at that!' I looked where Ajanthi was pointing. There was only rubble and the faint memory of a large house. 'Wasn't that used as a base by TELO?'

She was right. TELO was one of the original militant groups formed in 1979 alongside the Tigers. Like other militant groups TELO had seized many large residences, generally by force, and turned them into camps to house their members. This one on Old Park Road had been flattened to the ground.

A torn piece of fabric hung on an intact tamarind tree and an arm missing a body lay by the roadside, still wearing a watch. I realised that we were witnessing the aftermath of a tremendous explosion I had heard the night before. I remembered I had been woken up by an earth-shattering explosion, but I had soon dropped off to sleep again when I realised that it was someone else's house that was under attack.

As Ajanthi and I resumed our journey, a white Toyota HiAce van with tinted windows drove past us slowly. 'TELO and PLOTE are banned,' blared a faceless voice from the loudspeakers fitted on the roof racks. 'All their members and sympathisers must surrender to the Tigers, and anyone who resists will not survive.'

My heart sank. So it was true: the Tigers were eliminating their rival Tamil militant organisations. Until now, I had refused to believe the rumours as I had become so infatuated with the Tigers. They were our heroes—known for their impeccable conduct and discipline, ready to sacrifice their lives for the Tamil people. Unlike the other factions, the Tigers' code of conduct prohibited them from smoking, consuming alcohol and taking lovers, so it seemed ludicrous to me that anyone could suggest that they engaged in the murder and torture of fellow Tamils and Sinhalese civilians in the villages bordering Tamil-dominated areas.

There had been a few recent incidents suggesting a growing rivalry and struggle for supremacy between the militant factions that had once operated harmoniously. Now, as I witnessed the aftermath of the attack on the TELO camp and listened to the broadcast, I was left with little room for doubt. This troubled me.

'I feel sorry for TELO members,' remarked Ajanthi as we rolled our bicycles past the watchman at the school gate. 'They've fought for the same cause as the Tigers.'

The topic dominated classroom chatter over the next few days. 'My cousin witnessed the Tigers setting fire to their TELO and PLOTE captives alive, after they'd tied them to trees and hung tyres around their necks,' said one of the girls. 'How can they do this to their fellow Tamils?'

'Rasaak *maama* said it was because the PLOTE and TELO leadership was corrupt and we need a solid, united front,' answered another. Her Uncle Rasaak was a prominent member of the Tigers.

'Yes, I agree,' I added. 'We need sole representation, not a thousand corrupt factions.' It was well known in Jaffna that TELO, PLOTE and EPRLF engaged in kidnapping and extortion, collecting several million dollars in ransom. They had also done this in India, and several of their members had arrest warrants issued on them by the Indian police.

'But by killing fellow Tamils, the Tigers have now created enemies amongst us,' remarked another. 'We will never achieve our separate homeland this way.'

In the end, we agreed that if one faction was to remain it had to be the Tigers. After all, they were more successful in the battlefield than all the other rival factions put together.

I repeated this notion at home, when I heard our neighbours talk over the fence that evening, criticising the Tigers for their latest murders. They said Tiger leader Prabhakaran was paranoid that TELO and PLOTE were working with the Indian government to kill him.

'But *mahal* [daughter], the choice is being made for us and not by us,' explained Colombo Auntie, speaking mostly in English. She was one of those 'refugees' from Colombo who remained in Jaffna in her beautiful large house two doors down from us while most of the displaced had returned to Colombo or left the country as emigrants and refugees to the United Kingdom, Europe, North America and Australia. 'Creating one powerful entity is all well and good, but that's not democracy. Anyone who kills the voice of dissent is a tyrant.'

Having earlier cleared my doubts with the notion of solidarity, I was reluctant to let it be disturbed by any notion of democracy. In any case, if there had been such a thing as democracy in this country, the Tamils would not be in this situation in the first place. However, I did not voice my thoughts out loud. It was no use openly disagreeing with the grown-ups, because they would never understand and would label me defiant.

In May 1986, the Tigers were blamed for the bombing of a Tristar jet from Gatwick at Colombo airport, killing twenty-one and injuring forty-one. Over the following months the Tigers took full control of the city—flaunting their weapons and parading in jeeps, motorbikes and pick-up trucks, despite the fuel embargo imposed on Jaffna by the government. While the military remained confined to their barracks, the navy and the air force continued to dominate the sea and skies, and their artillery, cannons, bombers and helicopter gunships pounded the civilian areas.

Having defeated their strongest rival faction and gained control of Jaffna peninsula, the Tigers' desire for supremacy had become somewhat sated; for a time they seemed to let the less powerful, factional movements—PLOTE, EPRLF and EROS—continue their operations. So when, near the end of the year, Captain Benjamin of EPRLF—a distant relative of my mother—was captured by the Tigers during simultaneous raids on the PLOTE and EPRLF camps, we were completely taken aback.

Benjamin had occasionally paid us visits on his motorbike, always unannounced and accompanied by a bodyguard. It was difficult to imagine him as a combatant because he looked and behaved like a gentleman; he often talked in his gentle voice about social reform, books, art or cultural festivals, and this had earned him the nickname 'Dr Benjamin' in militant circles. I admired him and liked him and yet did not care for his allegiance to the EPRLF, because they were rivals to the Tigers. Although EPRLF was one of the prominent militant groups, in order of reputation among Tamils, however, they were the bottom of the rung—their recruits were mostly the poorest from rural villages and they had done the unthinkable by recruiting women for their military wing. 'EP' was now used as a derogatory term that described a 'loose woman' who hung out with men, called them comrades instead of brothers, and worked alongside them.

'What is wrong with being EP?' I had once asked my friends when they were teasingly calling each other 'EP'. 'They are the only ones who recognise women as equal to men.'

'Yes, but without the code of conduct to go with it,' said Vasuki, whose brother was a Tiger which made her the expert on the topic in our class.

Other girls with relatives in the Tigers agreed. 'The Tigers don't believe that women can fight alongside the men because it will be like placing a spark of fire next to cotton wool.'

'It's true,' added Ajanthi. 'This is what keeps the Tigers so strong and disciplined. Why tempt them?'

We were so in awe of the Tigers we managed to justify everything they did. We even excused Prabhakaran's recent marriage to his lover despite his earlier stance on lovers and marriages which had led to the breakaway faction TELO. We said that it was okay because his wife was not a fellow Tiger.

So as much as I wanted to become a militant, I could not bring myself to join the EPRLF and become the laughing stock of my friends or forgo my loyalty to the Tigers. So I spoke very little to Benjamin during his visits to our house despite liking and respecting him.

One December day in 1986, he picked up my poetry notebook as he sat down on the sofa and began to browse through it. A few minutes later he remarked 'These are good,' while stroking his groomed beard. 'I'd like to use some in one of our propaganda videos. Can I borrow this book?'

I wondered what it would mean for my reputation if the EPRLF was to use my material. Over the past few months, two of my poems had been published in the local pro-Tiger newspaper and another was due to appear in the next issue of the Tigers' official magazine, *Kalatthil* [*On the Field*].

Theeban's younger brother Mano, who was now a Tiger sympathiser, had helped me with the publications because he had connections in the Tigers' media unit. I wrote under my first name only and did not tell Amma about it. I was gaining the confidence of the Tigers, but if my poems appeared in an EPRLF video, the Tigers might question my loyalty. Even from mere sympathisers, Tigers demanded total devotion.

Seeing my unexplained reluctance, Benjamin had offered a compromise: 'Okay, I won't use them without your permission,' he had said, adjusting his black-rimmed glasses. 'But I will take this notebook with me and return it to you first thing tomorrow.'

I agreed, not realising what the next day had in store for him.

Benjamin had not arrived when I left for my chemistry tutorials the next morning. As Ajanthi and I headed towards the town centre, a van with loudspeakers attached to it passed us in slow motion once again. 'EPRLF is banned,' it bellowed this time. 'Members and supporters who do not surrender will face a bloody ending.'

My heart sank. 'Oh no! Benjamin anna!' I gasped. 'And my notebook!'

'Never mind your book,' said Ajanthi, pedalling her bicycle beside me. 'If the Tigers think that you have EPRLF connections, you will be in bigger trouble.'

As soon as we arrived at class, the friend of mine whose uncle was a Tiger approached me. 'Rasaak maama wants you to know that the Tigers have your notebook,' she said. 'He wants you to come to my house this afternoon so he can meet with you.'

I could not concentrate on my lessons that morning, worried about the interrogation I was to face in the afternoon. Although I had seen Rasaak before—often riding his motorbike without a helmet, his shoulder-length straight hair brushed back by the wind—we had never spoken to each other.

When I arrived at their house that afternoon, as arranged, Rasaak opened the door. The young man's towering presence made me anxious. He was in his early twenties.

'Come in and sit down,' he said smiling. 'It's nice to finally meet you.'

I was relieved. Rasaak was warm and friendly, enquiring about school and my interests. There was no interrogation, only a warning: 'Stay away from the EPRLF for your own good,' said Rasaak. 'Dr Benjamin is okay. He is being held captive at our Brown Road camp. Anyway, we liked your poems, so our media unit will be using them in our propaganda material.'

Amma opened the iron gate of the large two-storey house on Brown Road, and walked up to its front door along the path lined with the dense foliage of tall ashoka trees, which Shirani called 'upside-down trees' for their downward branches. I followed Amma. An earlier drizzle had released the smell of earth into the air and it was another warm afternoon. A young teenage boy with an AK-47 slung on his shoulder, stood at the door staring out to the street. As we approached him, he raised his chin as if to inquire what our business was.

'We are here to see Captain Benjamin of EPRLF,' replied Amma confidently. 'We have permission from your local area leader, *Muli* [bulging eye] Shankar.' Jaffna Tamils used adjectives in preference to surnames, giving little regard to their offensive nature. There had been a 'Fat Frida' and a 'Skinny Frida' in my school. Besides, militants used single *noms de guerre*, and it was the only way to differentiate two with the same name.

The young boy waved Amma and me on. It had been four days since the Tigers had attacked EPRLF bases and taken them captive. When Amma learnt that Benjamin was held in a house only a couple of kilometres away, she informed his family in Nuwara Eliya, a town in the Up Country, and went straight to the Tigers' head office seeking permission to visit him. The Tiger in charge was a man named Shankar, who had accompanied Theeban during one of his visits to our house. Since Theeban's death, he had occasionally visited us on his own and always unannounced. Making uninvited visits was one way the militants established and maintained contacts and support in the community via so called 'source houses'. More often than not, the head of these households were women or the elderly. Once the visits began you couldn't refuse them—that could be dangerous.

Since it was not proper for Amma to visit a militant base on her own, I volunteered to accompany her despite knowing that my association with Benjamin may now become obvious to the Tigers. I did so for two reasons: I was concerned about Benjamin's welfare and curious to see what the inside of a Tiger base looked like. So now as we walked through the living room, I glanced around. I expected to see ammunition and other combat paraphernalia. Disappointingly, the room was empty, devoid of furniture. We walked over to the garage at the side of the house. A few sarong-clad young men, who I assumed were EPRLF captives, were talking to their visitors. I was surprised to see these men wearing sarongs—it would normally have been considered disrespectful, like wearing your nightgown in public. Then I remembered that the Tigers had captured them while they were asleep. Amma and I sat down on some white plastic garden chairs. Minutes later, a bearded man wearing a blue sarong and a white shirt stepped into the garage.

'Thanks for coming to see me,' said the man, keeping his mouth covered with the palm of his right hand. His Indian Tamil dialect gave away his Hill Country upbringing: it was Benjamin. He was black and blue all over, his face swollen and his skin split open in many places. Both Amma and I were speechless. Benjamin sat down next to Amma.

'What have they done to you?' she exclaimed moments later. 'Tell me what happened?'

'I was asleep when the Tigers attacked my camp last Saturday morning,' said Benjamin, still keeping his mouth covered. I realised all his front teeth were missing and that he was embarrassed about it. My chest tightened; a big lump came into my throat. It was obvious to me that the Tigers had beaten him up. They had punished Benjamin simply because he belonged to another movement although it had fought for the same cause. Unlike PLOTE and TELO, the EPRLF had done nothing to provoke the Tigers, who were not without fault themselves. It made me feel terribly disappointed in the Tigers. I wished there was an explanation to what seemed to be their hypocritical and unfair behaviour.

'They brought me and a few of my comrades here, beat us up first and then questioned us,' continued Benjamin. 'Captain Vasu whipped me with his belt and smashed my face against the stairs, and that's when I lost my teeth. But now they've stopped all the torture. There's talk of releasing us soon.'

Then he turned to me: 'Niromi, I am sorry. They took your notebook and wanted to know how I knew you.'

I couldn't swallow the lump in my throat or stop the tears streaming down my face. I did not know why I was crying. Was it because I was sad for Benjamin, or disappointed in the Tigers? I could not tell.

'You'd better go back to Nuwara Eliya when they release you,' said Amma.

'Yes, I'm hoping to marry a girl I met recently and take her to the Up Country. There's nothing left for me here in Jaffna. EPRLF is over, and the Tigers will surely kill me if I continue with the cause. I've had enough of this freedom . . .' Benjamin was mid sentence when suddenly a massive explosion shook the ground, making us jump out of our seats.

'It's pretty far away,' said someone.

Totally unperturbed, Amma went back to the most important question in her mind: 'Who is the girl?'

'I met her while I was working on a community project. She's an epileptic, and no one would marry her.'

'Your parents will be disappointed,' said Amma without a second thought. 'Besides, pity is no reason to marry someone.'

'She's nice,' replied Benjamin simply.

I sensed that Benjamin wasn't marrying for love—not that many in our society did (most married because it was expected of them). It occurred to me that he probably didn't even know his bride-to-be very well. It was his last attempt to introduce social reform—marrying a girl with epilepsy from a poor family. Not many men would want to marry a girl like that, and especially not when the man was a young, attractive university graduate like Benjamin. Even the offer of a substantial dowry wouldn't persuade them.

For many years, I had pigeonholed Benjamin as simply another member of EPRLF, rivals to the Tigers. But now, for the first time, I thought I understood him. He was an utterly decent human being, and I felt proud of him. Before we left, Amma inquired about his release. The camp manager assured her that it wouldn't be long.

The following day we found out that the huge explosion we had felt had been the Tigers' failed attempt to blow up the Naavatkuli army barracks. Due to a technical error, the water carrier packed with explosives had detonated before it was driven into the barracks. Fifty civilians and sixteen Tigers perished, including Vasu, the very man who Benjamin said had bashed him.

Two months passed, and Benjamin's and his fellow captives' fate remained in the hands of the Tigers. *Muli* Shankar continued to visit us at home; Amma continued to visit Benjamin at the camp and Shirani would accompany her. I had decided not to visit Benjamin any longer because seeing him as a Tiger captive unsettled me. When I looked at Benjamin, I saw injustice staring back at me and demanding that I face it. That to me meant denouncing my loyalty to the Tigers. I wasn't prepared to do that, because without the Tigers there was no hope for the Tamils. This belief was the reason why, when one day Ajanthi suggested that we report an EPRLF member hiding in her street to the Tiger head office, I agreed, even if it wasn't proper for two young women like us to be seen there.

During this time, the Tigers launched their 'Gold Campaign' and demanded gold jewellery from every family in Jaffna. When two men came knocking on our door, Amma handed over her necklace, after a failed attempt to dissuade them. She told the men that the Tigers had most of her gold jewellery already, taken from the safe at the Peoples' Bank a few years earlier when they had robbed it. But, on seeing the television and the whitegoods in the house, the men thought us wealthy and demanded more gold. When Amma argued with them that she needed to collect dowries for her two daughters, I could no longer be silent: 'I don't need to buy a husband,' I said to her and with a suitably dramatic flourish I walked up to the boys and handed them my necklace and earrings, much to Amma's dismay.

Then, one morning in March 1987, news spread that the night before Tiger's Jaffna commander, Kittu—whom I had seen at Theeban's funeral—had been hit by a hand grenade as he left his girlfriend's house. Kittu lost a leg, and his bodyguard a finger. The assailant escaped and was not able to be identified, but the Tigers suspected it was the work of EPRLF.

When I arrived at Ajanthi's house, she was visibly distressed about Kittu's lost leg and she refused to come to school. In the past there had only been only two instances that had stopped Ajanthi from coming to school—when her pet puppy died, hit on the head by a falling coconut, and when her father accidentally stepped on her nose while she was asleep on a mat one very hot night. I reminded Ajanthi that we had our quarterly exams that day, and that she did not know Kittu personally.

'But I am very sad for him. He is a fine Tiger,' she said, wiping her tears away. On their front verandah, a cage full of budgerigars was making a noisy racket.

Ajanthi finally relented, after I convinced her that the Tigers would ensure Kittu was sent to south India where he would receive the best medical care. She was silent all the way to school. Many of my classmates were angry about the attack on Kittu and talked of boycotting the exams to show him our support. However, when our biology teacher walked in with the exam papers in her hand, everyone sat down without a word of protest.

'You should go and visit Benjamin right now,' said *Muli* Shankar to Amma that afternoon. He had arrived at our house unexpectedly and, although he did not say anything more, we felt something was not right.

Amma and Shirani hurried to the Tiger camp where Benjamin was being held. Two teenage boys were washing the floors. The dirty water was red with blood.

'Where is Benjamin?' Amma cried out.

'Dead and buried,' they told her and nothing more.

While Kittu was being sent to India for medical treatment via an illegal boat trip, one of the Tigers had taken revenge on their EPRLF captives, lining them up and shooting them dead.

Later that day Benjamin's aunt, who had arrived in Jaffna only the day before from Nuwara Eliya to accompany him home, came to see Amma. Benjamin's elderly parents couldn't have withstood the arduous travel to Jaffna by bus, through several checkpoints where the passengers were body searched and expected to carry their luggage and walk in the heat for several kilometres but Benjamin couldn't have travelled back home without a female accompanying him. Even if the military didn't know who he was, the fact that he was a young Tamil man on his own would've been enough for them to take him away, throw him in jail or worse, murder him.

The two women talked about Benjamin all evening and we mourned his death. 'How am I going to tell his parents that their only son, who had come to Jaffna for university with the promise of a great future, has been murdered by his fellow revolutionaries?' asked his aunt. 'They didn't even know he was a militant.'

I was sickened and distressed by Benjamin's murder. I wondered whether he even knew the reason he was being shot so unexpectedly. He did not deserve to die like that—no one did. I thought of the young woman he was supposed to marry—would she learn of his death, or would she be left to doubt his commitment for the rest of her life? I wondered why the Tigers considered their dead to be heroes and those dead from other factions to be traitors. Since when did the lives of some Tamils become less important than others? And what gave the Tigers the authority to carry out such acts against their fellow Tamils?

I didn't know the answer to these questions and I did not dare ask anybody, because I knew what my family and their friends would say: 'When low-caste, uneducated youths pick up guns, this is what happens.' And I didn't believe that that was the right answer. But it seemed to me no one was asking these questions of the Tigers either, perhaps fearing for their lives too.

'How did the Tigers know the assailant was an EPRLF member when they didn't capture him?' I asked Ajanthi the next day on our way to school. 'It's not like they don't have other enemies.'

It was a question that had bothered me since I'd learnt of Benjamin's murder. There were also rumours that the attack on Kittu was an inside job, because he was becoming more popular than the Tigers' exiled leader Prabhakaran himself. This was not only among the Tamils but throughout the whole country after he had struck up an unusual friendship with the enemy, Captain Kotelawala of the Sri Lankan army in command of Jaffna Fort Army Barracks. The two men had openly admired each other during a prisoner exchange and subsequently spoken of each other with great esteem.

'Who knows,' said Ajanthi, her voice distant. 'It was also pretty dark when it happened.'

Neither of us knew the answer.

We were silent after that and we never talked about the EPRLF or Benjamin again. But we had both concluded the same thing in our minds: for the greater good of a unified fight for Tamil Eelam, some sacrifices had to be made and some mistakes overlooked.

5

FOR THE GREATER GOOD

Corpses were turning up everywhere those days in Jaffna—by the roadside, hanging off lampposts or washing ashore on the Pannai beach I had frequented as a child. If we didn't see them for ourselves, we saw them on television.

Tigers, having taken over one of the television re-transmitting towers and setting up their own channel called Nitharsanam [Reality], transmitted the gruesome images of the washed-up mutilated bodies massacred by the Sri Lakan navy—among them were corpses of babies and young children. It also streamed other disturbing footage: the funerals of fallen Tiger heroes, civilians who had either died or been injured from aerial attacks and their wailing relatives, plus the spoils from Tigers' victorious raids on army camps, such as soldiers' body parts and confiscated ammunition. These telecasts would often conclude with images of young Tiger cadres at training camps and with the message that these young men were about to fight for justice for these atrocities committed against us—and so should the viewer.

While it seemed to me that everyone around me was carrying on as normal as possible amid this madness, I was being haunted by these disturbing images. It brought back memories of the men and women wailing at the Hatton railway station I had witnessed as a child some twelve years ago.

The dusk-to-dawn curfew and state of emergency continued. Schools and after-hours tuition classes were operating sporadically, but I felt little hope for a future. Over their fences, neighbours would continue to discuss current affairs; but it always ended the same way—'What can we do?' someone would say, and then others would sigh, at times muttering, 'Only God can save us.' I understood their concern over the day-to-day minutiae, such as the severe scarcity of food and fuel, but surely they realised that we could not continue to live our lives in denial, and in the hope of divine intervention? Surely they understood that it was up to each one of us to take a stand and save ourselves? All the peace talks between the militants, Tamil politicians and the government had led to nothing. The time for politics was over. The Tigers were right: the only choice left for the Tamils was to fight back. As we spent more and more time hiding in our bunkers from bombing raids and receiving news of more deaths and damage, I was becoming increasingly convinced that I should join the militants and fight this injustice. If I was going to die soon anyway, I might as well make myself useful in the meantime.

'So what's stopping you then?' Ajanthi would ask whenever I gave her such a speech. But we both already knew the answer: there was still no word that the Tigers were enlisting women for their military wing.

I was frustrated by my inability to put my thoughts into action, but I continued to hope that the Tigers would soon recruit women. The militants had already introduced much social reform among the Tamils in the north and east—they were doing away with caste, religion and other social hierarchies. In time surely they'd recognise that the role of women in combat was inevitable. I was convinced that it was only a matter of time.

So one Saturday morning, as I leafed through a pro-Tiger newspaper, I noticed something that got my heart racing with excitement: 'The hands that wore bangles now carry weapons . . .' read a poem. With this newspaper in my hand, I hopped on my bicycle and raced over to Ajanthi's house and rang my bicycle bell from the front gate. Ajanthi came out of the house and I showed her the newspaper. She read the poem and looked up at me: 'What about it?'

'It tells you that there are female Tiger militants.'

'Where does it say that?'

I pointed out the sentence, but she laughed.

I reasoned with her that a pro-Tigers newspaper would not suggest such a thing without good reason. But Ajanthi was not convinced, and I began to doubt it myself.

Within weeks, however, my suspicion was proven right. The official Tiger magazine, *Kalatthil*, featured a female Tiger in full combat gear. I raced to Ajanthi's once again.

'Now, that's more like it,' said Ajanthi.

But I still faced one problem. Having established the existence of female Tiger militants, I did not know how to become one myself. There was no official recruitment program and I couldn't walk into one of the many Tiger camps for information without someone finding out what we were doing there and informing our parents.

One weekend afternoon in late March as I was leaving the house, *Muli* Shankar arrived at the doorstep. Amma and Shirani were inside and, seeing that none of the neighbours were around, I decided to take the opportunity and ask him to enlist me in the Tigers.

'You are a child!' *Muli* Shankar exclaimed loudly, startling me. I was worried that someone's head would pop over the fence and instead of suspecting my real motive the neighbours would assume a romantic involvement between Shankar and me, which would be worse. *Muli* Shankar looked worried: 'Your Amma would be very upset if she knew what you are asking of me,' he said lowering his voice. 'Anyway, why don't you finish school first and maybe we can talk about it then.'

Having been called a child by someone barely five years older, I was too embarrassed to reason with him. So I gave up on *Muli* Shankar and decided to try my luck elsewhere. At that time, however, I hadn't thought of Muralie.

Muralie was the head of the Tigers' student wing, SOLT (Students

Organisation of Liberation Tigers). Late in 1986, a couple of months before the capture of Benjamin, they had begun galvanising support in the schools. When the Tigers demanded meetings with the students, the schools were powerless to stop them. Muralie was very popular among schoolgirls for his good looks and charisma—so much so that, when he held his first meeting at our school, our large auditorium was packed with girls just wanting a glimpse of him. But his charisma wasn't enough to sign up more than four members, Ajanthi and I included, from our affluent private college.

My friends had often spoken in support of the Tigers but, when it came to action, none of them raised their hands. I had no idea why. On our way back to class, I could not hold back my disappointment. 'What is the point of calling yourselves Tiger supporters if you won't even join their student wing?' I huffed. 'You are all hypocrites— mere admirers of the Tigers, and not of their cause!'

'I wish I could join,' said one. 'But I don't want to upset my family.'

'It's not proper for middle-class girls like us to join militant movements,' added another. 'Why do you want to ruin your reputation, Niromi?'

Before I could answer, someone gushed, 'But isn't Muralie anna cute!'

They all nodded in unison and began an excited conversation about their favourite Tiger men: 'Oh, I saw Rahim anna on his motorbike the other day, looking totally cool.'

At the time, I had taken a deep breath. Ajanthi had looked at me; she just shook her head.

Many months after we had joined SOLT and a couple of weeks after my failed encounter with *Muli* Shankar, Ajanthi and I were at Jaffna University, as members of the cast of a school play being staged there. The play was about the oppression of Tamils and the resultant uprising, written by a well known local poet, Seran. When I saw Muralie at the cafeteria there on his own, I decided to take the opportunity and ask to be enlisted in the military wing. Ajanthi followed me.

'We are members of SOLT from the Anglican Girls' College,' I said nervously.

'That's good to hear,' said Muralie as he set his cup down and turned towards us, smiling. 'I know it's tough to do anything in that school, but don't give up.'

His grey-brown eyes framed by long dark lashes narrowed with his smile. I realised why he sent many girls crazy. However, I did not let myself become distracted: 'Could you help us join the Tigers' military wing?'

Muralie's eyes widened for a moment and then he laughed out loud. 'Are you serious?'

'Of course I am,' I replied slightly annoyed at his reaction.

Muralie's facial expression stiffened. 'You are still at school. By signing up with SOLT, you have shown your support for us and that's enough for now. Perhaps we can discuss this again in a year or two.'

I was highly disappointed.

'Don't worry—I'll make sure I personally conduct regular meetings at your school, to keep you motivated,' reassured Muralie.

As promised, over the next few weeks Muralie had regularly conducted meetings after school even though we only had four members. Although my desire to become a militant was yet to be fulfilled, for now I was pleased to be part of the Tigers—pleased at gaining Muralie's confidence. The more I saw Muralie, the more I was taken with him: he was both charming and strong, and totally dedicated to the cause.

'I wish I had an older brother like Muralie anna,' I said to Ajanthi one day.

'I know what you mean,' agreed Ajanthi.

April 1987 saw some of the worst violence in the country: scores of Tamil civilians were murdered by the Sri Lankan armed forces in the north-west of Jaffna peninsula and in revenge the Tigers massacred Sinhala civilians in the bordering villages, near Anuradhapura.

Following a bomb explosion at the central Colombo bus station on 21 April 1987, which killed 113 people and injured nearly 300, the government launched 'Operation Liberation', its third major offensive on the Jaffna Peninsula. It was intended to wipe out the rebellion once and for all although the Tigers did not claim responsibility for the station bombing. Instead, the government appeared to be wiping out the Tamil population: the sound of deafening bombs and exploding artillery surrounded the city; smoke towers rose from distant villages; and the sun shone through an eternal haze. As the troops advanced from north of Jaffna city, the Tigers retreated into Jaffna itself. Everyone was speculating that within days the city could expect heavy pounding—the skies were already roaring with helicopter gunships and bombers. At times, these bombers were dropping 'barrel-bombs'—oil drums filled with TNT and other explosives, nails, rubber and human excrement.

'We are leaving for Kandy tomorrow, until this nonsense is over,' announced Amma, on 5 May.

I understood the reasons for Amma's decision but, despite feeling terrified of being killed, injured or raped, I did not want to leave. Ajanthi and her family were staying, and so was my father's family. They were still hopeful that the Tigers would protect the city as they had promised. Amma believed them too, but she had the option of returning to the Up Country whereas others had none. I argued with Amma that only cowards ran away. 'In that case, the brave will die and the cowards will survive,' she said to me. 'Do you want to live or die?'

That night, as we sheltered in our bunker listening to deafening explosions and strafing helicopters, I decided that I did not want to live in fear any longer. Being helpless and vulnerable was the worst feeling of all. The only way to take control of the situation was to fight this government. I would rather be brave, even if it meant living only one day. In the morning, I would go over to the SOLT office and ask Muralie to enlist me for military training, improper or not. If anyone was to be blamed for my decision, it should be the government. They were only creating more militants out of the innocent by their random violence against all of us in Jaffna.

I looked at Amma. In the dull light of the bulb, I saw worry on her face as she recited the rosary in silence. If I joined the Tigers, she would feel humiliated in front everyone. Appamma and my aunts would point their fingers at her again for my behaviour—rightly claiming that if my father was around I wouldn't have run away. I'd be labelled defiant and reckless, and my reputation would be tarnished forever, bringing a bad name to my family and my alma mater. Instead of referring to me by name, people would speak of me as the daughter of so-and-so and the pupil of such-and-such a school.

These thoughts made me feel guilty about something I was yet to do; but I recovered soon enough. I was not about to give up on my social responsibility, just because of the possibility of small-minded accusations. Once the initial shock wore off, my reasons for joining the Tigers would become obvious to everyone. They'd see that I had to do it out of necessity. You couldn't wait in hope that someone else was going to save you—it was up to every one of us to make a difference. I knew I had to do what had to be done, despite the personal consequences.

The next morning, Amma began making arrangements for us to catch the bus to Kandy the following day. The once four-hour bus journey now took nearly two days, with many army checkpoints along the way and stretches of roads damaged by landmines. The Yarl Devi train service had all but ceased since the Tigers destroyed Jaffna railway station after it had been used for transportation of the military. Both the Tigers and civilians had then pilfered many miles of railway sleepers in order to build bomb shelters.

After a lunch of red rice, tinned fish curry and fried okra with French shallots and green chillies, I went into Amma's bedroom, where she was sewing a secret compartment into her underskirt, so she could hide her jewellery there from the frisking soldiers at checkpoints during our journey. Many other women hid their valuables inside their elaborate beehive hair-dos or their bras—it was a time before metal-detectors had come into use.

'I'm going over to Ajanthi's to say goodbye,' I told her.

There had been a knot in my stomach all morning that would not go away. The ceiling fan was spinning rapidly, making a whirring noise.

'We have to say goodbye to Appamma, so I expect you to be at her place late afternoon,' she said.

I nodded. Appamma now lived at one of my aunts' houses not far from us, as Appamma's house had suffered artillery damage due to its proximity to the fort army barracks.

When I saw Ajanthi, I told her that I was going to Muralie's office. 'I'm going to ask him to enlist me.'

'Are you sure you want to do this?'

An artillery shell whistled and exploded a little distance away somewhere.

'No, I'm not,' I said, still feeling nervous. 'Besides, I am not confident that Muralie anna will be willing to enlist me. But I feel like I have to try.'

'I'll come with you,' she said and we set off to the SOLT head office, a two-storey house twenty minutes away near Jaffna University.

It was a typically warm, humid afternoon and—other than the sounds of distant bombardment, patrolling helicopter gunships and exploding artillery—the streets were relatively quiet. I was glad, because there was little chance of someone spotting us outside the SOLT office and finding out what we were up to. When we arrived there twenty minutes later, however, we were informed by Muralie's assistant, a young man named Rajan, that Muralie was out.

Ajanthi and I waited for nearly an hour under the mango tree outside the gate taking shelter from the heat, feeling restless the whole time, until we heard the rhythmic thump-thump of a motorbike arrive. A look of surprise passed over Muralie's face as he alighted.

'You are not here to bother me about enlisting are you?' he asked half-jokingly.

'No, Muralie anna, we came all this way to ask what you had for lunch.'

'Come into the office,' he said and we followed him into the house. His office was an empty room, except for a desk and four chairs. The day's newspapers lay on the desk.

Muralie asked us to sit down, and then he addressed us sternly: 'Look, children, this is a serious matter. You need to finish school . . .'

'But there's no school to go to,' I interrupted.

Muralie tried to dissuade me by saying that I was too young and not fit to endure the life of a militant. 'What's your hurry?' asked Muralie.

I told him that, apart from the fact that the war was intensifying, my mother was planning to take me to Kandy the following day and we were probably not returning to Jaffna.

'Yes, but I want to be enlisted too,' said Ajanthi, who had been silent 'til now, surprising both Muralie and me.

'Oh no, this is getting worse,' sighed Muralie, touching his forehead with his right hand.

After nearly half an hour, Muralie relented, having advanced every argument to dissuade us: '*Chari*, I'm calling Thileepan to talk to you.'

Saying this, Muralie left the room. We were stunned—we knew that Thileepan was the head of Jaffna's political wing. I hadn't realised we would have to convince the higher ranks.

I was feeling anxious. I did not want to miss this chance of enlisting in the Tigers—I was on the verge of realising my dream. I was prepared to say anything to convince Thileepan of my commitment. But while I felt excited, I was also distressed by what I imagined this was going to do to my family—they were going to be devastated at my betrayal. They would no longer trust me, especially Shirani.

Muralie walked back in with a walkie-talkie in his hand and sat down again: 'Thileepan will want to know how committed you are to the cause.'

Within minutes, we heard a motorbike coming to a stop outside, sending a surge of adrenalin through my body. The door opened and in came Thileepan. I had seen him on the streets before, wearing the same grey-and-black striped shirt and black trousers he was wearing then. I estimated him to be about the same age as Muralie—possibly mid twenties. There was no obvious trace of a guerrilla fighter about him: his build was slight and his movements gentle. He sat next to Muralie and smiled hesitantly, exposing his slightly protruding front teeth.

I was nervous with anticipation as Thileepan and Muralie sat down in front of us. So as not to prolong my agony, Muralie skipped the pleasantries and came straight to the point: 'Tell Thileepan what you told me,' Muralie urged us, looking at Ajanthi and me.

'Yes, tell me why you want to join our movement?'

Thileepan's gentle tone and demeanour reminded me that he had in fact been a second-year medical student when he gave it all up to join the movement. I told him that, like him, I had had enough of the treatment the Tamils were receiving at the hands of the government.

Thileepan raised his eyebrows behind his black-framed glasses. 'But how old are you?'

'Nineteen,' I lied, doing my best to appear truthful.

The two men laughed out loud.

'If you must lie, then make it appropriate,' said Thileepan, quoting a Tamil maxim. 'You are too young. Muralie tells me you did well in your exams. Don't throw it away—once you finish school, perhaps you could join us then.'

I was growing suspicious of the men's motives in conducting this interview. Were they doing it just to satisfy us, before they turned us down in the end anyway? Or were they genuinely interested in our answers?

'The war is intensifying and we don't have the luxury of time, Thileepan anna,' I said desperately. 'Please enlist us.'

'Thileepan anna, we want to fight for Tamil Eelam,' pleaded Ajanthi.

Thileepan told us that to be enlisted into the military wing the prerequisite was two years of 'area work', which involved propaganda in the community. 'We aren't actively recruiting women because we are yet to make a shortlist for our first training program from hundreds of girls in our political wing who already fulfil this criterion.'

'But you already have trained women Tigers,' I said, perplexed.

The female Tiger I had seen in the newspaper turned out to be one of the TELO and PLOTE recruits who had been trained by the Tigers. These women had been originally sent to India by their factions and were about to commence training when the Tigers annihilated their organisations. Uncertain what to do with them, the Tigers had offered them amnesty and allowed them continue their military training in India, and then shipped them back to Jaffna afterwards. So technically they were not Tiger recruits, said Thileepan.

At this point Muralie intervened and convinced Thileepan of our longstanding loyalty to the Tigers; he said we had participated in rallies and were members of SOLT. Although Ajanthi and I hadn't done anything particularly constructive as members of SOLT, we nodded in agreement with Muralie.

'I must warn you that the lifestyle of a militant isn't a bed of cottonwool,' warned Thileepan, and then he set out to give us a glimpse of what to expect. 'The movement that you see from the outside isn't the same on the inside. You see us with powerful weapons and fast cars; but what you don't see is the starvation, death and injury. You may be expected to do unpleasant tasks that you may not agree with. It is physically very demanding. As middle-class girls, I'm not convinced of your ability to cope. You have to do regular chores, like cooking and cleaning. You won't be able to keep your fashionable haircuts, clothes and shoes. There'll be none of the comforts you are used to.

'So I want you to go home now, and on your way I want you to think seriously about what I have said. If you still want to do this, then inform your families in writing. Muralie will take care of the rest when you return.'

Ajanthi and I nodded. The anxiety I had felt a few minutes ago was now replaced with exuberance. I was so excited that I could hardly speak. This was no longer a dream.

'Why is she crying?' asked Thileepan, looking at Ajanthi.

I turned to look at Ajanthi—she was quietly sobbing into her hands.

'What's wrong?' I whispered, lowering my head. 'You don't have to join me.'

'No, I'm fine,' she said, hurriedly wiping her tears and rising to her feet.

'If you decide not to return, it's perfectly fine. We can enlist you whenever you're ready,' reassured Thileepan as we headed to the door.

The sun was low in the sky as Ajanthi and I pedalled next to each other in silence towards home. A warm breeze brushed past us. I felt as if I was flying through the air. Although Thileepan had asked us to think about what he had said, all I could remember was, 'Go home and inform your families in writing.'

When we were completely out of sight from the camp, I turned to Ajanthi. Her eyes were fixed on the road ahead. I asked her why she had been upset earlier.

She hesitated for a moment: 'I was thinking of my Amma.'

It made me think of my own mother. 'Stay home then, Ajanthi, you don't have to come,' I said as I manoeuvred my bicycle to avoid a pothole. But in truth, I hoped she would join me: I could not imagine doing this alone, not sharing this immense experience with her, not seeing her every single day as we had done over the past ten years at school, or us riding our bicycles in parallel on the roads, chatting away, oblivious to the traffic chaos we were causing.

'But I'd miss you.'

I would miss her too. Although Ajanthi was a supporter of the Tigers and had expressed interest in joining them, I felt that she wasn't as single-minded as I had been about it. So I simply said, 'That is no reason to become a militant. I can always visit you.'

'No, I want to do this,' said Ajanthi.

I was glad. She was more committed to the cause than I had believed her to be.

We parted ways after agreeing to meet back at the SOLT office in half an hour. I was brave enough to head home—after all, I knew Amma was visiting Appamma to say goodbye before we left for Kandy tomorrow. She was expecting Shirani and me to come by after my visit to Ajanthi's. Ajanthi decided to go to one of our class-mates' house instead and write a note to her parents there, leaving our reluctant friend to deliver the note.

Amma,
Please don't come looking for me. I am leaving home, so my people
can have a homeland. My duty awaits me and, if I am to fulfil it, I
must leave. From now on, I am not only your daughter but the child
of an entire people. Amma, please don't pursue me because I choose
to leave.
Niromi

I left the note on the kitchen bench along with my gold earrings that I was wearing so that Amma would see it when she returned home from seeing Appamma. The news wasn't going to be easy on her and I did not want to think about how she'd react to it. Instead, I dashed over to my bookshelf and stuffed some of my favourite books into my school bag.

When I charged out of the front door, Shirani was sitting on her chopper bicycle in the driveway, looking at me curiously.

'What's the bag for?' she asked, knitting her eyebrows. 'We're only going to Appamma's.'

I hesitated for a moment, and then proceeded to lie: 'I'm going to drop these off at a friend's place along the way, so they'll be safe if the soldiers take control of the city again and raid our neighbourhood while we are away in Kandy.'

I couldn't tell her that I was about to run away to join the Tigers and that we might never see each other again. The scenario I painted for Shirani was plausible—in the past, when the Sinhala soldiers were in control of Jaffna, they raided Tamil houses without good rea-son. They would use the flimsiest of evidence to brand a family as militant sympathisers, such as a picture of a tiger on a postcard, any publication that mentioned prohibited words such as 'freedom' or 'motherland' (if the Sinhala soldiers couldn't read Tamil they forced a family member to interpret at gun point), or a photograph of a young person who no longer lived in the house. Then the soldiers might do anything—looting, or commit rape or murder. If Jaffna fell into their hands again as a result of this recent offensive, these atrocities would begin reoccurring. Shirani must have believed me as she said nothing more.

I felt a sense of relief but, within moments, that feeling was replaced by guilt—I was lying to my little sister, who, until now, had been my confidante. We had shared every one of our secrets; most mornings before school, I did her homework while she slept at her desk with a book over her face; and she couriered many unwanted letters and gifts from boys to me (although I had asked her not to), except when the gifts were sweets (many years later she was to admit that she devoured them in secret). Now, I was about to betray her.

Unable to look Shirani in the eye, I turned to our two dogs and ruffled their thick fur.

'Let's go, *Acca*,' said Shirani, her voice impatient.

As I closed the gate behind me, I glanced back at the house and its surrounding garden. It occurred to me that I might never see this familiar sight again.

The two of us set off towards Appamma's house in silence.

'I am going to drop this off first,' I said to Shirani when we were halfway to our destination, pointing at my bag of books and trying to sound casual. 'I'll see you at Appamma's.'

Shirani looked at me as I took a right turn, leaving her to continue on her own. Feeling exposed, I quickly averted my eyes after saying a hurried goodbye to her. Perhaps it was my own guilt that made me feel this way. As I pedalled away my earlier elation wore off, replaced now by the sickening sensation of my own act of betrayal.

6

AN ACT OF BETRAYAL

When I returned to the SOLT office with Ajanthi, night was falling and the cicadas were humming. The air was still warm. Muralie was seated at the table, reading a newspaper.

'I hope you're sure about this,' said Muralie looking up at us.

'Of course we are,' I replied excitedly. 'What happens now?'

'Follow me.' He folded the paper in half and tossed it on the table, picking up a bunch of keys as he walked out of the house with his assistant Rajan, and with us at his heels.

'Where are we going?' I asked, rushing after them.

'The first thing you must learn about being in the movement is not to ask questions,' said Muralie.

Minutes later we arrived at a bungalow set behind a tall wall with a narrow gate, in a lane in front of Jaffna University. A mango tree stood at the centre of the small front yard, surrounded by bushes of crossandra and four o'clock flowers. A short plump woman in a long housecoat was waiting on the verandah.

'So it was them you were talking about,' she said, and smiled at us welcomingly. Muralie informed her that Ajanthi and I were to remain in her house until further notice from himself or Thileepan.

'Ruby Auntie is like a mother to all of us,' he said, sitting down on one of the cane chairs on the verandah. I realised that Ruby Auntie was a single mother and this was a Tiger source-house.

As we sipped the sugary tea the woman served us, Muralie speculated that our families would come to the main camp first thing the next day. 'When they do, I'll fetch you.'

I was taken aback. I had thought the note I left for them was all I had to do. Now I wasn't sure if I had the courage to face my Amma and Shirani and stand my ground. 'Why do we have to see them, Muralie anna?' I complained. 'I don't know if I can handle it.'

'We want your families to know that we aren't keeping you here against your will. It will test your resolve.'

I realised that I had no say in this. I simply had do what was expected of me.

Once the men left, I felt awkward. We were at a stranger's house, knowing nothing about why we had been placed there or for how long. The woman they called Ruby Auntie had gone into the kitchen to make dinner, leaving the two of us on the verandah restless with anticipation. We sat there in silence, listening to the distant sounds of automatic gunfire. An artillery shell exploded now and then. A gentle breeze carried the shrill of cicadas and the scent from the hibiscus and jasmine bushes. The moon was rising.

Over a simple dinner of string-hoppers and *sodhi*, we learned that Ruby Auntie was a widow. In her house lived a student boarder from the university and Ruby Auntie's three daughters; the two older girls short and stocky like their mother. The eldest was nineteen, the middle one seventeen like us. The youngest one was only fourteen. The girls were members of the Freedom Birds, the Tiger women's political wing, which operated under Thileepan's leadership, and they confirmed Thileepan's earlier statement about hundreds of girls waiting to be shortlisted for military training with the Tigers. This was the first Ajanthi and I had heard of Freedom Birds. This group had not operated in our neighbourhood. Perhaps it serviced the poor communities. It made me realise how insular my neighbourhood was. I later realised that Ruby, which is what everyone called the mother, was in fact the name of the eldest daughter, and that she and second eldest, Chitra, were among those awaiting miliary training.

The girls speculated that due to heavy demand, it could be many months before Ajanthi and I received military training. I was disappointed, having had somehow assumed that as soon as we joined the Tigers we would receive training and then be given a weapon and sent to the battlefront. But I tried to remain hopeful. The girls and their mother were very kind to Ajanthi and me. The second daughter, Chitra, and I soon struck up a friendship. Unlike her other siblings, Chitra was outgoing and highly animated.

When we were shown to our room, it was bare, except for a hand-woven grass mat spread out on the polished concrete floor and two old pillows. Just as we were preparing to go to bed, I realised we had planned our 'running away' badly: all I had were books, and Ajanthi, nothing. In our eagerness not to miss the opportunity to realise our dream, we had failed to consider the essential details.

'Thileepan anna only told us to leave a note,' said Ajanthi and we burst out laughing.

I struggled to fall asleep that night on the grass mat. I wasn't sure if it was the sound of distant gunfire or the guilt of upsetting my family or the worry of facing Amma the following day that was keeping me awake. I had no doubt that Amma would have abandoned her plans to return to Kandy. She would be at the Tigers' main camp first thing tomorrow, pleading with them to send me home. But when it came to the Tigers, there was nothing she or anyone else could do other than to plead. The image distressed me—of her being reduced to pleading with strange men half her age.

'Ajanthi, are you asleep?' I asked, trying to distract myself from thinking of Amma.

'I was.'

'Don't start bawling when we see our parents tomorrow.'

'Mmm . . .'

I looked out the open window. The full moon was trying to hide itself behind the branches of a mango tree. Somewhere at a distance automatic gunfire continued to be heard. The Tigers were a brave brunch, no doubt, risking their lives at all hours to protect the Tamils from the brutality of the army. I realised that I was now their comrade. Well, nearly. I felt proud, although it had cost me everything I held dear. Everything except Ajanthi.

It was about half past eight in the morning when we heard the thump-thump of a motorbike. My heart began to pound heavily, expecting Muralie, but it was Rasaak who appeared.

Although I had only spoken to him the day Benjamin was taken captive, it was comforting seeing him now. But Rasaak looked at us disapprovingly as he sat down on one of the cane chairs on the verandah: 'I can't believe you did this,' he said, shaking his head in disbelief.

'How did you know where to find us?' I asked him.

'If all of Jaffna town knows you have joined the Tigers, it's hardly surprising that all of us in the Tigers know where you are,' said Rasaak. 'I'm not going to ask you why you joined the movement, although I am shocked. But I guess I don't have the right to ask you to return home either.'

'That's right,' I replied. It confused me that Rasaak did not approve of us joining the Tigers, despite being a militant himself.

He was silent for a while. 'Is there anything you girls need?'

I felt relieved. I was not prepared to listen to countless lectures from people telling us we should return home.

'Can you get us some clothes from home please?' I asked.

'And we forgot our toothbrushes,' Ajanthi chipped in.

Rasaak laughed. 'Didn't anyone tell you that, if you plan to run away, you must not forget your toothbrush?' He paused for a moment. 'Okay, so you want me to go to your homes and face your families? I'm fine to do that for you. But do you girls realise what you have done? Your lives will never be the same again. This is not . . .' Rasaak paused again and sighed. 'Never mind, I'll bring your things.' He rose to his feet and walked towards the door. We followed him outside.

'The boys at the main camp think Muralie and Thileepan have made a mistake enlisting two middle-class girls who won't last,' said Rasaak as he got on his motorbike. 'They are betting all kinds of favours against the two boys on this. So, if you two resign, Muralie and Thileepan will be condemned to a lifetime of either boredom or starvation—of endless sentry duty or having to give up their meals to others.'

'Whose side are you on?'

'For Muralie's sake, I hope you last. But I wish you weren't here in the first place.'

With these words, he kickstarted his motorbike and drove back down the lane.

'Mmm . . . Rasaak isn't happy about us enlisting,' I observed, as I watched him disappear into the distance.

'Correct, Einstein,' said Ajanthi.

I tried not to think of Rasaak's comments after he left. There was no point indulging in negative thoughts—I needed to keep my mind clear and open, to accept whatever the future held. But right now, I hoped the future did not involve facing Amma.

'I wish this day would come to an end,' said Ajanthi as we sat on the doorstep, feeling the heat. My stomach rumbled, but there was no sign of breakfast. All the girls in the house rushed about doing their own thing.

It was about eleven o'clock in the morning when Muralie arrived. We pleaded with him once again, not wanting to face our families.

'After all, we left them for you,' Ajanthi reasoned.

'Stop this nonsense and hurry up!' said Muralie without the slightest sign of relenting.

Feeling apprehensive, we arrived at the SOLT office once again. Out of the corner of my eye, I saw a few of our friends and neighbours outside the gate. Afraid of appearing nervous, I avoided eye contact and followed Muralie inside the house.

Shirani, Amma and Ajanthi's family were waiting in the same room in which we had been interviewed by Thileepan the evening before. They sat with tears in their eyes and distress on their faces. As soon as I saw Shirani, emotion flooded over me. My legs turned into jelly, and tears burst from my eyes and ran down my face.

The second I stepped into the room, Amma became hysterical. 'What have I ever done to you that you'd do this to me?' she sobbed. 'You were never left needing anything. And now you're throwing everything away—for what?' Tears ran down her face like rivers.

'I have everything, Amma, but the Tamils don't have freedom,' I tried to reason. 'We must achieve Tamil Eelam for everyone.'

'Who do you think you are, wanting to save the Tamils?' she shouted. 'This is not for you.'

Muralie's assistant Rajan, timing his arrival badly, walked in with a tray of glasses with green nelli cordial and offered it to Amma first. Amma sent the glasses flying into the air. Luckily Rajan had good reflexes, and ducked in time to avoid being splashed.

Over the next hour, while Ajanthi's family remained composed, although they too were distressed and tried convincing Ajanthi to return home, Amma continued to be frantic. Her rage, frustration and disappointment induced an emotion that came easily to me as a Catholic: guilt. Now I held on to my thirteen-year-old sister's reassuring presence. I knew that, although she did not approve of what I was doing, she supported the cause. 'I wish I could join you,' she muttered, holding my hands. 'But I have to look after Amma.'

Our families left after Muralie told them to be proud of their daughters and assured them that he would take good care of us. He then handed me an aerogram: 'I want you to write a letter to your father, taking full responsibility for your actions,' he said. 'I feel so sorry for your mother.'

'I thought you were on my side, Muralie anna.'

Muralie laughed. 'Yes, I am, but that doesn't mean I approve of what you've done,' he said. I knew he was only teasing, because of his tone. Muralie always spoke to me that way.

Later that afternoon, Muralie and Thileepan arrived at Ruby Auntie's house.

'I really thought this was the last day you'd be with us,' remarked Thileepan, as he sat down on one of the cane chairs on the verandah.

'Don't underestimate them,' said Muralie, winking at me.

I felt relieved. I had worried that my tears would have been considered a sign of weakness.

'You survived today, but this is not the end of the challenges you'll face,' said Thileepan seriously. 'It's just the beginning.'

Ajanthi and I had very little to do in the daytime, other than to assist the women from the neighbourhood, who gathered at the house in the mornings. They cooked two meals a day and these were taken on bicycles by their daughters to the young Tiger men at the watchposts around the fort army barracks. I observed that the meals were of very poor quality—often dry *pittu* with badly prepared lentil curry for the mornings, and then red rice with pumpkin, beetroot or string-bean curry for dinner. Ajanthi and I helped the women wrap the meals first in plastic sheets and then in newspapers. By the time the meals were distributed at the watchposts, they would surely have started to spoil in Jaffna's humid heat. Although I disliked doing this work, I helped out only because I was concerned that Thileepan would hear of it. Our chances of being sent for training could depend on this.

Over the next ten days Thileepan, Muralie and Rasaak regularly visited Ajanthi and me at Ruby Auntie's, and our families visited us at the Tigers' main camp. Amma had abandoned her plans to return to Kandy as I knew she would. On the morning of the eleventh day, a skinny, sunburnt girl with large white teeth accompanied Thileepan and Muralie. She wore a simple home-made cotton dress, a pair of rubber slippers on her dusty feet and a nervous smile on her face. I wondered where she had come from to have dressed like this. Wearing rubber slippers in public was not something my mother would approve of and neither would Ajanthi's. 'Mithila will take you to a house where you'll remain until further notice,' said Thileepan.

I did not ask the questions I was dying to know the answers to—how long, where and why. Muralie had already warned me, 'No questions'.

'Stay strong,' Muralie said winking, leaving me to wonder what he meant. When we made our farewells, Ruby Auntie and Ajanthi were sobbing.

Ajanthi and I followed Mithila out of Jaffna town on our bicycles. Nearly half an hour later, we entered a narrow dirt lane flanked by houses surrounded by palmyra palm fences. These houses were typical of those outside Jaffna town—their large yards were dotted with mango, murunga and coconut trees, and jasmine, crossandra and hibiscus bushes. A sunburnt, sarong-clad old man squatted by the roadside picking his teeth with a twig while a skinny street mongrel lay asleep beside him. The village smelt of dusty humid air. The sun was scorching and I was extremely thirsty.

Finally Mithila stopped in front of the wooden gate of a haphazardly whitewashed, little brick house at the end of the laneway, and opened the gate. A small crowd of women and children had gathered in front of the house. Poverty was evident in the topless, barefooted children with runny noses. A large fishing net was spread out in the sandy front yard. We hopped off our bicycles and walked towards the crowd, fixed by their unrelenting gazes. As we approached, I realised that all thirteen of them were members of the one family—the parents and their eleven children still lived under the same roof. 'Come in,' said one of the younger women, smiling.

Inside the house, the smell of dust, dirt and food hit me all at once. There was a wooden bench and two seats in the middle of the front room. Otherwise the room was empty—no radio, television or books. The floor and walls were dirty, even though the house seemed to be only a few years old. We were led into one of the three rooms in the house; it was devoid of furniture, except for a few rolled grass mats leaning against the wall.

'Your whereabouts must remain a secret,' cautioned Mithila. 'I don't want you stepping out of the house without me.'

After Mithila left for the day, the others continued to stare at us. When the older woman served us lunch, everyone watched us eat and then followed us around the house. When we asked them to eat with us they claimed to have already eaten, but looking at the way the young children stared at our food, I wasn't so sure.

'What are we going to do here?' I asked Ajanthi in exasperation, when we were finally left alone at the end of the evening. 'I'm worried that Thileepan anna might forget us now that we are out of sight in this village, far from the city.'

'He won't,' replied Ajanthi offhandedly. 'Thileepan anna is testing us. And I think Mithila is his spy.'

I sat on the dirty cement floor and looked out of a large hole in the wall, set in a frame—the window panes hadn't been fitted. The coconut palms in the backyard swayed in the breeze. I suspected Ajanthi was right about our test—we should have been sent to a women's base, but instead we were here in a fisherman's house.

By now the sun had set and someone turned the lights on.

'Thank God they have electricity,' I observed.

In the morning I went into the backyard in search of the toilet. I had slept well, considering the new environment and having shared the floor with four women. I ducked under the clothesline tied across two coconut trees and passed the well, where an old man was having a shower. Then I saw the toilet at the far end of the yard.

I opened the door and was hit by a horrible, stomach-churning stench. There was a hole in the ground and under it a metal bucket filled with human excrement. Flies buzzed. Horrified, I shut the door and ran back to the house, trying not to throw up.

'Is there a ghost in the toilet?' asked Ajanthi.

'Worse!'

'It can't be that bad—I'm going there now.'

Ajanthi came back at a sprint. 'We have to eat and drink less and when Mithila takes us out use the toilets there,' she declared.

In the days that followed, Ajanthi and I had a few new experiences: being constantly stared at; having a shower in the open (at the well, fully clothed); making *beedies* by rolling coromandel leaves over tobacco for the wholesalers (the occupation of the women in the house); and communal living (sharing the two-bedroom house with thirteen people and a puppy).

The family and their neighbours attended to us meticulously. 'Thileepan told us you are from well-to-do families,' said one of the women. 'He wanted to make sure you are looked after.' I realised that the family members were not eating as well as what they served us. When we asked Mithila about this she told us that Thileepan was paying the family to feed us well but the family couldn't afford to eat the same. Since then both Ajanthi and I made sure the children shared our meals.

Twice a week we usually visited the Tigers' main camp near the university, five kilometres away, to see our visiting families. Each time, I had to battle my emotions when I saw Amma and Shirani. Although relatively calm these days, Amma never stopped asking me to come home and I never stopped feeling guilty for upsetting her. Some days, Mithila took us to Freedom Birds camps in different villages. The girls there worked in their communities, encouraging cottage industries, organising loans, and overseeing disputes. I realised why they didn't operate in my neighbourhood. There was little need and no one would take them seriously.

On other days, we stayed indoors and I read and re-read some books I had picked up at a garage where Mithila had taken us after I asked her for some reading material. By then I had re-read the collection of poetry books I had brought from home so many times I knew them all by heart, and I had become bored to tears by the weapons manuals given to me by Thileepan, which were his idea of reading material. At the back of someone's house in a village nearby, there had been a garage used by the Tigers to store manuals on ammunition and other reading matter. Here I had found some amazing books: *The Diary of Che Guevara*, *Mother* by Maxim Gorky, Mahmoud Darwish's Palestinian war poetry, and a collection of poems by local poets.

Meanwhile Ajanthi played with the stray puppy she had recently adopted. The dog stayed in the room with us and I often found myself rolling into puddles of dog urine in my sleep.

Almost two weeks passed without any word from Thileepan as to our immediate future. The war was intensifying and the government troops were advancing on the city, bombing and shelling everything in sight. I was beginning to feel frustrated and also worried for Amma's and Shirani's safety.

But Ajanthi always kept me focused: 'You need to learn to cope with boredom,' she once said. 'Otherwise, if you're ever imprisoned, you'll divulge all the information without torture—just to do something.'

The fourth of June was a typically warm, humid day with little breeze. Some of the women in the neighbourhood were seated on the steps by the front door—their fingers rolling *beedies* and their mouths at work making idle conversation.

'It's quite fun, you know—you should try it,' said Ajanthi, who was sitting with them and also wrapping *beedies*.

I was seated on a wooden bench outside under the mango tree, reading, until I saw the youngest boy—a child with Down syndrome, whom they called the 'Brainless One'—trying to pull one of his teeth out with a pair of pliers. Horrified, I realised then why many of his teeth were missing. 'I can't see how pulling my tooth out could be fun,' I said absent-mindedly.

'You idiot! Rolling a *beedi*, I mean.'

'I have no desire to learn a trade in the tobacco industry.'

'I'd like to see you being so self-righteous when you are old and can't fight any more, and lack the skills to earn a living. At least I could make one of these and smoke it.'

'I'll be dead by then.'

Then we heard a dreadful roar. For a moment it seemed everything went still as we all stopped and looked up at the clear sky. I strained my eyes against the strong sun and saw a large silver fighter plane, of a kind I had never seen before. My heart dropped into my stomach.

The next minute, panic set in and everyone frantically began to scramble towards the dugout in the front yard, pushing and shoving each other. Once the whole family had hurriedly filled the small, stuffy underground hole, huddled against each other, there was no room for Ajanthi and me. So we crouched on the dugout's steps that had been cut into the earth. Mud from the un-reinforced walls was sliding into the dugout, covering the occupants with red dust.

Now the roar grew louder as three more jets entered the skies. I was petrified. My heart was pounding heavily and sweat began to trickle down my face. In the next few minutes—but it felt like hours—we held our breaths and waited for the sound of exploding bombs. The planes hovered around for less than ten minutes and then, to our intense relief, suddenly disappeared.

When the roar of the planes' engines had completely died away, we came out into the open, still confused by what had just happened. All of us ran out into the street hoping to find someone who knew something.

Within seconds, the entire neighbourhood had gathered. Everyone had an opinion about what they thought had happened when suddenly someone shouted, 'It was the Indians! Because the Sri Lankan government sent back the ships carrying aid from India to Jaffna just two days ago, the Indians have now decided to airdrop their relief!'

Suddenly there was jubilation on the streets and cheers for the then Indian Prime Minister: 'Long Live Rajiv Gandhi!' someone shouted, and others joined in. I heard comments such as 'We can win Tamil Eelam with India's help' and 'India will never abandon us'.

'Here's some of the Indian bread that was airdropped,' I heard someone say, and everyone scrambled for it, swarming around the boy who held the loaf. After the crowds had dispersed, I asked the boy how he managed to get hold of it so soon. 'It was stale bread from my house,' he grinned. 'I just wanted to see how stupid these people were.'

In the days that followed, more relief came to Jaffna from India by both air and sea. A small contingent of the Indian military also arrived to oversee the distribution of aid. The war-weary people of Jaffna welcomed the officers with traditional garlands of jasmine and crossandra, hence the operation was named *Poomaalai* (garland of flowers). Suddenly, the sounds and smells of war ceased. There was a general feeling among the people that this meant the end of the fighting: the Indian government had intervened in our ethnic conflict and would now surely demand a just resolution. I wondered what this would mean for the Tigers.

Two days after the airdrop, Ajanthi and I received an urgent message from Thileepan. We were immediately expected with our belongings at the Freedom Birds head office, five kilometres north in a suburb called Kalviyankaadu. I was delighted at Thileepan's request, but apprehensive about his reasons. Now that India had intervened in the political conflict in Sri Lanka, the war would surely end. This meant there'd be no need for fighters and no use for us. Was Thileepan about to send us back home? I was unsure.

As we bid the family farewell, Ajanthi was sobbing once again.

Ajanthi and I rolled our bicycles along the short driveway leading to the head office. It was an imposing building with fancy brickwork, rose-pink paint and a red-tiled roof; the second storey was wrapped around by a balcony. The front yard was dotted with bushes of white pinwheel jasmine and orange blooms of ixora and crossandra.

We left our bicycles under the shade of a mango tree and walked to the house, eager for relief from the midday heat. A young girl, about sixteen or seventeen, wearing a checked shirt and knee-length skirt, with her hair in two plaits, stood at the door watching the street. She ignored us.

We walked through the wide-open front door to be greeted by a male voice on the radio singing: '*Nee munnaalae poanaa naa pinnaalae vaaraen . . .*' [You keep walking away and I'll keep following you . . .] Inside, a few teenage girls lounged about on the marble floor of the living room, all dressed like the girl at the door—in checked shirts, knee-length skirts and their hair in a pair of plaits. Ajanthi and I, in our eighties-style belted dresses and shoulder-length bobs, made our way through the otherwise empty house to the backyard.

'Over here!'

Among a group of girls by a fire under a mango tree, I spotted Akila, towering above most, with the lively, skinny Kaanchana next to her, waving at us. Ajanthi and I had already made their acquaintance when we used to visit Freedom Birds offices with Mithila. We had found it easier to relate to these two girls because they were from suburbs of Jaffna and had attended Vembadi Girls' College, a school at the centre of town. The others were mostly from rural villages. When we had met Kaanchana and Akila before they had been living at home and working in their community, like their fellow Freedom Bird members. Only the morning before, nearly sixty of them had received the same message from Thileepan as Ajanthi and me: to be at the Head Office with our belongings.

Akila poured tea into two plastic cups from the massive cauldron on the fire and handed them to us.

'I'm glad you made it to the house too,' said Kaanchana, her large, restless eyes flashing. Akila smiled and nodded.

'So, do we know why Thileepan wants us all here?' I asked generally, taking a sip of the sweet tea made with condensed milk.

'Thileepan hasn't confirmed this, but I think we are being sent for military training,' replied Kaanchana excitedly. 'All of us here have made it to the shortlist, I'm sure.'

Ajanthi and I looked at each other and smiled. I was relieved.

That evening, Kaanchana and Akila invited us to join them in the room they shared with four other girls upstairs. Like the rest of the house, it was devoid of furniture. There were six plastic shopping bags in a corner, which I assumed contained all that these six girls owned. Each one had nothing more in it than a couple of sets of clothes and a hairbrush.

'What's that foul smell?' asked Ajanthi, wrinkling her nose as we placed our leather bags in the corner. I had smelled something too.

87

'We noticed it when we arrived last night. It was too late to investigate then, but I did think it came from the wardrobe,' replied Akila. 'Perhaps it is better left unopened. We don't want to see any skeletons.'

But in the meantime Kaanchana had opened the doors of the built-ins. We were taken aback at the sight of a dirty, blood-soaked pile of shirts, trousers and sarongs.

'Some government soldiers were kept prisoner here before they were shot dead and I think these are their clothes,' said Kaanchana, shutting the doors. 'And before that, this used to be a TELO base. The bullet holes on the wall here are a result of a shootout between our boys and TELO. All the TELO members died of course.'

It made sense. I had heard that TELO only took the grandest houses for their bases. The thought of murders being carried out in this very room made my stomach heave.

'Don't look so grave, Niromi,' laughed Kaanchana, exposing her large front teeth. 'The murdered men were our enemies. It was either them or us. Would it make you feel better if these clothes were laundered?'

Everyone laughed.

We turned off the lights and lay down on the cold floor, crammed next to each other. The girls talked 'til they dropped off to sleep, but I kept thinking about those murders. I could not erase the images of young men—both Tamil and Sinhala—falling down dead onto this very floor I was now lying on. How could anyone shoot someone at such proximity, especially unarmed prisoners? Then I thought of Benjamin—he had met death in the same way as these soldiers: unarmed and defenceless. I hoped I would never be asked to carry out such a task by the Tigers. The only enemies I was prepared to shoot were faceless, armed and in uniform, somewhere out there trying to destroy me and my people. I did not want them to be in civilian clothes, or in the same room as me.

Over the next few days, uncertain of our future, we continued to live a confined existence within the house. After I expressed my total dislike for housework, most of my household duties were taken on by Akila, who assumed the role of my fairy godmother. I had no idea why, and I wasn't about to question her. At eighteen years of age, Akila was a highly respected, longstanding member of the Freedom Birds and she was well liked by Thileepan. Her friendship with Ajanthi and me gave us some status in the house.

Yet I found communal living hard to adjust to because of some of my housemates' lack of inhibition—they did not bother to flush the toilet after themselves and peered through the bathroom windows while someone was having a shower. Worst of all, they stole my underwear and Ajanthi's sandals.

'You must understand that many of these girls hail from rural areas,' said Kaanchana, seeing me furious one day. I had just caught someone using my toothbrush. 'It's a shock to their system to go from mud huts to mansions.'

Thileepan and his assistants visited our house every day and spent a lot of time in the front room, which he used as his office, talking with some of the older girls, the founders of Freedom Birds. He oversaw the editorial committee of their monthly magazine and one day, much to my delight, he asked me to join the committee and contribute a regular column.

Now that visits from our families were prohibited, Thileepan had to deal with the parents of all new recruits at the head office. One day he remarked: 'You girls have strange families. Some come asking for your earrings or bicycles, but not for you. Others want to swap their son who has joined us for their daughter, reasoning that their son is more useful to them. And there are others, like Ajanthi's and Niromi's families, who are forever pestering for us to let you go.'

This news distressed me. The companionship of the girls around me had kept my mind off the world outside. Thileepan's words, however, brought back images of Amma and Shirani. They were taking longer to give up on me than I had anticipated.

On 9 June, Thileepan arrived at our base around 2am and asked us to gather in front of him. He was in his usual attire of a black-and-grey

striped shirt and black trousers; a thread hung loose from his sleeve and his hair was in a mess. His sixteen-year-old assistant, Navin, stood next to him in a crisp white shirt and blue jeans, with not one curly hair out of place.

'What kind of fighters are you going to make?' he complained, seeing us bleary-eyed.

'The ones who know the difference between night and day,' mumbled Kaanchana under her breath.

Then Thileepan announced something unexpected: that very night, he was sending us in small groups to Tiger watchposts outside various blockaded army barracks around the peninsula—for work experience, we assumed. I wondered about his reasons for this decision, but I remained silent, knowing he would prefer me not to ask. We had little idea of what was going on in the world outside our walls—our only source of information was Thileepan and he wasn't saying much.

Ajanthi and I were chosen for the watchposts around the fort army barracks with four other girls we hardly knew. Akila and Kaanchana were to remain at the head office, much to our disappointment. Thileepan instructed us that we were to spend our days assisting the men watching the army barracks, our evenings at the Freedom Birds' office learning first aid, and our nights at Ruby Auntie's house, where Ajanthi and I had begun our days as Tigers.

The following morning, as we prepared to head for watch duty, we received a message from Thileepan that we would not be starting at the fort watchposts until the following day. In the meantime, I was expected home for a short visit. We were perplexed, but did not question Thileepan's orders. There must be a reason why he thought it was important that I visit my family. I hoped it was nothing too serious.

I had mixed feelings about visiting home. As much as I was apprehensive about facing Amma, I did want to see Shirani and our dogs. When I opened the front gate after waving goodbye to Chitra, who had accompanied me, I saw Shirani out on the verandah wearing one of Amma's pale blue shift dresses, cut short and taken in. She ran towards me excitedly: 'Are you home for good?'

'No,' I said, hating myself for having to disappoint her. 'I just came for a visit.'

'Appamma is dead. I was just heading over to the funeral now.'

I was startled. Now I understood why Thileepan had sent me home.

'Appamma had been living with us for the past few weeks,' Shirani explained, surprising me. 'Her health began to fail after she hurt herself running to the bomb shelter during a raid. And, as you can imagine, Amma wanted to take care of her.'

So Amma had finally been granted her chance to prove herself a worthy daughter-in-law. It was what she had always longed for—to be recognised as the wife of the eldest of the sons, and allowed to perform her duties to her mother-in-law as she was entitled to. The responsibility of caring for an elderly parent always fell on the oldest son and, in the absence of my father, it was my mother's duty. Although another woman might have considered caring for her self-righteous mother-in-law a chore, it wasn't like Amma to think like that. I knew she would have considered this opportunity an honour, even though Appamma would have maintained her status in our home as if she was the head of the house, giving Amma orders—it was the house of her son, after all; she could assert her authority. I was glad that I had not been home to endure this strange interlude.

'Amma and I had to organise the undertakers and the transport of Appamma's body from the hospital to aunt's house,' said Shirani on our way to the viewing. 'The oldies expected me to do these things. I have no one to talk to—Amma is so upset all the time, and I have to look after her—it means a lot to me that you are here.'

I felt sorry for Shirani. She had just turned fourteen. But Shirani had always been good at taking care of Amma. Whenever Amma was unwell, Shirani had done the cooking and household chores and I had reluctantly helped her.

Shirani also warned me not to expect any of my aunts or cousins to speak to me at the funeral. 'They said they might have forgiven you if you had eloped with a low-caste boy.'

'Then it's such a shame I didn't,' I said, and we both laughed out loud. It felt good to be able to laugh with her again.

A small crowd of friends, neighbours and relatives had gathered at my aunt's house. As soon as I stepped in through the front door, the rosary recital stopped. Everyone was now staring at me, whispering and pointing their fingers. I looked at Appamma's body as she lay in a silk-lined oak coffin in the middle of the living room, dressed in a white silk sari. Her pale fingers held a rosary that had been sent to her by one of her daughters when she had visited Lourdes a year before. A transparent plastic vial containing holy water, also from Lourdes, in the shape of the Virgin Mary and with a blue-halo screw-top, sat beside her.

Appamma looked like she was asleep. I recognised the look of pride that had been ever-present on her face. She had good reason to be proud: widowed young, she had raised single-handedly her eight children to be well-educated, successful individuals who, with only two exceptions—one of them my father—she had married to arranged suitors. Appamma had certainly been an independent and capable woman, never relying on her affluent children for support, and preferring to return home after visiting them, whether in London or Sydney.

I now understood why my father had wanted Shirani and me to grow up under her influence. It was unfortunate that I had not been the recipient of her better qualities. However, perhaps without intending to, Appamma had instilled in me a strong sense of justice and, along with it, pride and determination—traditional qualities of an authentic Jaffna Tamil woman. For that reason, I felt immense gratitude towards her.

It was then that I realised that, as much as I felt alien in her house, it was because of Appamma that I belonged in Jaffna, the land of her ancestors and therefore mine. The irony of it brought a smile to my face.

I looked up to find all eyes still on me. Feeling that I had momentarily stolen the spotlight from Appamma, I walked out onto the back verandah, following Shirani. There I found Amma, resting on a chair beside the pergola of climbing jasmine. When she saw me, she burst into tears. I tried not to show any sign of undue empathy, which I knew would be mistaken for weakness and seized upon as a sign that I was prepared to relent.

Amma became hysterical: 'I can't cope any more. Everyone including your father is blaming me. You are so selfish!'

I stood in silence while Amma carried on accusing me of causing so much unhappiness in the family. 'We had been a happy family until you ruined it all for us,' she cried. 'Your father says he's never coming back until I get you back home.'

One of my father's cousins, Uncle Robert, took me aside after trying to calm Amma down and failing. 'Look, Niromi, what you are doing is honourable—but you *are* being selfish, forgetting your responsibility to your family. I'm a Tiger supporter and do a lot of community work for them back in our country town. I didn't have to run away to do this because I am still someone's father and someone's husband. My responsibility to them comes first. You are someone's daughter, Niromi.'

I liked Uncle Robert, so I listened to him without uttering a word in response. Although I saw the logic in his advice, I took no notice of it: that great man, Ernesto Che Guevara, had said that 'the true revolutionary is guided by great feelings of love', not selfishness. To think that my responsibility was only to my family would be more selfish.

Uncle Robert and my family and friends would never understand this because the only thing they were worried about these days was obtaining permanent visas to Australia, Canada or Europe. From those countries they'd then fund, with their Deutsche Marks, francs, dollars and pounds, the freedom struggle fought by those whose families had given their blessings to value the lives of their fellow Tamils above their own.

7

A TIGER NAMED ROSHAN

At daybreak, the day after my grandmother's funeral, very excited by the prospect of being at the front-line, the six of us made our way on our bicycles through the city centre. Our destination—the Tiger watchposts surrounding the seventeenth-century Dutch seaside fort and the adjacent multi-storey telecommunications department building where my mother used to work, both of which were now army barracks—was three kilometres away. The city was still asleep, except for a few people on bicycles out on the street.

Hospital Road was lined with flame trees and had once been a major thoroughfare. But it had been left with more potholes than tar. And though the carpet of flame-coloured blossoms spread in front of us was a welcoming sight, as we passed through the town centre we could hardly believe the current state of the once-busy city—it had mostly been reduced to rubble. Crows perched on the ruins, cawing anxiously.

Only a year before I had come here with my friends to farewell our friend Shereena, who had been moving to Canada. Hospital Road had been crowded with ringing bicycles and tooting cars, shoppers streaming in and out of colourful sari shops, fragrant spice centres and haggling fruiterers, and music blaring from speakers.

Despite being burnt down by the troops during the 1983 riots and then bombed and shelled in early 1985, it had been rebuilt after the Tigers took control of Jaffna. Now the area resembled a ghost town.

As we approached the Tiger watchposts by Pannai beach, the road disappeared, so we alighted from our bicycles and rolled them over the planks that had been laid across the large craters created by aerial bombardment. Then we saw the first sign we were nearing the watchposts: three young boys, armed, prostrate on the ground, testing a self-loading rifle. I was astounded. These boys were merely children, no older than fifteen or sixteen, and some as young as nine or ten. They gave us the directions to where we could find the man in charge.

We turned into a narrow lane flanked by moringa trees infested with hairy caterpillars; from them dangled 'drumsticks', their distinctive pods. Soon, on one side, the trees disappeared, and were replaced with a tall concrete wall with sandbags stacked in front of it. The wall had tiny peepholes, through which the young Tiger boys were watching for any movement of the soldiers confined inside the fort barracks.

The air smelt of the sea as we arrived at one of the beachside bungalows set in the middle of a coconut grove along the seashore. However, another tall concrete wall blocked our view of the ocean. The houses surrounding the barracks and along the beach had been abandoned and were being used by Tigers keeping vigil: the barricaded soldiers were always trying to find ways to get out and infiltrate the city. Although these homes were nestled in the most idyllic spots among swaying palms on the golden sandy beach, they were badly damaged—riddled with bullet holes, their roofs and windows broken. Some houses had been reduced to rubble.

On the porch of one of the less damaged houses, a few young, baby-faced boys were lounging on stacked sandbags. They were armed with a range of heavy weapons—from AK-47s to G3s. These weapons were as big as some of the boys. I wondered why *Muli* Shankar, Muralie and then Thileepan had been calling us young— these boys were far younger than us. Perhaps our age was not the real issue and they actually thought us 'sheltered' or naive.

One of the boys rose to his feet and approached us. 'Who are you?' he asked.

'Thileepan anna sent us here,' explained one of the girls in our group. At twenty-one, she was the oldest among us and this automatically gave her the authority to appoint herself our spokesperson.

'You need to see Roshan anna. He's in charge of these watch-posts,' said the boy, fiddling with the black thread that held his *kuppie* around his neck. 'He's out at the moment, so I'll send him a message.'

I wondered if this was the same Roshan who had come demanding Upstairs Auntie's house the year before. Since that incident, I had frequently seen him drive at high speed around my neighbourhood, beeping at me whenever I was on my own, something I ignored. Whenever I was with my friends on our bicycles as a group, he would swerve his black pick-up truck at us. Then he would laugh out loud when he saw us nearly crash in fright by the side of the road.

'Roshan anna is on his way,' said a boy with a walkie-talkie in his hand. 'Just warning you—the man has a foul temper and swears too much.' The other boys laughed and nodded in agreement. 'So what brings you here?'

'Thileepan anna wanted us exposed to the front-line before our training commences,' replied the oldest girl, though she was just guessing.

'Front-line exposure,' repeated the boy with a sigh. 'It's not what you think it is. No one knows or cares who we are until we die. Then they print a poster with our picture on it. Not our own poster, mind you—just lumped with the lot that died that month. Stick them on lampposts—that's all there is to our lives. You see the big shots on the streets riding their motorbikes, jeeps and all—they're the ones who acquire titles at their death and fanfare at their funerals.'

The others nodded in agreement. I was astounded at the boy's honesty.

'But then,' he added, 'I suppose your experience might be different, because girls are better taken care of than us.'

'I haven't seen my Amma in three years, because I'm from Batti-caloa,' said another. 'All my requests for leave have gone unanswered.

It's like blowing a horn at the deaf. If nothing changes over the next month, I'll have to do it the only way I can—give *thundu* [a resignation note].'

We were awkwardly silent. Tall coconut palms swayed in the sea breeze, making a swishing sound.

There were many such moving stories from the boys. I felt sorry for them. At an age when life should be carefree, they were carrying the burden of a nation. If only the adults were not so self-serving, children wouldn't have to take responsibility for claiming their own future.

'So what still keeps you all here?' asked Ajanthi in her cheerful voice.

'Probably Kittu anna,' said one of them. I had expected him to say it was the desire to save his people, or something along those lines. 'When he was Jaffna's lieutenant colonel, he often visited us with new sarongs and soap. But now that he's been injured and sent to India, I wonder how things will be.'

Just then we heard the telltale thump of a motorbike and all heads turned towards the laneway. Wearing the caramel shirt and black trousers I had seen him wear previously, and with his curly hair ruffled, Roshan left his motorbike by the side of the laneway and headed our way. But he walked straight to the house, just nodding in acknowledgment as he passed us. He showed no sign of recognising me and, to my surprise, I was disappointed.

The boys dispersed. We waited outside, unsure of what to do. Nearly ten minutes passed before Roshan came out to meet us, this time in a change of shirt and his hair neatly set in place. Leaning against the door frame and crossing his arms, he assessed us one by one, saying nothing. When it came to me, he swiftly moved his eyes from Ajanthi on my left to Dharani on my right. I was confused— why won't he look at me? Either he was rude or I was mistaken.

'Follow me,' he said abruptly and began to make his way down the front steps.

As I followed the others, I decided my first explanation had been correct—he was rude.

We walked through the beachside watchposts and discovered a vast network of trenches, burnt-out vegetation, large craters left by bombardment, and blood-stained walls. Empty cartridges, metal pieces, unexploded shells and large bombs littered the area. The air smelt musty from the damp hemp sandbags stacked along the way. Throughout all this, Roshan talked; he constantly warned us to follow his steps exactly, because parts of the track were marked with landmines, and he explained how the intersecting trenches connected the six major watchposts. Our role, in case of any attack, was to assist in removing the injured, so they could be transported to the nearby Jaffna hospital.

As we passed through various posts, armed young boys wolf-whistled at us, not doing their ferocious image any favours. 'Excuse them,' said Roshan. 'These boys haven't seen the outside world in months—in some cases years.'

All the while he spoke, he did not once look at me.

On returning to the original house-turned-watchpost, he split us into three pairs, and sent two of these off to nearby posts. That just left Dharani and me. He looked at my bright-eyed companion standing next to me and addressed her directly: 'You can stay here with me at this post. See you later.'

At this Roshan walked to his motorbike, leaving me furious.

Our mornings at the watchposts were spent hanging out at one of the empty houses at the post Roshan had allocated for Dharani and me, listening to gunfire, exploding artillery and the gentle sound of waves crashing on the shore as we chatted desultorily. The previous occupants must have fled with all of their belongings for the only things left in the house were some wall hooks. The boys at this watchpost occupied one of the neighbouring houses. By mid morning, everything became silent except for the sounds of unceasing waves and the swishing palms.

The young men complained bitterly about the quality and poor timing of the meals from Ruby Auntie's house delivered to them by Freedom Birds members, but ate them out of desperation and a lack of any alternative. For this reason it was hardly surprising when, one day, they risked their lives for a decent goat curry.

One morning, I saw some of the young boys gathered outside their house talking excitedly. When I came out to investigate, I realised they were watching and egging on two boys who were crawling towards a grassy plain about 100 metres away to our left. It was a no man's land since the army at the telecommunications building had a direct view over it. I was astounded when I realised the boys were heading towards two stray goats grazing there. Suddenly a few gunshots rang out in automatic—the soldiers had shot the goats.

'The army must have thought the goats were tigers,' laughed one of the boys standing beside me. 'They saved us the bother of killing them after capture.'

I asked why they hadn't shot them themselves. The boys explained that their bullets were rationed and each boy had to provide a weekly account of usage to Roshan—shooting goats wouldn't go down well with him.

Then we heard more gunshots. The soldiers had spotted the boys dragging the goats back and opened fire at them. The bullets hit the ground beside the two boys and raised dust, but the boys were determined. Cheered on by their fellow comrades, the two of them made it to safety with the goats and were treated to applause as if they were sporting heroes. Later that afternoon, an excellent spicy goat curry was sent to all the watchposts.

Contrary to my expectation, Roshan was hardly ever at our watchpost. He would arrive from time to time, spend an hour or two lying on a hammock tied between two coconut trees many metres away from the house where I was stationed, and then disappear. I was baffled as to how someone in charge of the watchpost could be mostly absent from it. I was also bothered by Roshan's indifference towards me. When I had first seen him on the streets, he had attempted to draw attention to himself but I had ignored him. Now he was ignoring me, and I could not stop thinking about him.

An encounter one morning changed everything, even though outwardly I carried on as though he did not exist. The twelve-hour days at the watchpost felt long as there was nothing for us to do and the boys mostly kept to themselves. Ajanthi and I were at least able to visit each other's watchposts twice a day, as we were only a five-minute walk away, but my sentry partner, Dharani, who was a year older than me, was a shy, quietly spoken girl and I found it difficult to keep conversation going with her for the rest of the time. On our third day, anticipating boredom, I had bought the newspaper and my walkman, which Shirani had brought for me during one of her earlier visits with Amma to the main camp. In the mid morning, a motorbike approached and the sound drowned out my walkman's Tamil movie song. Rasaak parked his red Yamaha 20 metres away from the house and made his way towards me, hopping over the network of trenches. Surprised, I rose to my feet and walked out to meet him.

'I won't ask how you knew that I was posted here,' I said, shielding my face from the strong sun.

'Don't then,' laughed Rasaak, now standing in front of me with one hand on his hip and the other sweeping away his straight hair that fell over his forehead. 'I took a detour on my way to carrying out an important errand, so I could see you. I'm sorry I haven't visited you all this time. After you left Ruby Auntie's house, Thileepan refused to tell me where he had moved you.'

Rasaak said Amma and Shirani continued to visit the main camp, despite being told they wouldn't be allowed to see me for many months. Hearing this news made me unhappy again.

We talked on for half an hour, before he had to go: 'I'll come back as soon as I have time,' he said. 'I want to make sure you are all right here. When I'm back, I want to see more weight on you. You won't be able to carry a weapon if you remain this skinny.'

This was a comment that I had endured all my life—at school my friends jokingly called me 'Miss Ethiopia'.

'No chance of that,' I said, laughing as I watched Rasaak stride back to his motorbike. 'Have you tried the food here?'

'What a fit body he has!' I heard Dharani comment quietly behind me.

When Rasaak visited the following day, he brought me some music tapes and asked me whether we were happy.

I immediately began to complain—Roshan was ignoring us and not teaching us how to handle weapons. The previous evening, on our way to first-aid class, the other girls had talked excitedly about having learnt to operate automatic rifles at their posts. Here, no one even spoke to us.

'I'll talk to him,' said Rasaak.

'No, don't do that,' I said quickly. 'I'm told he has a foul temper.'

Rasaak tossed his head back and laughed, 'I'll have to bring in my 50-calibre to teach you then,' he said and turned on the ignition and kickstarted the motorbike.

I headed back to the house. But when I realised that the motorbike had not yet left, I looked through the window and saw Rasaak talking to Roshan. I picked up a newspaper and sat down on a sandbag opposite Dharani, hoping that he wasn't telling Roshan about my complaint.

Minutes later I heard footsteps approach the house. I looked up to find Roshan standing in front of me, with both his hands in his pockets. He tilted his head slightly to the right, as though he were speaking with a child: 'What did you tell Rasaak?'

My heart sank. Luckily, he continued without expecting an answer: 'I wish you had come to me about wanting to learn to use firearms. We don't need a third person between us. I didn't want to teach an innocent girl like you to kill people. But if that's what you want, it's fine by me—I'll do anything to make you happy.'

'That's okay,' I said blushing, aware of Dharani's presence in the room. 'I can see that you are busy.'

'I'm never too busy for you, I say,' he said, smiling. I noticed a small chip in one of his front teeth. 'All you need to do is to ask. In future, come straight to me. I don't want to hear it from others—understood?'

I nodded, realising that this was the first time we had spoken to each other.

'I've got to go now, but I'll teach you how to operate an AK rifle this afternoon.'

As he made his way out the door, Roshan turned around for a moment and glanced at me sideways. Then he disappeared.

'I'm never too busy for you, I say,' I murmured scornfully, making Dharani laugh.

'I think he has a crush on you.'

'Whatever makes you think that, Dharani?' I barked at her. 'He's been ignoring me 'til now, and all he talked about were firearms. That sure sounded romantic.'

'Don't get all upset with me. It's plainly obvious.'

'I'm not interested in such an arrogant man.'

'I didn't say you were,' said Dharani and went back to reading the paper. I was certain I could see a smirk on her face. That annoyed me.

True to his word, Roshan returned that afternoon carrying an AK. He sat cross-legged on the floor in front of us. 'Before I begin, I'd like to know your names,' he said like a new schoolteacher. 'I'm Roshan.'

The man finally introduces himself a week after we first met him here at the watchpost, I thought.

We told him our *noms de guerre*. 'Shenuka,' I said when it was my turn. Thileepan had asked us to choose our own when we first arrived at the women's base. Despite Ajanthi's warning that most of our comrades wouldn't pronounce it right, I decided on this Sinhala name simply because I liked it. Ajanthi chose her mother's name. The list had been submitted to Prabhakaran, who approved most of the names and changed Pistol, Rocket, Artillery and Bazooka to more conventional female names, like Prema, Radha, Arthy and Bama.

'But I will call you Niromi,' said Roshan to me, ignoring Dharani.

I was baffled. How did he know my real name? I did not realise then that he had known everything about me, for nearly a couple of years.

'Please call me by my *nom de guerre*, Roshan anna.'

He laughed and picked up the rifle. 'Okay, Niromi. As you know this is an AK-47,' he said. 'T-56 and AKMS are variations on the 47 model.'

That night, as I lay on my mat, I caught myself thinking of Roshan. Then I wondered why I was thinking about him. I could not possibly be attracted to him; he wasn't suave or friendly like some of the boys I knew from school. In fact, he was their opposite. I concluded that perhaps my attraction towards him was merely a distraction. Roshan was like 'a shade in the sun'—keeping me amused during these boring days, nothing more.

One morning in mid June, about a week after we had arrived at the watchpost, Rasaak appeared on his motorbike, shouting, 'Happy birthday, Niromi!' as Ajanthi and I were heading to my post. The sea breeze had died down and, despite the shade of the palm trees, I felt the heat.

'Thanks. How did you know?'

'Your mother sent a feast to our main camp for you. But the boys devoured it before I even heard about it. I'm really sorry.'

In Sri Lanka birthdays were an occasion to be made a huge fuss over and were celebrated with much enthusiasm. For my birthday, every single year up 'til then, Amma had always made an elaborate cake and held a lunch party for my relatives and a tea party for my friends. This would be the first time that I had not had a cake, party or presents.

Just then I saw Roshan a few metres away lying on his hammock with his hands locked behind his head, watching us. It was unusual for him to be here this early. Sunlight filtered through the swaying coconut palms, casting fluid patterns over his bare chest.

Our eyes locked. It sent my heart racing.

I turned back to Rasaak, trying to ignore Roshan. Rasaak must have seen Roshan too, for I sensed uneasiness in him.

'You have a nice birthday, if that's possible here,' he said hurriedly. 'I'll see you later.'

Ajanthi and I continued towards the house, stepping over the trenches.

'Niromi, Roshan is coming this way,' whispered Ajanthi.

'Niromi, wait! I have to speak with you,' called out Roshan, walking towards us.

Ajanthi headed to the house alone. I stopped and turned to face him, crossing my arms. I did not like his commanding tone. His shirt hung loosely over his shoulders, unbuttoned, exposing his chest. Most men would consider that inappropriate in front of a woman, but not Roshan.

'Is it your birthday today?'

He stopped on the other side of the trench. Sand trickled from beneath his feet, into the digging.

'Yes.'

'Why didn't you tell me?'

'Was I supposed to make an official announcement?'

'I didn't say that,' he said, lowering his eyes. 'But what's wrong with letting me know, I say.'

'Why would I come up to you and tell you that it's my birthday? I don't even know you,' I said. I was feeling flattered, but I didn't like it—it seemed that he was far too much in control of my emotions already.

'It would've made me happy to hear it from you,' he said, thrusting his hands into his pockets. 'You could've at least given me that.'

'Now that you know about it, what are you planning to do? Throw a party?' I asked laughing.

'Perhaps if the circumstances were different I would have made the day a real celebration. But I could still get you a small present.'

I was taken aback at the sincerity of his tone. I had thought we were engaged in banter.

'I don't want anything from you,' I said hurriedly and headed to the house, feeling my heart flutter. When I reached the front door, I turned around to find him gone.

'What's the matter with him?' asked Ajanthi.

'Ah, he just wanted to know if it was my birthday today.'

'I think he likes you.'
I shrugged. 'Who cares?'

Some hours later, Little Anton, the youngest boy in our company, was at the door. He was carrying a large jug and some tumblers. The AK slung on his shoulder scraped the ground behind him.

'*Falooda* everyone!' he announced.

'What's the occasion?' asked Ajanthi.

'Roshan anna organised it,' replied the ten-year-old as he poured the cold milkshake mixed with rose syrup, mint leaves and tapioca seeds into the tumblers. 'All the guards have received their share.'

'Roshan anna is in a very happy mood today it seems,' added one of the other boys. Ajanthi looked at me and I turned to Roshan, who had just walked in through the front door.

'What's the special occasion, Roshan anna?' I asked casually, holding in the smile that threatened to break out on my lips.

'Nothing,' he said grinning at me.

After the young boys had left, Roshan opened his wallet, pulled out a pocket-sized laminated picture and handed it to me. 'This is very dear to me, and it's my birthday gift to you.'

It was a picture of Ernesto Che Guevara. 'How did you know that I was an admirer?' I asked, pleasantly surprised.

'I didn't. But I admire the man greatly.'

'In that case, you should keep it.'

'Don't disappoint me twice in one day,' said Roshan, looking forlorn. 'I want you to think of me whenever you look at it.'

'Don't get your hopes up,' I said laughing. I was feeling more relaxed now that there were only the three of us in the house. No one was going to tell on us.

'And there's another thing I want you to remember,' said Roshan, this time sounding serious. 'My birthday is on the second of December.'

I sat on the floor of our watch house, trying to write a poem honouring the lives of the boys at the watchposts. It was a particularly warm afternoon and the sea breeze carried the heat inside the house. Dharani had gone over to visit Ajanthi and her companion at their post leaving me on my own. I thought about the young boys' comments on our first day here—how they might end up as one of the faces on a poster. Then I remembered seeing Roshan looking at one of the twenty-two young faces on a poster stuck on the wall inside the house—one among many others there. This one had been titled 'Fallen Heroes of April 1987'.

I heard footsteps approaching the house and knew they were Roshan's. None of the other boys at this post wore sandals—some wore rubber slippers; the others went barefoot. My heart began to race, but I did not look up. My eyes fixed on a single word on my notepad, while all my other senses became acutely aware of his presence in the room.

'I've been meaning to talk to you, alone,' he said.

I felt a thousand butterflies take flight in my stomach. Hiding my anxiety, I casually looked up at him. He looked equally nervous.

'You may have noticed that I feel differently towards you,' he said as his voice dropped to a whisper. 'It's a feeling that I haven't felt for any other girl.'

Little droplets of perspiration appeared on his forehead. Our eyes locked and I tried to inhale, but it was as if there was no air around me.

Moments ticked past before I caught the sight of an armed boy walking by at a distance. I realised where we were. I did not want Roshan to say anything more because, if he did, I would have to acknowledge his feelings and respond. It would seal my fate—once a commitment was made, Tamil society expected it to be honoured with a marriage one day. The only commitment I was prepared to make was to the freedom struggle. I had been single-minded about it until now; I did not want to ruin it by becoming someone's girlfriend. In an organisation where relationships were frowned upon and required the approval of our leader Prabhakaran Veluppillai, now a married man with children, I wanted to earn my kudos first. Besides, Roshan was all wrong for me; my family would never approve of him. I did not want to end up with him and humiliate my family even further. My father's family would say that I had joined the Tigers for some Hindu, low-caste man and not to fight for Tamil Eelam.

'Is that why you've been ignoring me, Roshan anna?' I asked teasingly, hoping to change the mood.

It worked. He laughed, and I breathed a sigh of relief. I knew the moment had passed.

'I never did that,' he protested.

'So you have a poor memory, in addition to the bad temper I've been warned about.'

Roshan looked surprised. 'That's not true. But whatever I am, everything changes when I see you . . .'

Just then, to my relief, Ajanthi and the other two girls walked into the house.

'So I hope you remember the three classic firing positions I taught you yesterday,' Roshan said, trying to appear casual. 'No Rambo-style shoot-outs.'

The girls smiled at me, knowingly.

When we arrived at my watchpost at dawn the following day, some of the boys were brushing their teeth and splashing water at one another at an outside tap, the only source of running water. Seeing Roshan among them brought a smile to my face. He was wearing a pair of shorts and a towel on his shoulder. His brown skin glistened in the morning light, exposing his toned body.

Dharani went into the house and I decided to go up the stairs along the side of the house to watch the sunrise. As the first floor was in direct view of the Telecom army barracks, I sat halfway up the stairs and looked out to the sea, over the concrete wall. The gentle morning breeze carried the sea smell to the shore. Behind the diving seabirds and gigantic, menacing naval vessels, the sun was just rising out of the water to its full glory.

'I'm glad to see you this morning.'

I jumped with a start and turned to find Roshan at the bottom of the stairs. Blood rushed to my face. 'The helicopters fired here all night. I didn't get a wink. Did you have a good night's sleep?'

My eyes met his. It set my heart racing again.

'Yes,' I said flatly, having instantly lost my ability to think.

'Can I read the poem you were writing the other day?' he asked after a few minutes of silence. 'What is it about?'

I told him.

'I lost a friend in a battle last April,' he said. 'He was chosen for the ambush in my place while I was out.'

'Oh.' So that was why he had been looking at that poster so intently.

'I'll be at the Pannai seaside watchpost this afternoon. Please come and see me with your poem . . . I love your name, Niromi.'

'Please call me by my *nom de guerre*.'

'You are Niromi to me. It's the real you that I want.'

My lips seemed to be stuck together. I began to feel anxious about our being seen together on our own, fearing it might trigger gossip and lead to my expulsion. Roshan did not seem to care for his own reputation—he didn't have to. He had been a Tiger for four years now, since Black July 1983—long enough to prove his loyalty. I, on the other hand, had joined the organisation proper only four weeks earlier. I rose to my feet and went down the stairs, passing Roshan. When I stepped into the house, I did not look back.

By mid afternoon I had changed my mind and decided to take my poem to him. As I headed to the seaside watchpost where two of the other girls had also been stationed, Rasaak arrived. He paid us a visit at least once a day. At times he continued his dangerous work, detonating the unexploded 55-kilogram bombs that littered the ground around the watchposts; but, at other times, such as today, he did not even alight from his motorbike.

'Where are you off to? Want a lift?' he asked.

'Don't be cheeky,' I laughed. 'There are enough eyes here to make a *thahadu* [Tiger slang, meaning an accusation against somebody] against us and have us expelled.'

'You're a fast learner,' laughed Rasaak. 'How is Roshan treating you these days?'

'Okay. I'm on my way to see him now.'

'I see why you didn't want a lift,' said Rasaak, revving his motorbike. Then he drove away in a cloud of dust. I couldn't work out whether his tone was teasing, contemptuous or indifferent.

When I reached my destination after a ten-minute walk through houses turned into rubble, the boys stationed there pointed upstairs. I climbed up the stairs and knocked lightly on the door.

'Come in!' I heard Roshan say.

As I pushed the door open, the afternoon sun forced its way in behind me, lighting up the little room. There was a faint salty odour of sweat. Roshan lay on a mat on the polished concrete floor of the empty room, wearing only a pair of black jeans. A thin layer of perspiration covered his bare chest. He propped his head with his right arm and strained his eyes against the sunlight. I regretted walking into the room—I hadn't realised that he was all alone, and asleep 'til now.

When he saw the piece of paper in my hand, he reached his hand out to me. I noticed that his eyes lacked their usual spark. Without exchanging words, I gave him the piece of paper and walked out to the balcony. The vast Indian Ocean stretched in front of me, dotted with distant naval ships. The fear of random cannon charges meant that no one lived by the coast any more. I realised that the relative freedom of movement we enjoyed inland was only possible because the Tigers controlled it. Total freedom was nowhere nearby.

I turned around to find Roshan still in the same position, staring at my back. The piece of paper with the poem on it lay on the floor next to him. I wondered if he had read it, or whether he had been looking at my rear the entire time.

'What did you think of it, Roshan anna?'

'It's good,' he replied in a tone that was hardly convincing. 'You could do with less use of cliché. Can I keep it?'

Although I was taken aback by his forthright comment, I had already noticed that he seemed uncharacteristically melancholy in my presence.

'I'll rewrite it and bring it back to you,' I replied and walked over and crouched beside him to pick up the piece of paper, all the while feeling his gaze on me.

In that split second, I suddenly felt the small room turn into a furnace. My pulse quickened. I raised my eyes and met his; I felt my blood drain away from me. Neither of us spoke. His lips slightly parted, as if he was about to say something, and a thin film of saliva glistened on his bottom lip. I thought I could feel the warmth of his breath on the wrist of my left hand.

I knew that this was the moment that could change everything. My body wanted to collapse and submit to the situation, but my mind was saying *No*—a definite *No*.

I wilfully averted my eyes, rose to my feet and walked out of the room. I went down the stairs quickly, nearly stumbling over the steps, still feeling weak at the knees.

'Was Roshan anna okay?' asked one of the boys when I reached the bottom of the steps, catching my breath. The girls Duwaraka and Sanjika were talking with them.

'Not his usual self. Why do you ask?'

'We're guessing that today is his last day here at the watchposts,' replied the boy. 'An hour ago we had a visit from someone from the senior ranks, and there were some discussions.'

Resisting the urge to run back upstairs to see Roshan, I said goodbye to the boys and headed back to my post with the girls, still feeling lightheaded. It was nearly time to head back to the Freedom Birds' HQ for our first-aid course.

That evening, while we were at the Freedom Birds' head office, Thileepan informed us—without giving a reason—that there would be no more visits to the watchpost. He was sending someone to fetch our belongings. All the girls sent to various watchposts around the peninsula would also be called back. I wondered if this had anything to do with India's presence in the country on a diplomatic mission, but I did not ask him.

After just over two weeks, our time at the fort watchposts came to an abrupt end. 'We didn't even get to say goodbye, or thank those wonderful boys,' said Dharani later that evening.

'Thileepan anna doesn't see the point,' replied Ajanthi, wiping her tears away.

I realised then how much I had looked forward to visiting the watchposts every day, even if it was life-threatening. As much as I did not want to admit it to myself, I knew it was because of Roshan. I did not know if I'd ever see him again. But for now the only thing I needed to worry about was what my future in the Tigers was to be: being sent home or to a military-style training base.

8

A MILITARY-STYLE TRAINING BASE

Over the next couple of days, Thileepan recalled all the girls back to the Kalviyankaadu Freedom Birds HQ. Now nearly one hundred of us occupied two large houses in the neighbourhood, including a young girl of fourteen years.

'What's that child doing here?' I exclaimed, seeing the girl in the backyard picking flowers. She was Shirani's age.

'She's the daughter of Tiger *Panna kaai* [Top fruit], Bashir Kaka,' began Kaanchana, trying hard to appear sincere. 'I think Thileepan convinced him to send her into training. So now we have her to represent the Muslim minority—and you to represent the Christian minority.' The rest of them were Hindu.

'And you must be the representative of the know-it-all majority!' Ajanthi teased her back, making us laugh.

One day ten armed female Tigers, all of them in their early twenties, arrived from their base camps. These female militants had been housed separately from the Freedom Birds since their return from India, where they had been trained. While nearly ninety young women had trained initially, only about sixty of them now remained—many had deserted or married. Although Thileepan gave us no information, we suspected that we were about to be sent for training because these women from the military wing wouldn't be with us otherwise. Our group was therefore to have the honour of being the first group of Tiger women to be trained on home soil.

With the absence of Roshan and an uncertain future, I had been feeling melancholy, but this possibility gave me a sense of elation and anticipation. We guessed it was likely that these new arrivals—who spoke in strange eastern and western provincial Tamil accents, their hair in two braids and strutting around in their checked shirts, denim jeans, chest-holsters and automatic rifles—would be in charge of our training program. Although I found them friendly, I thought their speech distasteful—they spoke to us with great familiarity (using singular pronouns!) and swore without inhibition, neither of which I had been familiar with until then. No one I knew spoke that way.

One evening, Thileepan asked us, the would-be trainees, to queue up outside a room in a house down the road. Our enigmatic leader, Prabhakaran—or Anna (older brother) as we called him—who had been in exile in south India until a few months earlier, was to interview us, one on one.

Prabhakaran had returned to Jaffna six months earlier in January 1987, via an illegal boat trip after the relationship of convenience between the Indian government and the Tamil militant groups stationed there had begun to sour. Misusing the patronage offered to them by the central and state governments and the people of India since 1983, many of the militant groups engaged in criminal activities. After a PLOTE leader shot and killed two local men over a fight for an auto-rickshaw, the presence of these groups in India became public knowledge and India could no longer pretend to Sri Lanka that it did not foster the Tamil militants on its soil. As a show of its stance India began to clamp down on the militant groups, arresting some of the leaders, confiscating their ammunition and communications equipment and closing down the training camps that it originally helped to set up. While other militant leaders were apprehended, Prabhakaran protested his innocence and, backed by India's Tamil Nadu state government, emerged as the most powerful of the militant leaders.

Yet, paranoid that the central Indian government might assassinate him to show allegiance to the Sri Lankan government, Prabhakaran returned to his homeland. Jaffna was safer for him now, as his men effectively controlled the peninsula, performing military and civil administration. Perhaps now Prabhakaran would tell us where all the political manoeuvring was heading and what it meant for us.

I walked into the room as if I was about to meet God: there was no doubt that Prabhakaran was our saviour, our hero. He was going to save the Tamils from destruction and gain for us an independent homeland.

The small room was warm, and dull in the twilight. Prabhakaran sat behind a desk in a short-sleeved white shirt and black trousers. His large, dark eyes glistened in the golden light of the hurricane lamp on the table. The hollows of his round plump face were in partial shadow, giving him an eerie aura.

'Sit down,' he said, pointing to the chair across the table. 'How is it that you and your friend were born only fifteen days apart?'

Prabhakaran smiled widely, making me feel that, after all, the fearsome guerrilla leader was only human. I sat on the edge of the sagging Dutch-style woven chair and smiled uncertainly, unsure if it was a statement or a question.

'I know that Muralie recruited you and your friend from SOLT,' Prabhakaran continued, waving his stubby hands. 'You'll be the first two SOLT members to go for military training. I want you to set an example for others with your dedication to the organisation.'

'Yes, Anna.'

I could feel bedbugs biting at the back of my thighs.

'I congratulate you and your friend for joining the movement because your neighbourhood is one of the most difficult for us to recruit from. Most girls here are from rural towns, where they're used to hard work, from pounding rice to chopping fire wood. You wouldn't be used to such things, so no doubt training is going to be hard for you. Are you prepared for that?'

'Yes, Anna.'

I could feel the bugs tasting my blood now. I resisted the urge to jump out of my seat.

'Muralie spoke very highly of you and I'm confident that, despite being brought up in a well-to-do family, you'll withstand the rigorous training. Is there anything more you'd like to discuss?'

I understood that this last question translated as 'Do you have a boyfriend?' because the senior girls had warned us that Prabhakaran did not tolerate secrets and, in particular, romantic relationships among his followers. He reserved the ultimate decision on who married who.

'About boys . . .' I began, now wriggling in my seat.

'You're too young to think about boys,' interrupted Prabhakaran. 'At your age, your only focus should be fighting for Tamil Eelam and that's all you should think about.'

But all I was thinking about at that moment was the feast the bedbugs were going to have that evening—there were another eighty young girls still queued up outside the door.

'Don't hesitate to kill yourselves with this at the earliest opportunity,' joked Thileepan as he distributed the cyanide capsules to our long line. 'Because the coveted title of first female Tiger martyr is still up for grabs.'

Stars were beginning to appear in the twilight sky, and the noise of croaking frogs swelled in a well nearby. A thousand zizzing mosquitoes, and the cloying fragrance of crossandra and jasmine, besieged us. Thileepan's bodyguards stood outside the gates, chatting beside four Toyota HiAce vans and a pick-up truck. There was a sense of anticipation in the air. Although Thileepan, as usual, had told us nothing, we knew our destination was a training base somewhere. It was the way the Tigers operated: the less you knew, the safer everyone was. My inquisitive nature had all but vanished over the past few months.

After handing out the *kuppies*, Thileepan took some submachine guns (SMGs) from the back of the pick-up truck and began to hand them out. There were only twenty of them, so I felt honoured to receive one and accepted it with reverence. Holding my very own lethal weapon sent a shiver down my spine. But the feeling of pride did not last long.

'Don't try shooting helicopters with those things,' laughed one of the senior girls.

'And wait 'til the enemy is tapping you on your shoulders,' commented another. 'Or you'll hit no one with them.'

The senior girls giggled because they had heavy weapons, AKs and M16s; I understood that our SMGs were much inferior.

'Treat them like your boyfriends,' Thileepan said. 'Don't let them out of your sight, even in your sleep.'

'But I never had a boyfriend,' murmured Kaanchana.

'We aren't allowed one,' I whispered.

'And as if we'd ever get to sleep with them,' added Ajanthi.

'Shh . . . enough of your complaints already,' cautioned Akila. 'Thileepan anna has never been anyone's boyfriend either—he was just drawing an analogy.'

'Oh, really? Sorry, we took it literally,' mocked Kaanchana, making us laugh.

All 120 of us were loaded into the five vehicles with our weapons and our belongings in a shopping bag each. Ajanthi and I had our leather bags. I was in a van driven by Thileepan, and filled, as we all were, with quiet anticipation. Thileepan drove in total darkness, without headlights, through backstreets where there were no streetlights, to avoid being fired upon by helicopter gunships. Due to the fuel embargo, motor vehicles hardly operated in Jaffna now, and the few that did belonged to the Tigers. In order to minimise our time on the road, Thileepan drove at high speed through streets full of potholes—quite a feat, considering his poor eyesight. The other vans followed.

Nearly an hour and a half later, the vans turned onto what sounded like a gravel road and then came to halt after a few minutes more. A tractor stood across the road and an armed young man greeted us.

'*Chari* girls, do your training well and make me proud,' said Thileepan as he helped us into the trailer attached to the tractor. 'When you return, I hope you'll continue working for the movement in a different way than you're used to.'

Although I could hardly see Thileepan's face in the dim moonlight, I felt the emotion packed into his voice. As the head of the Tigers' political wing, Thileepan had guided the Freedom Birds since their inception. After many years in waiting, now these girls were leaving to become Tigresses. I thought that Thileepan must feel like a proud father.

But for some reason, I also felt sorry for him then. He worked tirelessly day and night, and took hardly any care of himself. He was all skin and bone—he had lost most of his large intestine in a battle injury and had difficulty eating. He was mostly serious, and he behaved so responsibly all of the time that it was easy to forget that he was only twenty-six years old. He was a great example of a fine Tiger.

'Thileepan anna is a softie,' remarked Kaanchana.

The tractor started on its way and we waved to the receding silhouettes of Thileepan and his bodyguards behind the screen of dust. We held on for dear life as the tractor lurched up and down on the uneven road.

About twenty minutes into the journey, our nostrils were filled with the sweet smell of ripening and rotting mangoes. It was pitch dark around us. Finally, the tractor came to a sudden halt in front of a large farmhouse. A hurricane lantern hung from the ceiling on the verandah, and beneath it a few boys were seated on the floor.

'Come on, boys!' shouted our driver. '*Makkal* have arrived!' *Makkal* [people] was a slang word used by the Tigers in reference to their untrained female counterparts. The boys stirred themselves and left the premises, disappearing into the dark, possibly to another house on a nearby farm, leaving this farmhouse all to ourselves. Because this was now an all-female training base these boys would guard the outer periphery of it.

Soon after our arrival, the base's female commander, Theeba, announced that all of us were being rostered onto half-hour sentry duty starting that night; Ajanthi and I were rostered on at 2am. The twenty-four-year-old Theeba had graduated from training in India at the top of her class. She and our co-commander, Sugi, looked the part in their military-style camouflage uniforms and red berets, with their pistols tucked into their hip holsters. We all proceeded to find places on the floor of the old farmhouse where we could sleep until woken up for sentry duty.

At dawn, I could see at last that the house was set in the middle of a vast mango orchard and that adjacent to it was a coconut grove. I wondered whether the Tigers had received this property as a donation, or taken it by force.

We were each rationed to one cup of water in the morning, for brushing our teeth and washing with, because there was hardly any water in the four-metre-deep well and it needed to service the entire camp for at least six months. We were instructed to build twelve huts, using sticks, dry coconut palms, ropes and some primitive tools. After two days, we completed this work and then our camouflage uniforms, sarongs and grass mats were rationed out. We were now ready to commence training.

It began on 1 July, at five o'clock in the morning with a wash at the well using a cup of water; then we proceeded to the coconut grove for our oath of loyalty. The very first time I repeated the oath after Theeba, my hair stood on end. I had dreamt of this moment for many months now. I already knew it by heart, having watched videos of training camps on the Tigers' television channel:

I dedicate my heart, body and soul to fight for the sacred cause of our revolutionary movement, which is to attain a free, democratic Tamil nation and, as I say this, I wholeheartedly accept the guidance of our leader Prabhakaran and promise that I will dutifully work for him with honesty and dedication, and begin my training. Tigers thirst for Tamil Eelam motherland!

The oath was followed by a gruelling four-hour exercise regime. A standard breakfast of boiled red beans and a cup of sugary tea were served mid morning. We had no cutlery or water to wash our hands and plates afterwards. Until midday, we worked on building a commando base and digging trenches around the encampment. After a lunch of red rice with beetroot or pumpkin curry, our lessons commenced under the large canopy of a mango tree, followed by target practice. Dinner was always vegetable semolina pilaf. While the entire training base was run by young women, lessons on politics, explosives and combat tactics were provided by visiting male instructors. I enjoyed these lessons more than the physical training, but most of my comrades slept through them.

'Can you repeat what I said five minutes ago?' Yogi Yogaratnam, our politics lecturer, once asked a girl he had caught sleeping during the lessons. He was popularly known as Yogi Master within the organisation.

'In 1948 we attained freedom,' replied the bleary-eyed girl.

'Then what the hell are you fighting for?' barked Yogi Master, making us laugh. He punished us all with fifty sit-ups on the spot.

The senior girls were not comfortable issuing punishment and we got away with receiving only a few reluctant beatings with serrated-edged palmyra leaf stems, or with a few hundred sit-ups or squats if we did not accurately carry out their orders. I was only punished once, with 200 squats in the middle of the night, for not taking one of my boots with me into the trenches during a midnight alert whistle, unable to find it in the dark. Outside of training sessions the senior girls, without exception, were sociable and kind to us. In general, everyone at the camp got on well with each other but remained in small cliques, generally determined by which part of Jaffna peninsula we were from.

During our rest time, we were allocated light duties around the base—sweeping the ground, peeling coconuts or occasionally slaughtering a goat for lunch or dinner—which Prabhakaran ordered to be added to our vegetarian menu after hearing how many had fainted during training sessions. Knowing my reluctance to participate in this last task, my vegetarian fairy godmother, Akila, took my place at the slaughter when the senior girls weren't looking.

One sunny morning I was outside the farmhouse on leaf-sweeping duty when suddenly a jeep and a van drove in at high speed. They came to a screeching halt in front of the house, sending dust and my pile of dry leaves into the air. I was annoyed until I saw Prabhakaran and his entourage of bodyguards step out of the vehicles.

'Keep up the good work,' said Prabhakaran to me, smiling as he walked to the house.

I nodded politely, wondering if their reason for their speed and the abrupt halt inside a safe compound was just to show off!

That afternoon chocolates and sweet treats were rationed out.

'Anna is just like a father to us,' Akila said. I was shelling the husks off coconuts with an iron rod at the time—and Akila was peeling off the fibre when I had finished.

'Well, he's too young to be your father,' commented Kaanchana. 'Or maybe you're too old.'

'Look who is talking, *kilavi* [old woman]. You're so ancient that you should be kept in a museum.' At nineteen years of age, Kaanchana was the oldest one of the four of us.

'I'll show you who the *kilavi* is,' said Kaanchana and chased after Akila, who ran off. But as she did, she hastily threw away the coconut in her hand, hitting one of the trainees and knocking her down. We were given extra chores for a week as punishment.

Prabhakaran visited us regularly with his entourage of bodyguards and he sometimes stayed overnight at the farmhouse. His wife Madhivadhani and their two young children—three-year-old son Charles Anthony and one-year-old daughter Dhuwaraka—accompanied him at times. Prabhakaran would supervise our training regime, particularly target practice. He showed keen interest in making us good shots, often displaying his accuracy and encouraging us to aim for perfection. Although I did not find any of my bullets on the target on the first two days I soon improved, hitting the bulls-eye a few times, and earned a brand new AK-MS, which was awarded only to the top twenty shooters.

Prabhakaran also spoke to us at length about topics that mattered to him, discipline and Tamil Eelam, and we listened admiringly to his monologues. A self-trained man, he wanted us to develop exceptional patience and mental strength which he claimed to have achieved as a young boy by staying inside a sack in the sun all day (no ordinary achievement, considering Jaffna's heat), by inserting needles under his fingernails and by torturing insects. He knew he was one day going to fight the Sinhala regime, he said. He had grown up seeing the discrimination against Tamils that began eight years before he was born, in 1954. Luckily, he did not expect such displays of commitment from us.

Prabhakaran criticised the Tamils who had fled overseas, calling them traitors. 'When we achieve Tamil Eelam, they'll be back and I'll settle them in border towns where they'll suffer in the hands of their Sinhalese neighbours,' he said. 'That'll be their punishment for abandoning the fight.' We laughed, not realising it was these 'overseas traitors' who were funding our fight, including our uniforms and weapons. He was also passionate about Hinduism; about equality in caste, education and gender; and about building a Tamil nation, where the purest form of the language would be exercised. It all sounded good to me, except for the Hinduism part; I hoped he was not expecting us to convert. The nuns had warned us against 'St Peter's syndrome'—Christians who, amid people of other religions, disown Jesus. Conversion was the worst sin of all, they said.

'I'm keen to involve you girls in the new Black Tiger Squad,' said Prabhakaran one day as the ninety-six of us sat in front of him on the dirt shaded by the canopy of a mango tree. The Jaffna commander, Kittu, who had lost his leg in the grenade attack eighteen months before, sat beside Prabhakaran on a chair, his crutches resting on the tree trunk. Only a week earlier, on 5 July, a twenty-one-year-old comrade called Miller had driven a lorry packed with explosives into Nelliyadi Army Barracks, in the first-ever Tiger suicide bombing attack. Prabhakaran had bestowed on him the title of 'captain' posthumously. Miller was the first ever Black Tiger, the suicide squad of Tigers. The whole concept was new to us.

Our training camp was located over 20 kilometres south of Jaffna in a region called Thenmaraadchi, and Nelliyadi, where the suicide attack had taken place, was in Vadamaraadchi, north of Jaffna. I wondered why the hostilities had resumed despite India's recent presence in the country. Perhaps they were only interested in supplying relief to the Tamils and not in solving the political problem. Typically, I did not question Prabhakaran about this—no one did, because that would be disrespectful.

'How many of you would like the opportunity to prove yourself as the true movement's faithful and become a hero of heroes?' Before Prabhakaran could finish his question, many voices around me shouted: 'Me', 'I', 'Can I?'

I turned around to find many raised hands and eager faces. Most of them were from Vadamaraadchi, where Prabhakaran hailed from. I looked at Ajanthi and Akila, and then Kaanchana. Their hands were resting on the rifles in their laps. I was relieved.

I tried to visualise what it must have been like for Miller to turn on the switch, knowing his young body was about to explode into smithereens and take many other lives with it. The thought sent a shiver down my spine. I understood the benefit of a suicide bomber—one militant could kill many soldiers, minimal outlay for maximum outcome. It also avoided unnecessary civilian casualty. I admired Miller's gallantry, and I wished I had his courage. However, I knew that there was no Black Tiger within me; I was not brave enough.

Prabhakaran laughed and continued. 'I'm glad to see that you are eager. Not everyone can become a Black Tiger though. I will hand-pick the ones with the inner strength and dedication of Captain Miller to carry out a task of that nature. Miller is a *maaveeran* [hero of heroes].'

I felt somewhat disappointed, knowing that I could never be a member of Prabhakaran's hand-picked, elite group.

'At the moment we have eight Black Tigers, all of them boys. Thiyaagu here is one of them.'

All heads turned admiringly to Thiyaagu, one of Prabhakaran's bodyguards. The tall, good-looking fellow smiled coyly. I had thought being Prabhakaran's bodyguard was a suicide mission enough.

'I would like you girls to complete your basic training before being considered for the squad. Speaking of dedication and courage, you might have heard that some well-known figures of our organisation were asked to resign recently for abuse of power. I reward *iyakka visuvaasihal* [the movement's faithful], those who tell on their comrades when they see them doing wrong. I hope that is a lesson to everyone.'

Then he named a few of those who had been dismissed or forced to resign, one of them being Rasaak. I was startled.

'I know this must come as a surprise to you,' continued Prabhakaran. 'Power is a potent drug, *makkal*. This is why I bestow ranks only posthumously. One joins a movement like ours to struggle for a common cause, no matter the personal loss.'

I wished Prabhakaran would be more specific about Rasaak's resignation instead of talking so generally. One of the girls, Dora, raised her hand and, much to my annoyance, changed the topic: 'Can Kittu anna, who was so successful in the field, give us some advice?'

Kittu, silent until then, smiled and murmured, 'What advice can a legless commander give budding fighters?' and said nothing more.

I heard Kaanchana mutter under her breath, 'How about a lecture on self pity?'

By the end of the second week of our training, dirt and grime had begun to build up under our fingernails, and then gradually on our skin, our uniforms, our plates and cups and everything we owned. Our heavy uniforms, which we never changed out of, smelt of stale sweat.

But now we were promised a wash and change of uniform. The wash, however, turned out to be a douse with half a very small bucket of muddy water at the well, followed by a brief rub with a bar of mud-caked soap, and then finished off with another half a bucket of muddy water before we made way for the next in line. One more bucket of muddy water was provided to each of us for washing our heavy uniform. I struggled with washing the heavy uniform when Akila once again came to my rescue, bargaining with another girl for her half bucket in exchange for doing one of her nights of sentry duty and washing my uniform for me in the extra supply of muddy water.

The primitive conditions at our training camp meant there were many accidents. Girls fell from the top of our makeshift climbing-pyramid, slipped off the climbing ropes, tumbled into the well and dugouts or ran face first into the wall of railway sleepers we were meant to climb over. Ajanthi managed to burn her eyebrows and some of her hair when she ran through the fire created after an explosion we set up. 'The idea is to wait for the fire to die down and enter under the cover of smoke,' our explosives lecturer explained to her afterwards. I was often found vomiting and disoriented after handling powerful explosives such as gelignite and TNT bare-handed, packing them into containers.

But I endured all of it, except for the toilet pit. The three-metre-deep regular army toilet was at the far end of the training base. You were meant to squat on the railway sleepers laid over the rectangular trench, which was fenced off by coconut palms. I was put off by the lack of privacy, by the smell and the noise as your own contributions caught up with their predecessors, and by the flies that nosedived into its abyss and then ascended to perch on my face.

One day I accidentally looked down and saw the large pool of faeces and urine, filled with wriggling huge maggots. Horrified, I ran outside and vomited. From then on, I ate only a tablespoon of my meals and emptied the rest onto Akila's plate when no one was looking. I'd never had a big appetite anyway.

Although everything we did at the camp was regimented, there were a few things I continued to enjoy: sleeping under the stars, Sunday afternoon entertainment, where I had the opportunity to write plays, act, sing and recite poetry with my friends; my secret journal, in which I wrote my own fiction by the light of the hurricane lamp when everyone was sound asleep (all reading materials, including newspapers, were prohibited); and thinking of Roshan during night-time sentry duty.

A month into our training, Prabhakaran redesigned our program to reduce commando training and lessons, and increase target practice and explosives lessons. We were not aware of the rapidly changing political climate outside our little world and had not noticed that over the past few weeks the skies had gone silent, except for the occasional helicopter. We did not understand the significance of the regular nightly congregations of Tiger political heavyweights at our base—Anton Balasingham, Yogi Master, Lawrence Thilakar, P. Nadesan and Thileepan. While they sat around a hurricane lamp on the verandah of the farmhouse and talked for hours on end—their deep discussion sometimes interrupted by loud laughter—we sat in front of our huts in total darkness, playing a game of 'guess the laugh' and not realising that history was in the making. Unbeknown to us, our lives were about to change forever.

One evening Prabhakaran called a meeting at the usual spot, under the mango tree in front of the farmhouse. His deputy, Mahathaya—whom the boys called *Mudhalai* [crocodile] behind his back—and Kittu sat on either side of him. While these two men kept an eye on us with a light grin plastered to their faces, Prabhakaran began speaking.

'Children, there has been a new development on the political scene . . .' He went on to say that the Indian government was facilitating a peace deal between the militants and the Sri Lankan government. Prabhakaran said that the Sri Lankan government had made a huge mistake in allowing the Indian government to intervene in the country's internal affairs. He believed that India was taking control of Sri Lanka and IPKF (Indian Peace Keeping Forces) deployment wasn't part of this plan. Years in India had taught him not to trust the Indian government because it was India which encouraged the militancy in this country, and now it pretended to play peacemaker.

'Like the Americans in Vietnam and the Russians in Afghanistan, the Indians in Tamil Eelam won't last,' said Prabhakaran. 'If they don't behave themselves, they'll learn a very sorry lesson.'

I was pleased to hear of the attempt at a peace deal facilitated by a third party, but felt that if Prabhakaran did not trust the Indians then the negotiations were bound to fail. 'Will we participate in elections?' questioned Theeba, our base commander. Only she or her co-commander Sugi had permission among the women to ask Prabhakaran a simple question without antagonising or undermining his authority in any way.

'I'm not a politician. That's Mahathaya's job,' replied Prabhakaran and laughed out loud, looking at Mahathaya. All heads turned to Mahathaya, whose grin turned into a contrived smile; but he said nothing. For a second I wondered if Mahathaya did not like what Prabhakaran had just said about him. Then I dismissed it—the men were cousins and childhood friends and no doubt understood each other well. Prabhakaran continued: 'Recently, three of your fathers have complained to the IPKF commander that we had kidnapped their daughters and provided training. The visiting international media got hold of the story and went public with it. It's unfairly given us a bad name. You know that none of you are held here against your will?'

I was glad my father was in Dubai so he couldn't have been one of them. I would have hated it if he had caused such grief to Prabhakaran.

Two days later, our training came to an abrupt end. After breakfast, we were ordered to change into our civilian clothes, pile our uniforms in the middle of the yard. Fifteen minutes later, we were packed like cattle into the back of the old lorry and driven out of the base. After enduring a nauseating half-hour trip—with little air, intense heat and the pungent smell of sweat and body odour—I was relieved when we suddenly jerked to a halt.

We had been dropped off at the town of Suthumalai. Here we followed Theeba along with masses of people all headed in one direction. None of us dared to ask where we were going. I was glad to be in the midst of civilisation—I had felt rather cut off from the real world at the training camp.

When we reached our destination, the Suthumalai sportsground, it was packed with tens of thousands of people, all eagerly facing in one direction. 'In a few minutes, there'll be some speeches,' said Theeba, stopping in the shade of a mango tree—it was a scorching hot day. 'I expect all of you to return promptly to this spot when they're over. Stay in groups and no talking to the public, even friends or relatives.'

There was a makeshift stage at one end of the grounds, which was occupied by senior officials from the IPKF, and by Prabhakaran and the Tigers' political leaders. We managed to nudge our way through the crowds to about 10 metres from the cordoned area in front of the stage, which was occupied by international journalists, camera crews, photographers and more IPKF officers.

'This is Anna's first ever public appearance,' said Kaanchana. 'No wonder there's such a massive turnout.'

As the speeches progressed, it became evident to us that a peace accord between the governments of Sri Lanka and India had been signed already. As a result, Tamil would be recognised as a national language alongside Sinhala, Tamils would have the chance to elect representatives for their autonomous north-east region and Tamil militants would receive amnesty and be expected to participate in the democratic process.

What we were witnessing was the historic first weapons surrender ceremony. But all this was news to us—Prabhakaran had said nothing to us about giving up our weapons. We'd only know the truth if our leaders briefed us privately—Thileepan had once warned us that the movement was not what it appeared on the outside. While my fellow trainees and I watched the podium, we did not wonder about the truth. As true foot soldiers we had become unquestioning of our leader, caring little for true knowledge and ready to do as ordered.

As a result, we were unaware that both the Tigers and the majority of the Sinhalese were against the signing of the Indo–Sri Lankan peace accord because they felt India was forcing the deal to maintain control of Sri Lanka's politics. In the south, the Sinhalese were staging mass protests and the Marxist Sinhala extremist group JVP (Janatha Vimukthi Peramuna) was becoming deadly, having assassinated leading Sinhala government politicians. The Sri Lankan government didn't trust the Tigers to surrender their weapons and made it a condition for releasing hundreds of Tamil political prisoners held in detention without charge for many years. As for the Tigers, they were reluctant to surrender arms while government-sponsored Sinhala settlement continued in the Tamil stronghold of the eastern provinces and unhappy about sharing power with formerly exiled militant groups such as TELO and EPRLF, who were now joining the political arena. Of course, at the heart of all these concerns was one overriding desire: Prabhakaran wanted the Tigers to be the sole representatives of the Sri Lankan Tamils and himself to be their unchallenged leader.

On the podium Prabhakaran rose to speak. He did not look his usual relaxed, confident self. I wondered if he was uncomfortable appearing in front of such a large gathering, after years of reclusiveness. Perhaps he was not pleased with the peace deal.

Prabhakaran spoke in pure Tamil in a moderate tone, looking uneasy. 'True peace is often elusive,' he said. It was in good faith that he had agreed to give up the armaments that had been used to defend the rights of the Tamils. He was now surrendering the wellbeing of the Tamils into the care of the Indian government.

When the masses applauded in response to this, I was certain I saw an expression of annoyance flash across Prabhakaran's face. While he said he was entering a peace deal, he nonetheless proclaimed that 'the struggle for Tamil Eelam will continue'.

We were growing very tired in the simmering heat. When the speeches finally ended, a few Tigers walked up onto the stage and, kissing their rifles, handed them over to an IPKF officer.

'Now I get it!' exclaimed Kaanchana. 'This is why Thileepan told us to treat our rifles like our boyfriends. You use it and abuse it, then kiss it goodbye before you hand it over to someone else.'

Just then I saw and recognised a black Isuzu pick-up truck parked on the periphery of the gathering and the man leaning against it, facing the stage. It was none other than Roshan. What a miracle—to have found Roshan in this ocean of people! My heart began to race.

But I quickly remembered the state I was in, and hid myself behind the other girls—I did not want him to see me, not with my skin caked in dirt and my hair covered in dust. Minutes later, I peeked in his direction but he was gone. Then I felt disappointed.

When the symbolic gesture of the arms surrender was over, we once again followed Theeba on foot. People stood along the sides of the road and watched us jog past in a single file. A brave citizen shouted, 'Now that your boys have surrendered their weapons, what are you poor girls to do but run, run, run for your dear lives!' This caused a cascade of laughter among the spectators.

That night, we were made to wait at an abandoned Portuguese-era mansion, which had once been the residence of Suthumalai's member of parliament, while Theeba attended a meeting with Prabhakaran. We were no longer certain about our future.

Finally Theeba arrived in her jeep and said: 'Girls, we have to return to the training base. You have a few more months of training to go yet.'

I was disappointed that we were heading back to the training base. The mere thought of the dirty uniforms and the hard work made me feel ill. And what about the peace accord and the arms surrender we had just witnessed? 'Just because that's what Anna said in public, it doesn't mean that is the truth of the matter,' reasoned Kaanchana.

Four hours later—on that warm moonless night—with the aid of a hurricane lamp we were searching for our uniforms among the huge, foul-smelling heap in front of the farmhouse. I managed to find some of my belongings, because I had marked them with my name, but the others picked out whatever they could find. Kaanchana and Ajanthi were pragmatic about having to wear someone else's dirty, smelly clothes.

It was 2.10am. We had just gone to sleep on our mats outside our huts when a loud whistle shrilled through the night. Within minutes we were sitting crossed-legged on the dirt outside the farmhouse, bleary-eyed once again. Prabhakaran sat on a wooden chair in front of us, flanked by his bodyguards. The flame of the hurricane lamp that hung on the branch of a mango tree nearby cast shadows on his face as it swung in the wind. The leaves rustled.

'How did Anna manage to have children if he's always surrounded by bodyguards?' whispered Kaanchana in my ear.

I observed Prabhakaran. The expression of annoyance I had seen as a momentary flash earlier in the day had now become permanent on his face.

'*Makkal*, what happened today might have come as a surprise to you,' he began. It certainly had, I thought. 'I have agreed to the peace accord under a few conditions: the northern and eastern provinces must be merged with limited autonomy and a referendum held one year later, and the Sinhala government must comply with agreed resettlements and release the Tamil political prisoners they are holding. But I doubt that they will honour these conditions.'

So he was sceptical. The deal was only a temporary measure, and our training would continue in the meantime.

'All our good ammunition was stashed prior to the surrender. We'll continue to hand over the rest.'

I was astounded. I thought of the young man who had kissed his rifle before handing it over to the IPKF. If I was an outsider, I would have believed in the Tigers' arms surrender and been sure that peace was here to stay.

Our training program resumed the next day and continued for a further two weeks. While the rest of the nation believed in the ceasefire, the arms surrender and the peace accord, we still had our AKs and SMGs with us.

'Things will be quiet on the battlefront for a while,' said

Prabhakaran, one afternoon, after coming to our camp and taking up his customary position under the mango tree. 'I'd like you to return home until such time as I need you again. I'm certain it will be no longer than a month or two. Keep in touch with our bases. For those who are unable to return home, I'll organise a base. The decision is totally yours.'

I was excited. I didn't have to make a decision: I wanted to return home. It was just for a month, and I could make my family and friends happy. Most of all, I could have decent showers, wear clean clothes and be rid of the scourge of the camp—head lice.

Two-thirds of the trainees were returning home. When I realised that Ajanthi, Kaanchana and Akila had decided to remain at the base, I was disappointed. 'I don't want to upset my family twice,' reasoned Ajanthi.

Around this time, Prabhakaran called me into his office in the farmhouse for a chat. 'I would like you to return home, although I'll leave it up to you to decide,' said Prabhakaran, when I sat in front of him. 'If you do, then pretend you've come home for good. I also want you to go back to school and educate other students about us. You'll probably be the one to face the most challenges when you return home, because the people in your suburb are all for this accord and have befriended the IPKF leadership in next to no time. They may even throw parties for the officers. Although you can't stop them, do your best to educate them. Keep in touch with Muralie, so you stay in the loop.'

When the time came for us to go our separate ways, my friends made a last-ditch attempt to convince me to remain with them. 'There's still time to change your mind,' sniffed Akila as I climbed into the van that was to take me home.

'If you are not back in a month, I'll find you and shoot you,' threatened Kaanchana. Ajanthi was crying into her hands again.

The van started on its way and I looked out the window and saw my waving friends growing smaller and smaller, then disappear completely into the coconut grove. The van sped along dirt lanes and finally made it onto a tarred road.

As we went, I thought of Roshan and the possibility of seeing him again—since the last time I had seen him at the watchposts around the fort two months earlier, I hadn't been able to shake him off my mind. Then I thought of Shirani and the surprise I was about to give her. It brought a smile to my face.

9

THERE'S STILL TIME TO CHANGE YOUR MIND

'My daughter is back!' exclaimed Appa as he opened the front door.

I had expected either Shirani or Amma to answer the door, to watch their faces bloom in surprise. Had I known that Appa was home from Dubai, I might have chosen to stay at the base with my friends and a head full of lice. His presence in the house would certainly make it difficult for me to keep in touch with the Tigers or to leave home when the fighting resumed.

Appa was by no means a tough man. He had never once spoken harshly to Shirani or me, but then we had never given him reason to. We respected and trusted his opinion on our clothes, hairstyles and how we conducted ourselves, and never once asked for anything—not even pocket money. He encouraged us academically and was proud of all our achievements—one of his most treasured possessions was a brochure advertising my role as conductor of our junior school orchestra.

By Jaffna's standards, Appa was a modern father—open-minded and forward-thinking. It was because of him that I had escaped a particularly embarrassing ritual when I reached puberty. At the onset of menstruation, many of my girlfriends, Hindu and Christian alike, were kept confined to their houses for two weeks and given daily doses of raw eggs and neem oil (which they believed balanced female hormones); at the end of this confinement a public ceremony was held, in which the girl was subjected to the rituals, crowds and costume of an elaborate Hindu wedding—but without a groom. Appa had reasoned with our disgruntled Amma: 'Look at the westerners—they don't make their daughters do such things.'

Appa had a penchant for the western way of life. He preferred the London *Telegraph* and the *Guardian* over any local newspapers; he enjoyed English music and movies; and had convinced our vegetarian Amma to make beef stews and baked dinners once a week, and while we ate them he taught us formal dinner-table etiquette. Appa could be highly persuasive about certain things, and he was particularly cynical about activities that offered no tangible reward. I had found this out about five years earlier, when he had applied his remarkable logic to make me give up my hobby of collecting pictures of the Indian Bollywood actress Sri Devi. I had returned home from school one day to find my treasured scrapbook of Sri Devi missing. 'Collect pictures of Mother Mary!' advised Appa, who was home on holidays at the time. He laughed as I stared at the empty space on my bookshelf in disbelief: 'At least she will know of your devotion and secure you a place in heaven. What is that Sri Devi going to do for you?'

Appa's list of other such Useless Activities included: reading novels, owning pets, watching Tamil movies or listening to Tamil songs (English movies and songs were okay, because they improved your language skills), painting, writing and singing (well, those were okay if you won some prizes for them). I had no doubt that 'fighting For Tamil Eelam' would certainly have made it onto that list. Neither he nor anyone in his family was particularly interested in politics, let alone in militancy. Other than Christianity, the only thing they believed in was gaining a higher education and self-improvement through hard work.

So when I returned home from the training camp and saw

Appa at the door, the thought of getting back on my bicycle and fleeing crossed my mind. But it was too late—I was locked in his embrace. Then Shirani's, then Amma's. Such displays of affection were extremely rare.

Within minutes, the news of my return had spread in the neighbourhood and all the Aunties on our street turned up to welcome me. 'We are so glad to have our Niromi back!' exclaimed Colombo Auntie. 'I'm throwing a dinner party at my house to celebrate, with Niromi's favourite *lumpries* and *vattilappam* on the menu!'

After months of eating poor-quality, mostly vegetarian food, the thought of ovenbaked rice and meat parcels wrapped in banana leaf and a fragrant dessert of jaggery and coconut milk custard made my mouth water.

By late afternoon, my family had taken me to three churches, just to be sure, and each time made me light candles and swear on the Bible never to return to the Tigers. I went along with it outwardly, having little control over the situation. In my mind, however, no one was going to jeopardise the allegiance I had sworn to Prabhakaran—not even God Almighty.

The mood at the party that evening was vastly different to that among the Tigers—everyone here was optimistic and jubilant about the peace accord. Munching on entrées of deep-fried meat and potato pastries, crumbed and fried spicy fish cutlets, and Dutch meatballs called *frikandels*, they talked as if they had won the lottery, their eyebrows raised and smiles wide.

In their eagerness to see the end of hostilities which nearly wiped them out only weeks earlier, these war-weary Tamils failed to see the political game that was being played out in front of them. Their desperate hope for a normal life made them blindly optimistic about the intentions of the parties to the accord, who they believed were genuinely committed to peace and to the welfare of the people. Even the moderates, having let the more extreme elements take control over their lives in the past, continued to be dangerously apathetic towards the country's political agenda. Peace was finally here and the Tamils were not about to question it. So thankfully, no one, including my parents, questioned my intentions either. They did not even ask me about my time with the Tigers or why Ajanthi had remained at the base camp. They were simply glad for the return of their prodigal daughter.

'This is no time-buying ceasefire. It's real peace. Can you believe it?' asked someone.

'I never thought Prabhakaran would agree to peace or to surrendering weapons. I must admit the man has gone up in my opinion,' remarked another.

I thought of Prabhakaran's words: 'All our good ammunition was stashed.' If only these people knew the truth. The Indian government was not to be trusted, Prabhakaran had said, and the war would resume. But I would say nothing to them—let them enjoy their temporary fantasy of permanent peace.

So when Ajanthi's mother and sister came to see me the next morning, I maintained the lie: Ajanthi had been given an important assignment in communications and was unable to return home, despite her desire to do so. 'It's okay, Niromi, you don't have to protect her,' said an intuitive Mala Auntie. I noticed that her eyes lacked their usual spark. She rarely smiled these days.

Jaffna was beginning to enjoy relative normality. The sounds of exploding bombs and gunfire had been replaced by Hindi, the foreign language spoken only by the Indian peace keepers. A few foreigners—even a few foolhardy Sinhalese, including Buddhist monks known as Bhikkus—entered the once-forbidden city. No one in Jaffna gave these Bhikkus any of the recognition or respect normally given to members of the clergy and they generally ignored their preaching. Most Tamils—as well as Buddhist moderates—believed that these socially and politically powerful clergy had poured petrol on the flame of ethnic division by preaching their unique Sri Lankan-style Buddhist extremism and intolerance, claiming Sri Lanka was a sacred land of Buddha and his followers, which were of course all Sinhala, and had sought to mobilise the mostly Buddhist Sinhala masses against the religious minorities such as Hindus, Christians and Muslims.

In 1959 the Bhikkus had taken responsibility for the assassination of the country's prime minister, Solomon Bandaranaike, because he failed to satisfy their Sinhala nationalist agenda. What he had done up to then hadn't been good enough for them—even though he had converted from Christianity to Buddhism, introduced the discriminatory *Sinhala Only Act* of 1956, and turned a blind eye to the Sinhala mobs during the 1958 anti-Tamil riots during which some 300 Tamils died. Now the Bhikkus were here in Jaffna, everyone said, trying to reclaim Jaffna for the Sinhalese. But there was little chance that would happen.

A week after my arrival from the training base in September, Appa decided that he would return to Dubai. He had come to Jaffna to rescue me from the Tigers and, now that I was safe at home, he felt confident I would remain there.

I felt relieved at this news. I was, however, unhappy about my family's decision to accompany Appa to Colombo, to see him off at the country's only international airport. Our visits to Colombo in the past had often been a month-long affair because Amma's extended family and her friends lived there. Since many of them were Sinhalese, they knew nothing about my connection with the Tigers and I would have to lie when they asked me about school and the rest of my life. And there was another thing: I guessed my parents would be making secret plans to enrol me in a boarding school in Colombo because, if I were them, that's exactly what I'd do.

My protests did not convince my parents to leave me behind, so I accompanied them unwillingly and tried to prove a point by being sullen all the time. Once in Colombo, Shirani did her best to cheer me up with various stories—she puzzled about why half-Dutch-Burgher Deidre Auntie used a tea-cosy despite the eternally hot Colombo weather; was amused by Latha Auntie's oh-so-light string-hoppers becoming airborne when the ceiling fan was turned on; and wondered about how the 'clever' Sinhala army weeded out the 'trouble-making' Jaffna Tamils from the other Tamils at Colombo checkpoints by asking them to repeat the name of the Sinhala town, Galkissa—unable to pronounce the sound 'Ga', the Jaffna Tamils called it 'Kalkissa'.

My parents, with the help of my aunts and cousins, tried to impose on me the material pleasures I had shunned over the past few months—visits to the hairdresser and beautician, and shopping. I hated every minute of it. The Tigers had preferred us females to have long hair, but despite my protests, my parents had my hair cut short again. As far as my family and society in general were concerned, I was still a child, at seventeen, with little control over even personal choices.

'Duwa [daughter], that pretty dress will suit your figure,' said Deidre Auntie in her native Sinhalese, picking a floral dress off the rack in a women's boutique. 'Unlike those boyish shirts you've taken a liking to lately.'

'Leave her alone, my dear,' said Uncle Raj to his wife, winking at me. 'She's allowed to wear what she wants to.'

'Am I too?' jumped in my young cousin Sonaali, seeing her opportunity. 'What about this mini skirt for me then, Thaathi?'

'You have mistaken a hanky for a skirt, Duwa,' observed Uncle Raj.

Some of my mother's friends tried a different incentive: 'My son Nimal would be keen to meet you', or, 'Asanka is going out with his friends tonight—why don't you join them?'

I did not care for pretty dresses or going out. Whatever their inducements, all I wanted was to return to Jaffna and to be there when the war resumed. I was never going to disappoint Prabhakaran, Ajanthi, Muralie or Thileepan. So I smiled politely, said nothing in reply and spent my time buried in a book or the newspaper.

When Appa waved us goodbye at the airport he was clearly holding back tears, and my sense of relief was momentarily replaced by sadness for him because I knew he'd rather remain in Sri Lanka. Nearly twenty years ago, Appa had been posted in Kandy on his first assignment as an engineer. Away from his family, he had met and fallen in love with my mother and married her shortly afterwards, against the wishes of his family. Even a couple of my schoolteachers had remarked how, as a well-known young cricketer, my handsome

Appa had been desired by many young women, who had been disappointed when he married an outsider.

I had long suspected that he had done so as an act of rebellion against the expectations placed on him by the high-achieving women of his family. Yet he wanted both Shirani and me to become like his mother and sisters because they were the very people he admired and respected. Their disapproval of his choice of wife must have been difficult to endure over nineteen years. Added to that was his concern over his two daughters' education and dowries, and then there was the matter of my latest behaviour. Now he was once again leaving for a country where he did not particularly enjoy living.

Dubai of the 1980s was a desert full of men from all over the world, building a new country founded on oil. While it ostentatiously displayed its wealth, this conservative Middle Eastern Arab country was no place for young women—even the locals kept theirs covered up, Appa said. Despite his well-paid, respect-earning career, which included a personal chef (who, Appa claimed, was a better cook than Amma) and a coveted alcohol permit, he was only there out of necessity, as were the fathers and older brothers of many of my friends who lived and worked away from their families.

As Appa walked into the airport's customs area and the door closed behind him, I stood there thinking that if we had our own independent homeland Tamil families would never have to be split up like this again.

Soon after Appa left for Dubai, Amma decided to return to Jaffna, believing peace was permanent. After all, the boys had surrendered their weapons, everyone said. I tried to hide my relief when we finally boarded the coach to Jaffna.

As I sat by the window with a book, I saw Ben, a boy I knew, with some friends outside the shops near the coach terminal. Someone had informed him that I was there. Ben and I had first met in Jaffna when he arrived as a refugee from Colombo after the Black July riots. He and his family had since returned to the capital, but he continued to write letters to me and returned to Jaffna during school holidays to see me. I liked Ben; he was my age, a nice boy from a good Catholic family who attended a private Catholic boys' school—the kind of boy my family approved of. But to me he was still a boy—carefree and wanting to hang out with his friends. The state of the country didn't seem to matter to him.

Now one of his friends approached my window: 'Ben is heartbroken that you joined the Tigers.'

I looked at Ben, who was standing at a distance watching me with forlorn eyes. It was like him—too shy to approach me himself, out of respect for my family.

'I'm more passionate about my duty to my people than to anything or anyone else,' I replied. 'Tell him it would make me happy if he too joined the Tigers.'

Then I turned my attention to the book I was reading. The bus started on its way to Jaffna.

'But he hates the Tigers,' I heard his friend yell out.

Soon after I arrived back in Jaffna, I visited Muralie to ensure he knew I was back. 'I thought we'd lost you,' said Muralie, looking pleased.

I told him that if it wasn't for my father, I would've visited him sooner.

Muralie said he understood, because it had been my father and Ajanthi's who had complained to the IPKF a while ago, that the Tigers had kidnapped their daughters. This news made me flush with embarrassment. Muralie and Thileepan had avoided going anywhere near the office because our fathers had stalked it, holding the two men responsible for the loss of their daughters, and pounced on them every time they saw them there.

But without Mauralie's help, I may have not returned to school. Initially Amma and I had sought permission from the school's principal but she had refused to re-admit me, reasoning that a prestigious private school such as hers could not have students who were militants. It was a far cry from only a year before, when my teachers and peers thought me a model student, and it had reduced Amma to tears.

'Don't worry, I know just the person to fix this,' I said to Amma, and I'd gone straight to Muralie. I was reinstated within ten minutes of his visit to the principal's office. No one defied the Tigers, even during peace time. All Muralie needed to do was to ask, although he did that behind closed doors, while I waited outside.

My friends had been welcoming, as if nothing had changed. Some were curious about my time as a Tiger, mostly asking to see the cyanide capsule that I continued to wear on the black thread around my neck, under my school uniform.

One school-day morning in mid-September Shirani and I sat down for breakfast, to find waffles with honey and banana in front of us again instead of the more traditional fare such as *pittu* with fruit, or fried eggplant and potatoes, or *dhosai* with coconut sambol, or string-hoppers with creamy *sodhi*.

'One more week of waffles and I am throwing that waffle-maker out,' said Shirani rolling her large eyes at Amma.

Amma had bought the waffle-iron during our trip to Colombo (an appliance never before seen in Jaffna until it was introduced by Colombo Auntie a year or so previously), and now we were having sweet waffles for breakfast and savoury waffles for dinner almost every day.

Amma laughed, tucking a strand of curly hair behind her ear, knowing Shirani would carry out her threat—only a month before she had set fire to Amma's favourite nightgown in the backyard after warning her that she would do so if Amma did not stop wearing the old thing. Luckily Amma was not in it at the time!

As I went to pick up my schoolbag, I heard a bicycle bell outside the gate. 'It's Muralie anna's assistant, Rajan,' shouted Shirani, looking out to the gate through the window. Then she asked me if they were twins. 'With those round faces and curly hair, they look so much alike.'

I replied that at eighteen Rajan was nearly eight years younger.

As I stepped out, Amma came to the door. 'Promise me that you will go to school.'

I promised. I had been back at school for barely two weeks now.

'Muralie anna wants to see you at the SOLT office now,' said Rajan.

When I arrived at his office, Muralie told me to sit down. 'Thileepan begins his hunger strike in a couple of days and I want SOLT members to mind the crowds at the venue. You'll be rostered on duty, given identification badges and further instructions. Anyway, while we wait for the other SOLT members to turn up, I'll let you pick the spot you want to mind.'

A few days earlier, I had been invited to a meeting held by Thileepan at the Freedom Birds' head office by Ruby Auntie's daughter Chitra, with whom I kept in regular contact. Like me, she too had returned home during the peace. At the meeting I had hoped to see my fellow trainees, in particular Ajanthi, Kaanchana and Akila, but none of them attended. I was told they were housed in the southern town of Chavakacheri, some 20 kilometres from Jaffna town centre, a significant distance considering the poor roads and transport. Although they were at an all-women base, they were dependent on the local Tiger men for every supply or piece of communication, and they required permission of their local area leader, Dinesh, to leave base or receive visitors. After realising this was the same Dinesh who was named *movement's faithful* by Prabhakaran for telling on his then area leader, I was glad to have chosen to return home—it sounded like my friends were under house arrest.

At the meeting, Thileepan had spoken excitedly about his impending hunger strike. 'We in the political wing don't have the opportunity to prove our commitment to the organisation,' he had said to the handful of young women gathered in front of him. 'This is my chance. I'm optimistic it will achieve something, whether I live or die. We must force the Indians out of our land.'

After Thileepan left, the girls told me that Prabhakaran had chosen Thileepan from a large number of volunteers, and that he'd had heavy competition. It made sense to me that the Tigers should now show their discontent of the peace accord by non-violent protests, but it made no sense that Thileepan was chosen for it—he was too physically fragile to withstand it and too intelligent to be sacrificed this way.

When the twenty-six-year-old Thileepan began his hunger strike, refusing food and water at Nallur Hindu Temple on 15 September 1987, I went straight there in my uniform, without the black-and-red striped tie that would identify my school, to begin my crowd-control duties. I watched Thileepan being welcomed onto the makeshift podium with Prabhakaran's deputy, Mahathaya, by his side.

The renowned Hindu temple dedicated to Lord Murugan, son of Shiva, sprawled across large grounds that had very little greenery. The grand entrance of the main temple was topped by an elaborate clock tower depicting many Hindu deities in various poses, and many other smaller towers. The outer walls of the temple were painted in large stripes of red and white. The Tigers had chosen this 700-year-old site due to its significance to the people of Jaffna. There were many speeches and Thileepan, in a white shirt and black trousers, took up his position on a seat and smiled at the masses who had turned out in support of him. The Tigers hoped that, in the minds of these people, Thileepan would be elevated to the state of a god.

I spent many eight-hour days at Thileepan's hunger strike. On the days I was rostered on for crowd-control duty, I would leave home in the mornings, pretending I was going to school and carrying my schoolbag; I returned home in the late afternoon, when school was finished. Although my teachers had a word with me about my frequent absences, they did not dare do anything about it, for fear of having to face the Tigers.

The crowds at the hunger strike were generally well behaved and required little 'controlling'. So, sheltering from the scorching sun by huddling against the walls of the temple, I spent my time watching vast numbers of people arrive in buses and trucks from distant villages to show their support, and listening to poignant songs played on the speakers or to the passionate sentiments expressed in very lengthy speeches. I kept an eye out for my comrades and for Roshan.

It had been nearly three weeks since I had returned from Colombo. I had not seen Ajanthi in that time and constantly scanned the crowds at the temple looking for her. I had seen Roshan once, but only fleetingly. He had been driving in the opposite direction to me as I was cycling along with a friend from school. Although he had stopped by the side of the road for me I had continued past, overcome by a sudden coyness that I regretted later. Now I hoped to see him to apologise for my behaviour.

One evening after crowd-control duty, I was about to go home when I heard a male voice call out my name from the crowd. Suddenly Roshan appeared in front of me, and rested his left arm on my bicycle handle. I felt out of breath and my heart began to race. Although I was thrilled to see him, I was once again engulfed by anxiety—there were too many prying eyes around us. 'Why did you ignore me the other day on Palaali Road?' he asked.

'I didn't see you until it was too late,' I mumbled. This was not what I had intended to say.

'Don't run away from me like that again. Don't I have the right to speak to you? I thought I was special to you.'

Butterflies fluttered in my stomach. I wondered where he got the idea that he was special to me. Perhaps he was testing me to see how I'd respond.

An awkward silence hung between us as he held my gaze. The hustle and bustle of the crowds seemed to have momentarily vanished around us. All I could see was him in the glow of the afternoon sun, and all I heard was my thumping heart.

Then I noticed his new clothes and sandals, his short haircut and the soft scent of an after-shave that surrounded him: 'Whatever happened to you, Roshan anna? You are a new person.'

He smiled. 'What do you think? Sometimes someone comes along in your life and inspires you.' He dropped his voice and continued, 'I find it hard to sleep or eat these days.'

I thought of Thileepan and said, 'Yes—me too.'

'You sit in my head day and night, and I can't focus on anything any more.'

I realised he wasn't talking about Thileepan. 'What do you mean?' I asked, knowing very well what he meant.

He said nothing in reply but kept looking at me. Being with him always made me feel incredibly nervous, but excited at the same time. That awkward silence returned between us again.

'I must go,' I said finally, not really wanting to leave him. But I did not know what else do to—we couldn't be seen talking like this. Neither my mother nor the Tigers would approve of it.

'When can I see you again?' he asked as I got on my bicycle.

'Don't you have anything better to do?'

'Other than movement work—no!' As I pedalled on my way, I heard him shout. 'I have to see you. Can you tell me when?'

'When fate has its way,' I shouted back.

One day as I was returning home from a Tiger meeting at the university, I saw Rasaak. He had called out my name from the verandah of one of the houses by the road, where he was playing cards with three other men. I remembered that he was no longer with the Tigers having been, as Prabhakaran had put it, forced to resign.

'How are you settling into civilian life after being the Tigers' 50-calibre Man for nearly four years?' I asked him as he walked towards me, closing the gate behind him. The Rasaak in front of me looked healthier and fresher than his former self, and yet there was a kind of world weariness in his eyes.

'Okay,' he replied without enthusiasm. 'I've been applying for driving jobs and spending quality time with my cousins who you saw on the verandah. We've all resigned from various movements, forming a Coalition of the Disenchanted, if you like.'

Rasaak invited me to his house around the corner. I deliberated for a moment as to whether I should accept or not. I had only known Rasaak as a Tiger; now that he wasn't one and I was, I was confused about how I should relate to him. I did not know what the Tigers' etiquette was about socialising with past members. Then I decided it was okay, it was a time of peace after all. Besides, we'd be out of prying eyes if I visited him at his house.

I pushed my bicycle as I walked with Rasaak. We turned into a nearby laneway and entered a lovely garden, dotted with coconut trees and bushes of jasmine, four o'clock flowers, crossandra, hibiscus and ixoras. At its centre was a modest bungalow.

'I still can't believe that you are not with the movement,' I said as he opened the front door. A lanky middle-aged woman in a sari popped her head from around the side of the house.

'Amma, can you make some tea for us?'

The woman smiled and nodded and disappeared.

Over a cup of sugary tea Rasaak denied knowing the real reason behind his expulsion. 'Many didn't expect it. I only resigned out of principle, because I was punished without being given a chance to explain. Someone had made a complaint that I frequented the fort watchposts too often after you girls were posted there, and that I was romantically involved with a female comrade.' Rasaak laughed, but his eyes betrayed his sadness. I recalled Roshan at the watchpost, staring from his hammock whenever Rasaak came to talk to us. I wondered if Roshan had anything to do with the complaint against Rasaak—but I said nothing.

Rasaak had been a dedicated man—to the cause and to the movement. Now, over a rumour, his dreams and ambitions had been shattered. To me, he seemed disillusioned and lost, and this made me sad. 'Please visit me whenever you can,' were the last words I heard from Rasaak. After I stepped out of his house that day, I never saw or heard from him again.

'Is Thileepan inviting Death? Does he need to, at this young age?' sang a female voice through the loudspeaker as I stood watch at the hunger strike. The lyrics of all the songs expressed the same sentiments:

Thileepan's dying wish was to see the foreign army, the IPKF, defeated. As Thileepan deteriorated right in front of our eyes, the emotional momentum around him was building rapidly. Women and children at the venue shed tears listening to the poignant sentiments expressed in songs and speeches. As the monsoon clouds gathered in the skies above Jaffna, I could feel the mood darkening.

One hot afternoon while on duty at Thileepan's hunger strike venue, I saw a large group of girls get down from a lorry and head my way to take their seats in front of the podium. Just as I realised they were my comrades, I saw Ajanthi. Calling out my name, she came running towards me. Behind her were Akila and Kaanchana. We embraced and shed tears of joy. I had not seen or heard from any of them since I'd left the training camp over a month before.

'I miss you very much,' said Ajanthi, tearfully. 'Why did you have to go home?'

'You must return to the base with us,' insisted Akila.

I noticed that the crowd was staring at us. Even Thileepan was watching us. Realising we had stolen the spotlight from him, I returned to my position and the girls sat down in front of the podium. I promised the girls I would join them as soon as there was a call from Prabhakaran, which should be any time soon.

As I headed home that evening I realised how much I missed my friends, especially Ajanthi. I missed her listening ear and the calm influence she had on me. I had so much to share with her. It was strange not doing everything together. I consoled myself that in a couple of more weeks I would be joining them again and that I could enjoy my relative freedom in the meantime.

A week after Thileepan began his hunger strike, Muralie acceded to my request that I might visit Thileepan up on the podium. By that point in time Thileepan had been lying on a bed placed on stage for a few days, having become too weak to sit up. He mostly kept his eyes closed. I could not imagine the excruciating agony he was going through. Apart from starving to death he also had no privacy, as he was surrounded by large crowds, bright lights and loud music 24 hours a day. It made me feel anxious that I might never see him again face to face. I wanted to say some encouraging words to him.

'I don't want to see any signs of weakness from you when you are up on stage,' warned Muralie as I headed towards the podium. 'I heard that you and your friends created a scene here the other day, crying and carrying on. When a fighter sheds a tear, he or she should do that in private. Only show your strong side to the public, then they'll trust you to do great things. Otherwise you are just a kid pretending to be fighter. That will not inspire any confidence in our movement.'

A voice sang through the loud speaker:

A sweet-smelling flower is withering
It cannot speak, it cannot walk
Will Thileepan anna's desire be satisfied?
Won't the foreign army flee?

As I climbed the steps to the podium, I wondered how Thileepan could bear to listen to this day and night. When I reached his side, I looked at the limp, helpless figure that lay in front of me. My heart broke into a thousand pieces—Thileepan was just skin and bone, his yellowing eyes were sunk into their sockets and his teeth protruded out of his hollow face. He resembled a dark skeleton. His dry lips were split in many places and saliva had dried around them, leaving a white stain.

I wanted to scream out loud that this was not the Thileepan I knew—not the man who had enlisted me, handed me my first rifle and *kuppie*, and who had never known the difference between day and night when it came to his dedication to the cause. Tears welled in my eyes and began to roll down my face. Words totally abandoned me.

Thileepan turned his eyes slowly towards me. 'Have you gone back to school?' he asked. His voice sounded like he was speaking from the depths of the earth. He could hardly move his lips, which seemed to have stuck to his teeth.

I felt as if I had forgotten any form of language I knew. I stood there, simply staring at him and sobbing.

'Don't spend all your time here. You need to get an education,' said Thileepan, whispering the words with great difficulty.

Just as a wail was about to break out from my throat, Muralie came up and ordered me to go home.

As I headed through the crowds I wondered why, of all the volunteers, Prabhakaran had chosen Thileepan for the hunger strike. Thileepan was going to die, there was no doubt about it. Prabhakaran must have believed that Thileepan's demands would be met and that he'd survive, because there was no way he'd have knowingly sent Thileepan to a slow, agonising death. Only a day before, my neighbourhood political analysis team of aunties were saying that the 'Tigers are getting desperate and that poor fellow Thileepan is just a pawn in the game'. I had dismissed their words.

Suddenly, a white van appeared from nowhere and screeched to a halt, almost knocking me down. Some bystanders screamed, thinking I was hit, but I had already recognised the driver. Roshan stuck his head out of the window and grinned: 'What do you think of my driving?'

'You'll find out when your van gets confiscated.' I walked away without expecting a response from him. I was in no mood for silliness when Thileepan lay there dying.

The following day, I only took to school my books for the first lesson. Muralie had informed me that a student rally was being organised for the day and he would personally come to our school to obtain permission from the principal so we could join in. My classmates all agreed that we should join the procession, except for one, the girl who sat next to me. Her father was the government agent (GA) of Jaffna district.

The position of government agent—a civil servant appointed by the central government to govern one of our country's twenty-five districts—was established by the British during the colonial era, and in the past it had been a prestigious position. But in 1987, being the GA of Jaffna was a hazardous job—he was viewed by some Tamils as the Sinhala government's representative and therefore as a traitor to the Tamil cause. The rally that day was planned to end outside his office, making demands to unconditionally release the Tamil students held in custody by the Sri Lankan government. These students had been captured over the past few years in different parts of the country. Many still had no charges against them. But my classmate said she did not want to protest against her father.

'Just because the GA is your father, you don't need to agree with everything he does,' I told her. 'At home he can be your father; but outside, he's the government's agent and you should treat him accordingly.'

Neither of us then knew that the GA only had a few months to live. Like the recent GAs before him, he was murdered by unidentified gunmen. Everyone suspected the Tigers to be the killers.

I sat close to the window in the biology laboratory, keeping an eye on the street below. 'Oh, there's the van!' I exclaimed when I saw the white Toyota arrive. All the girls ran to the window, dropping whatever they were doing so as to see Muralie. He climbed out of the passenger seat and, to my surprise, Roshan stepped out of the driver's seat. I hadn't realised they knew each other. As they walked towards the school gate, Roshan looked up and saw me and smiled.

'Now that must be Roshan,' giggled one of my friends. 'Legend has it that when King Rama walked into the city of Mithilai he looked up and saw Seeta at a balcony and it was love at first sight.'

The girls laughed.

'Sorry to say that he's not King Rama,' I replied. 'Nor I his Queen Seeta.'

'It's love nevertheless,' teased another.

My entire class, minus the GA's daughter, lined up near the school gate with most of the school population behind us. Minutes later Muralie and Roshan came out of the principal's office and walked towards the van. Seeing the two Tiger men created a lot of excitement among the girls.

'Wait 'til the boys' school joins you,' Muralie said.

Although I felt Roshan's eyes on me, I tried not to look at him while Muralie spoke. The two men then drove off.

Suddenly our music teacher came running towards us, her sari fluttering in the wind around her skinny frame. She was shouting hysterically, as if an artillery shell had hit her house. 'Children, you are a disgrace to our school! I know a man is dying out there, and you can go there after school and die with him for all I care. But I won't let you do it during school hours. Our principal has become the hand puppet of the Tigers. You girls will leave over my dead body!'

She was still alive when we joined the march with thousands of students from all over Jaffna. We walked in the stifling heat, shouting slogans until our voices gave out. When we reached the fort, which was now the barracks of the Indian peace keepers, I handed over to their commanding officer a petition on behalf of the students, as Muralie had requested me to do.

The procession then headed to the GA's office, back towards my school. Here, many student leaders, using a handheld microphone, spoke out against the presence of the Indian peace keepers in Jaffna. Suddenly Muralie thrust the microphone into my hands: 'Say a few words in English on behalf of the SOLT,' he said.

I was startled but I didn't want to disappoint Muralie, so I spoke of the need for students to unite together to show our collective power, even though we might be thought of as young and inexperienced. I concluded with the SOLT slogan, 'Let's fight for our education and let's educate ourselves to fight.'

I was flattered when I saw Muralie smile.

On our way back, I became separated from my friends. I was too tired to look for them, so I walked home, totally exhausted, looking forward to a cold shower and a nap. When I came out of the shower, Shirani was snapping her fingers and insisting '*You've gotta have faith!*', egged on by George Michael singing on the stereo.

Suddenly there was a male voice at the door: 'Is she home?'

Shirani and I went to the lounge room to investigate. I was taken aback to find Roshan at the open front door and Amma standing in front of him looking perplexed.

'Thank God you're here,' he sighed, seeing me. 'Why didn't you tell anyone you were going home?'

'Tell whom?' I asked, wondering how he knew where I lived. My friends would never have given that away.

He did not answer my question immediately. He looked at me for a few seconds, shaking his head. Amma returned to the dining room, keeping a watchful eye on us from a distance.

'Your friends told me you were missing. So I drove all the way back, finally ending up at your school. Then I decided to check here. And you're asking me "Tell whom?"'

'I'm sorry,' I said apologetically. 'But I don't know why they bothered you with it. I only lost them when I was a twenty-minute walk from home.'

Roshan looked confused for a moment, but recovered quickly. 'Either way, you shouldn't have walked in that hot sun. If only you had bothered to ask me, I would've driven you home.'

I laughed. 'It's the movement's vehicle and should not be used for private purposes.'

'You *are* in the movement—have you forgotten that already? *Chari*, I'll see you later.'

'Who is he?' asked Amma, as soon as Roshan left. 'He walks straight in, asking for you without having the courtesy to introduce himself. Isn't he the same man who came asking for our neighbour's house a while ago?'

I nodded. 'But I didn't know him then.'

The following morning Theeban's mother came knocking at the door with the day's newspaper in hand. 'Niromi's picture is in the paper,' she announced and handed it to Amma. It was a photograph of me handing the petition over. I looked at Amma. Her eyes were filled with tears, of either anger or disappointment, maybe both. I picked up my schoolbag and walked out of the house without uttering a word in response. Although I felt guilty for walking out on her, I told myself that I was no longer really answerable to her because I answered to the Tigers.

No sooner had I entered the classroom than all my friends had something to say. I had expected they would tease me about Roshan after he had taken their mock concern seriously and gone looking for me.

'I wish I had a boyfriend like yours,' one of them said, with a wide grin on her face. 'Even before I could finish telling Roshan anna that you were missing, the white Toyota vanished. Now that's love!'

'Couldn't you find anyone better than Roshan to go tell?' I asked, trying hard not to smile and pretending to be annoyed at them.

'No,' they replied in unison and laughed.

'I understand your disapproval of our course of action,' said one of them, pretending to be very serious. 'I was going to make an announcement that you were missing. And that we'd give you as a reward to anyone who found you. But these girls convinced me to tell Roshan instead.'

They laughed again, only stopping when our physics teacher walked in.

Saturday, 26 September was another hot and humid day. As I neared the Nallur Temple, I detected tension in the air. A sickening feeling rose in my stomach. I hurriedly locked my bicycle on the side of the road and pushed my way through the crowd towards the stage. Everyone else was also pushing and shoving to get nearer to the podium, raising dust everywhere. A voice through the loud speaker asked for calm. When I finally got close enough to see the stage, I saw someone examining Thileepan with a stethoscope. As the crowd anxiously waited, the man removed his stethoscope, touched Thileepan's feet with both hands and bowed as a sign of respect. One of Thileepan's assistants cried, '*Ayyo*, Thileepan anna . . .' and threw himself on top of his body.

Thileepan was dead.

My knees turned to jelly. I felt dizzy with the heat and from being crushed by the large wave of people who were wailing and pushing towards the stage.

I believed this was the tipping point for the Tigers. With his life Thileepan had paved the way for war.

'Everyone get away from the stage!' shouted the voice over the speaker. 'We need to take him to the hospital.'

I joined my comrades in forming a guard of honour along the path of the ambulance as it carried Thileepan's body out of the suburb to the General Hospital. By late evening, after an outpouring of grief, the crowd gradually dispersed. I returned home physically and emotionally exhausted, feeling the loss of a big brother.

Later that evening there was a knock at the door. It was Kaanchana and Ajanthi. A bus was waiting outside, in the laneway. They had managed to convince Amma that I was needed to play in Thileepan's funeral band. An hour later, the twenty of us in the bus were dropped by the side of the road, where an equal number of boys were practising the marching drill. I realised that Kaanchana and Ajanthi had told the truth—we were here to make music, not war.

In the dim light of the street lamps, I noticed a handsome young man with short curly hair, towering above everyone, striding towards us. He introduced himself to me as the leader of the marching squad. Then he took us to a house and showed us some instruments in a room. 'Ajanthi tells me that you were in your school band and played the piano accordion,' said the young man, looking at me. He hoped I would teach the band a tune or two. It had to be simple, because no one here had touched a musical instrument previously.

So, starting at midnight, I tried to teach my comrades *When the Saints Go Marching In* as we practised marching up and down the street, making a mighty racket until the early hours of the morning. But I failed in the attempt. It was only the next morning that I realised why no one had come out from the houses along the road to complain—we were the Tigers and no one was game enough to say anything against us.

Later that morning I was disgruntled to find the boys dressed smartly in black trousers and shirts with the Tiger emblem printed on the back, while we were wrapped in cheap, bright red traditional saris and midriff-exposing blouses. But I had to go along with it.

Starting on that day and for the next week, we accompanied Thileepan's funeral procession through every town and village in the Jaffna peninsula, under the scorching sun, clanking our instruments and drowning the wailing and lamenting that swept along the dusty streets. On the upside, the sound of the band was often gentler by midday, because many of the band members dropped like flies as we marched along. By the evening, we were often reduced by half.

Thileepan did not have a traditional Hindu cremation. Instead, his body was taken to the Jaffna University medical faculty, to which he had donated his body. As Tamils would say, he was worth a thousand gold in life and worth a thousand gold in death.

Amma, although unhappy to see me still literally marching to the Tigers' tune, was more than accommodating when I returned home at the end of each day. By not questioning me openly, she made it easier for me to ignore her silent tears. This allowed me to enjoy the best of all worlds while I lived at home—time with Ajanthi and my other comrades, as well as the companionship of my school friends and occasional chance meetings with Roshan.

In the days that followed Thileepan's funeral marches, an eerie silence prevailed over Jaffna. The Tigers and the IPKF appeared to be getting on well: they posed for press photos together and IPKF officers were invited to the weddings of some of the more prominent Tigers. Many mistook this silence for peace.

'Perhaps Thileepan died in vain,' said my neighbourhood political analysis team of aunties. 'The Tigers have no choice against the political pressure from Rajiv Gandhi.'

'Yes, Indian intervention has brought us peace like no other.'

I thought of Prabhakaran's words: 'War will resume in a month or two.'

Four weeks had already passed, so four weeks remained—at the most. Silence or peace? Whatever it was, I knew it wouldn't last forever.

10

I KNEW IT WOULDN'T LAST FOREVER

'All these dead men give me nightmares,' complained Shirani, watching me stick posters of Thileepan on my bedroom wall among the pictures of many other fallen Tiger heroes. 'Why can't you admire the living?'

Shirani's room was adorned with posters of Rick Astley, Madonna and George Michael. Although she liked Michael Jackson, he had been sidelined because his *Thriller* video had scared her.

'Do you realise the trouble I have gone to collect these?' I asked her. 'You can't just buy them, like posters of pop stars, you know.'

'I know the trouble you went to,' laughed Shirani. 'You got that tragic, Roshan anna, to source them—to drive all the way here and deliver them to you.'

She was right. Posters of Thileepan had been very hard to obtain because of his immense popularity, so I had paid a visit to Roshan's camp one afternoon. But it was Shirani's idea anyway. 'If anyone has curd in their hands and is searching for ghee, it's you. Why don't you ask Roshan anna?' she had suggested.

The sentry at Roshan's base told me that he was asleep after working all night. When I explained the reason for my visit, the young man had laughed out loud. 'Don't count on getting the posters,

Thangatchi [little sister]. Even we here at the Miller House [named after Black Tiger Captain Miller] haven't been able to get any.'

'That's all right,' I replied, feeling embarrassed. 'Just tell Roshan anna that I came by.'

I had left without seeing him, but that very afternoon, as I was doing my homework, the doorbell rang. I didn't know why I was bothering with homework, considering I was due to return to the Tigers soon, but I couldn't help myself. I had never once been to class without doing all the work required of me.

'I was disappointed that you came all the way to my base and left without seeing me,' said Roshan at the door, beaming at me. I had never seen him happier.

Both you and me, I thought, but said, 'I didn't want to wake you.'

'I should be so lucky to be woken up by you. Next time simply demand that you see me, no matter what the boys tell you.'

Whatever made him think there was going to be a next time? I wondered.

'I have something for you,' said Roshan and headed towards his van parked outside the gate. I followed. He opened the passenger door, took out rolls of paper and held them out to me. I could hardly believe my eyes when I unravelled so many different posters of Thileepan. I looked up at him gratefully. He was leaning on his van watching me, still glowing.

'You must have gone to some trouble to get these for me, because I know they are hard to come by. I really don't know how to thank you.'

'Seeing the surprise on your face is enough for me,' he said and climbed into his van and turned on the ignition. He then reversed the van out of the driveway and took off, all the while keeping his eyes on me.

One early October day, nearly two weeks after Thileepan's death, there was news of suicide attempts by seventeen high-ranking Tigers who tried ingesting cyanide while in the custody of the Sri Lankan navy. Twelve of them died. They were part of a group of men who had been arrested at sea for transporting armaments, and were due to be transferred to Colombo, to face criminal charges for crimes committed during the period of armed conflict. But arresting them during the peace accord breached the amnesty provisions of the accord. In protest the men chose to die because even the IPKF could not guarantee them a fair trial.

That evening, Kaanchana and Akila came on their bicycles to see me at home. Prabhakaran had requested that all the cadres from our training camp assemble at the Freedom Birds' head office. We speculated that fighting was about to resume so, trying to be better prepared this time, I packed a couple of shirts, trousers, underwear and toiletries in a small bag and smuggled it out while the girls engaged Amma and Colombo Auntie in conversation.

Many of my comrades had gathered at the office when we arrived there. Ajanthi came running over to me and we embraced. 'I am sorry I didn't come to pick you up,' she said. 'I wouldn't have been able to convince your mother to let you come. Besides, seeing her and lying to her makes me feel guilty.'

I was excited to be back in the company of my friends and at the prospect of Ajanthi and me fighting side by side.

There was no telling exactly at what time Prabhakaran would arrive, so Kaanchana suggested that we go upstairs and look through the piles of photo albums and read the personal letters of a well-known Tamil politician of the TULF, now exiled in India, to his wife in Jaffna.

'Why do we have these letters?' I asked.

'Apparently the Tigers have been blackmailing him, threatening to go public with the contents; so he'll never set foot in this country again,' said Kaanchana. 'The letters are full of juicy personal matters and *karuvaadu* [dried fish] politics.'

The girls immediately scrambled upstairs.

'Of course you're all only interested in the boring political information,' laughed Kaanchana following them.

The letters and photographs were very entertaining indeed. Ajanthi just read the juicy bits from the letters, and then tossed them away.

There were thousands of photographs of Tiger leaders, mostly taken in India when they were exiled there. The Tigers were obsessed with pictorial documentation of themselves—they photographed and videotaped themselves going about everyday matters as well as battles and ambushes. Prabhakaran must have been the only exiled guerrilla leader who allowed so many photographs of himself in circulation. He certainly seemed to enjoy posing: with powerful weapons, staring into the camera, contemplatively looking at the trees, lying on a hammock, or with his blushing bride or awe-struck cadres, all taken in India.

Kaanchana found an album with many pictures of Roshan. 'It appears that your man likes himself as much he does you, Niromi,' she observed. 'There's a whole album of him.'

'He's *not* my man, Kaanchana. Anyway, I don't understand why these men enjoy posing for photos with weapons—they are incriminating evidence.'

'Oh, look who's feeling protective of him!' Ajanthi teased.

'When the war is over, I think you should obtain Anna's permission to marry Roshan,' advised Kaanchana. 'I know for a fact that his family isn't as well off as yours, and of lower caste. He's Hindu and you are Catholic. So your union would be considered a positive change in our society, and Anna would welcome that.'

I realised that she was no longer teasing. 'Inter-religious relationships may sound romantic,' I replied loftily. 'But they are not worth the trouble they bring. Besides, if I wanted to be married I wouldn't have joined a militant organisation.'

Just then we heard Prabhakaran's jeep arrive. It was nearly 2am.

'I don't know why we can't have meetings in daylight, at least during peacetime,' muttered Ajanthi, and everyone made their way downstairs. Taking advantage of the distraction Prabhakaran provided, I quickly slipped a photo of a sullen-looking Roshan posing with an AK-47 into my bag when no one was looking.

Prabhakaran walked into the house with his entourage, wearing his usual short-sleeved white shirt and black trousers. We sat on the marble floor in front of him half asleep. But Prabhakaran was all fired up.

'The loss of my best boys is a great tragedy for our movement,' his voice thundered, slicing through the still night. 'We have lost more leaders in peacetime than war. The Indian government engineered the so-called peace process as a plot to gradually eliminate us. The death of my men has to be avenged, so yesterday I ordered my boys to finish off any Sinhalese who have come to claim our land using the peace as an excuse,' he said as his voice rose with every sentence and his face flushed with rage.

So now the Tigers were going to kill the Buddhist monks and other Sinhala visitors in Jaffna, I thought. 'Children,' he instructed us, 'never shed tears to lessen your sorrow. They wipe away your grief. You must turn your despair into anger. Bottle it up and let it explode! If the enemy kills ten of my men, I'll chop ten thousand heads off his men.'

He continued talking into the early hours of the morning, about death and revenge. I had never seen him so angry. I did not recognise the man in front of me as the Prabhakaran I had known until now. It scared me a little. I much preferred the happier Prabhakaran.

He left in the morning, after informing us that war would resume after the funerals of the recently deceased. I decided to head back home with my bag, and wait until I was called again.

The anxiety I had felt when listening to Prabhakaran had all but vanished by the time I reached home. I told myself that he was right: we must avenge the death of our men. Thileepan's sacrifice must not be in vain—I must remember to bottle up my sorrow and anger and use it against the enemy.

The public cremation of the ten men was held in the northern village of Valvetti. As the Tiger marching band was required at the funeral ceremony, I was summoned once again to play the piano accordion. As previously, Kaanchana and Akila came to pick me up. By now, the two girls had earned Amma's trust and affection, so she no longer questioned them.

When the van carrying the twenty band members and our musical instruments arrived at the cremation site mid morning, the large oval was already packed tight with heads of black hair. We stood alongside the corpses, which had been laid on logs. By midday, while the never-ending line of mourners paid homage to the men, we had grown tired and thirsty standing under the blistering sun. Near the end of the evening, the band was reduced by half—most of the girls had fainted from the midday heat and possibly from the nauseating stench of body odour. Unfortunately, I had remained standing.

It was around midnight when the bodies were doused with petrol and the fathers of the deceased torched their sons' bodies (a poignant reversal of the usual custom). Each of our band members played whatever they thought the tune was. Despite all the practice, no one seemed to remember what I taught them, and I had given up trying to get the band to play in harmony. I resolved never to join the band again, unless the funeral was Prabhakaran's.

The firewood crackled and the fire became a large blaze lighting up the entire oval, fanned by a heavy breeze. Flying embers burnt little holes in our saris. Sweat and tears poured out of everyone. Family and friends of the deceased wailed, holding onto each other. In their grief, some of the young wives of the dead men—widowed in less than two months—attempted to enter the fire and had to be restrained. They had all been married during the peace, after Prabhakaran, for the first time ever, had approved the romantic relationships of some of his loyal cadres and permitted their union. Until then, he had been the only man married after becoming a Tiger. An intense heat rose from the flames; dust and cries of sorrow filled the air, followed by the stench of burning wood and flesh. Amidst all this chaos, our band played its final discordant cacophony.

The following morning, the Tigers dumped for public display at Jaffna's central bus terminus the bodies of the five Sinhalese army personnel and three policemen they had captured during a battle before the peace accord and then imprisoned. After Prabhakaran had authorised the murder of all Sinhalese in Jaffna, all these captives had been shot dead.

I went to see the bodies; curiosity had got the better of me. One corner of the bus terminus was crowded with men. I was taken aback when I first saw the gore at the centre of the throng—the bodies of the sarong-clad soldiers lay in a pool of blood, diluted by the morning rain. Flies perched on their slightly open mouths and eyes; their hands were tied to each other's with hemp ropes. Each man had two bullet wounds, one in the forehead and the other in the chest. Their shirts and sarongs were still wet with fresh blood. I realised that the soldiers must have been alive when they were brought here this morning. I felt a sickening sensation rise in my stomach.

'This is the Tigers' response to the funerals yesterday,' speculated the crowd.

I recalled the lamenting family and friends of the dead Tigers around the pyres the night before. Then I thought of the Sinhala soldiers' wives, parents, siblings and friends. As I walked away from the scene, I felt unsettled. I wondered if the families and friends of these soldiers would see their bodies. I felt sad for them for a moment before I remembered Prabhakaran's words: 'If the enemy kills ten of my men, I'll chop ten thousand heads off his men.'

Yes, they started it first, I told myself, and so the Tigers were right in teaching them a lesson. It was the only thing left for them to do.

Over the next few days more of the Sinhalese in Jaffna were murdered and the rest, including the monks, fled from the peninsula. Apart from a very few military personnel remaining with the Indian peace keepers, Jaffna once again became a Sinhala-free zone.

One afternoon, I was cycling home from school when a jeep heading in the opposite direction veered towards me and came to a halt. I quickly applied my bike's brakes. Roshan turned his engine off and smiled at me.

'You are such a bad driver, always running people off the road,' I chided him.

'Not people—only you,' laughed Roshan, tossing his head back.

'It won't be so funny if I get hurt.'

'I'll never hurt you,' said Roshan. Then he dropped his voice:

'Why haven't you come to visit me again? Have you forgotten me already?'

'Do you think I have nothing better to do, Roshan anna?'

'I like to think that I'm your priority.'

I laughed. 'You are always overestimating yourself, judging by all the photos you've posed for. You must think of yourself as handsome.'

'Oh, so *you* must think that I am handsome,' said Roshan, making me laugh. 'I have one complaint, Niromi. When I come to see you at your house, I don't want to have to get your mother's permission. I have the right to speak to you, don't I?'

'You ask for the impossible,' I said. 'She's my mother, and there's no changing that.'

'I feel like I have to keep driving around your neighbourhood to see you. I would die if I didn't get glimpses of you like this,' said Roshan and fixed his gaze on me.

I felt light-headed. I managed to hold his gaze for a few seconds before looking away.

'Anyway, can you get me photos or posters of the recently deceased Tigers, Roshan anna?'

'Of course, anything for you.'

'I better get going, Roshan anna,' I said finally. 'And don't forget the photos.'

'My photo, right?' laughed Roshan, turning the ignition on.

'Why would I need yours?' I replied. After all, I already had one.

I visited Roshan at his base only one other time, with a friend in tow, before the war broke out, although I had told myself I wouldn't. However, there was a good reason—I had to inform him that I was about to join the war. I told myself that I did not want him to waste his time driving around the neighbourhood looking for me, or visiting home and bothering Amma.

Our conversation this time was no different to any other: silence filled the gaps of our disjointed conversation; he tried to discuss us and I did everything to avoid it.

❖

It began harmlessly enough, but 10 October 1987 turned out to be a day of momentous significance. That morning, I had joined a 20-kilometre protest march against the presence of the IPKF in Jaffna from the Old Park to Palaali Airbase. I noticed a few Tigers, including Mahathaya and Yogi Master, in the background.

Around mid afternoon, when we reached Palaali, a village north-east of Jaffna, we found the whole town flattened to the ground so the army at the airport would feel safe from the Tigers sneaking up on them. Although totally exhausted, we stood outside the gates of the domestic airport turned Sri Lankan air-force base turned IPKF camp, shouting slogans.

Suddenly Muralie arrived on his motorbike, parked it by the roadside and hurried towards the crowd with a walkie-talkie in one hand. 'Everyone please go home,' he announced into a borrowed handheld microphone. 'There are buses waiting in the next street—they'll take you to your destinations.'

I pushed my way through the crowd to reach Muralie: 'What's the matter, Muralie anna? Why are you asking us to leave?'

'The soldiers opened fire at the crowds protesting outside the fort army camp. We are worried that the same thing might happen here.'

I hadn't known that confrontations between the Tigers and the peace keepers had begun the day before when the peace keepers decided to forcibly disarm the Tigers by attacking their camps, con-fiscating communication equipment and closing down the offices of newspapers sympathetic to the Tigers. That day it had escalated to a dangerous level when the two groups engaged in an armed con-frontation in Kopaay, a village outside Jaffna. It claimed the life of twenty-year-old Tigress Malathy, who became the first female Tiger martyr. I had not met her. At the same battle, the enemy captured two other female Tigers and Akila, who was part of this unit, nar-rowly escaped.

The following evening I was back at the Freedom Birds' head office, having left home for good. Kaanchana and another of my comrades had come to my house earlier and told Amma and me that I was needed for the band again, but while Amma was making them tea Kaanchana asked me to pack my bag, because I wouldn't be returning home. The Sri Lankan government had repealed the amnesty given to the Tigers, and Prabhakaran and his followers were once again on the wanted list. That night, Prabhakaran came to our base to confirm this. We were fortunate to be personally briefed by him so regularly—most of the men in the organisation were yet to meet him. He certainly showed preferential treatment towards the women in the organisation, possibly because we were still a novelty.

I was happy to be back with Ajanthi, Kaanchana and some of the other girls who were now at the Freedom Birds headquarters. Akila was still at the battlefront in Kopaay with two all-female units. The girls had been split up randomly by our training-base captains Theeba and Sugi—some joining groups that were sent to battle and others waiting for their share of weapons.

Leaving home this time was easier for me than the last because my loyalty now was to Prabhakaran and to Tamil Eelam, but I did feel sorry for walking out on my little sister again. Shirani seemed more introspective these days. Her best friend had recently migrated to the United States with her family; and her only other confidante, me, was now abandoning her once more. She was only fourteen, and I worried that she would become lonely; perhaps Amma, too wrapped up in her own grief, would not give Shirani the love and affection she so desperately needed at this time. But then, I reasoned, Shirani was loved by everyone—her beauty and her outgoing nature had often made me look and feel wooden next to her. In the end I persuaded myself that she would be all right.

I was also anxious about something else—the increasing number of people opposed to us. Not only did we need to confront the Indian forces—the world's second largest army—and the Sri Lankan government forces, but the exiled factions—TELO, PLOTE and EPRLF—had been legitimised under the peace accord and they were ready to avenge themselves. Worst of all, much of the general public now believed that the resumption of hostilities was the Tigers' fault. Deep down, I thought so too. I felt that everyone concerned, including the Tigers, had not given this accord a real chance.

To add to that, the odds against us seemed huge. After all, we were only a rudimentary guerrilla force, comprising a few thousand young people, and with little firepower. We had previously surrendered much of our weaponry and we lacked significant land, air and sea capabilities to fight such powerful enemies. It seemed to me that no one and nothing was on our side, and that we were going to wage this war on hope alone.

'How can we win against such odds?' I asked Kaanchana one day. 'Especially if the Tamils don't want this war, shouldn't we try our best to resolve this conflict politically? After all, it is for them we are fighting.'

'We are mere foot soldiers, Niromi,' reminded Kaanchana, regarding my reflection as she plaited her hair in front of the mirror. 'We aren't privy to all the facts like those at the top of the hierarchy. We have to trust Anna because he's never wrong.'

I conceded.

We spent the next two days listening to a walkie-talkie, which emitted a steady stream of commands and profanity from the battle-fronts at different villages, but mainly from the Jaffna university. Like us, most of the female units were on stand-by because our stashed weapons were yet to be unearthed. We believed the boys' units would receive priority; until some ammunition trickled down to us, we were confined to the Freedom Bird's head office.

While others enjoyed listening to the walkie-talkie, I was troubled: 'Why do you want to listen to the walkie, anyway?' I grumbled 'No one's talking to *us*.'

'You'll be at a battlefield very soon, so you need to get used to the field language,' reasoned Kaanchana. 'You must desensitise yourself to it, so you don't find it offensive or distracting.'

'Fuckers! Hit it! Hit it!' crackled the walkie-talkie.

'Profanity conveys no meaning and is therefore ineffective in communication,' I offered.

Kaanchana turned to me: 'I'll give you meaning. Say you find your unit completely surrounded by the enemy. Your unit commander needs you to fire and break out. In scenario one, he says to you "Niromi, please shoot" and in scenario two he shouts "You damn mother-fucker—fire!" Get the picture?'

I did.

The following day, Kaanchana and I were asked by our female base leader, Kala, to visit Prabhakaran to collect funds to purchase combat-ready clothing for the girls. There was no time to have uniforms organised, so it would have to be jeans and shirts. So that afternoon Kaanchana and I went to a house behind the university. We opened the three-metre-high gate and let ourselves in. In the small, leafy front yard, Prabhakaran stood next to a pick-up truck onto which a 50-calibre machine gun was being fitted. Some of his bodyguards stood nearby. I was amazed at the low security around him—there was not even a sentry at the gate.

When Prabhakaran saw us, he strode towards some outdoor furniture and took a seat under the shade of an umbrella, motioning for us to sit down too. I once again noticed his stubby fingers—a palm reader who had come to our house had said that such fingers denoted an aggressive, violent and obsessive nature.

'How much money do you think you'll need, children? About 20,000 rupees?'

'I think that'll be enough, don't you?' Kaanchana looked at me.

'That's a bit much. Only thirty-five of us have returned to the fight.'

'I'll give you the lot anyway,' said Prabhakaran, grooming his moustache with his right forefinger. 'You can give the change to your base leader.'

Prabhakaran then turned to a man standing beside him.

'Manmadhan, could you get me the money?'

Kaanchana kicked me under the table as I tried hard to stop myself from giggling. In Hindu mythology, Manmadhan was the very handsome god of lust, melting women's hearts. I thought that this Manmadhan on the other hand was quite his opposite. Tigers sometimes did this—gave their new cadres ironic *noms de guerre*. (At this stage women were still allowed to choose their *nom de guerres* because there were only a few of us.)

'Children, choose only dark colours. Dark denim is good. Don't hesitate to ask for more money if you need it.'

Manmadhan returned from the house and handed Prabhakaran bundles of hundred rupee notes. I tried not to look at him for fear of breaking into laughter. Prabhakaran counted the notes and handed them over to me.

'When will you send us into the field, Anna?' I asked boldly.

Prabhakaran smiled. 'Once the dumped rifles are unearthed, then you'll be out there right away. That 50-calibre was taken out only this morning.' He gestured to the pick-up. 'Can you see the grease on it?'

After a fleeting glimpse of peace, the sounds, smells and sights of war returned to Jaffna. The skies were roaring once again with low-flying helicopter gunships and bombers. They strafed and bombed the Tiger bases, which were in residential areas. But the bombers' accuracy could hardly be relied on and civilians were often affected. The IPKF was also receiving reinforcements from India now that their role had changed from peacekeepers to active soldiers. The people of Jaffna dubbed them the 'Indian People Killing Forces'. At least on ground, the Tigers were in control.

As I sat on the front steps of the old SOLT office in my jeans and checked shirt (attire considered suitable for a Jaffna Tamil female only if she was a guerrilla), I watched the men and women, the children and the elderly streaming towards the Nallur Hindu temple for temporary refuge from the bombs, carrying their meagre valuables. In their faces I saw sadness, indifference, disappointment, fear, and above all, I saw anger. It flashed in their eyes whenever they saw any Tigers.

Six of us—Ajanthi, Madhana, Nora, Nihintha, Kaanchana and I—had been dropped off at the now-empty SOLT office near Nallur temple, where Thileepan had held his hunger strike five days after the war resumed. Having trained together and being of similar age, we got on very well. We were waiting for weapons so we could join the war; but in the meantime we kept ourselves entertained by people-watching, chatting and taking shelter from the bombers down the road, knowing our house had been marked.

When we had arrived at the SOLT office, Kaanchana had informed us that murders had been committed in this house too—nearly two years earlier the Tigers had executed PLOTE's Jaffna area leader here, and later some EPRLF members.

'Oh, every house we stay at has stories of murder,' I sighed. 'Besides, how do you know so much? You're like a walking Tiger encyclopaedia'.

'Like I've said many times before—unlike you, I've worked with the movement long enough to know many things. I didn't join on a whim like the two of you.' Kaanchana always liked to stir us for fun.

'Whim or not, we are all in the same boat now,' defended Ajanthi. 'What's the use of all this knowledge when you are dead on the streets tomorrow?'

Ajanthi and Kaanchana got on very well and shared a similar sense of humour. As Tigers, we weren't allowed to discuss personal matters or politics with each other, so all that was left for us was superficial conversations and banter, and the two girls made the most of it.

'Fair point,' conceded Kaanchana, but only for a minute. 'But I'd be more glorified in my death than you would be,' she said, hoping to have the last word.

'I'll see you in hell either way,' laughed Ajanthi, as she went into the kitchen. 'Tea, anyone? I'm going to ask the boys to get us some.'

Whenever we heard a bomber overhead, we scurried out of the house and took shelter at a little shop a few blocks away. The shop's owner—and occasionally another sympathiser—had been supplying our meals once a day. One time, an elderly woman had brought us a box of chocolates: 'My son, about your age, lives in Switzerland as a refugee,' she said. 'I'm certain he'd be pleased to know that you had them.'

One afternoon Ajanthi's parents came to visit us. The SOLT office was only about 2 kilometres from Ajanthi's and my homes. Someone had seen us and told them where we were. Ajanthi and I met her parents at the gate but we did not invite them into the house—there was no furniture for them to sit on anyway. 'How could you break your mother's heart twice?' Mala Auntie asked me. 'She's so disappointed in you that she refused to come here with us.'

'I'm a member of an organisation now and I must do what the organisation expects of me,' I replied.

'If you had any respect for the people who brought you into this world, you wouldn't be able to change your loyalties so easily,' said Uncle Jerome, scornfully.

'We love and respect you, and that's why we're sacrificing ourselves,' Ajanthi replied. 'Can't you see that?' I was astounded at her tone. I had not heard her raise her voice like that before. However, I could understand her frustration—over the past six months, every time we had seen our families and friends, we'd been forced to explain ourselves and justify our actions.

'Do you think we're willing to die for no reason?' I added. 'It is to attain freedom for our people. Only Tamil Eelam will give them that. All our sacrifice will be worth it then.'

'What makes you think that you are going to attain Tamil Eelam?' Uncle Jerome asked.

'We'll never know if we don't try,' I replied.

For a few minutes, silence prevailed. I couldn't be certain if our families wanted Tamil Eelam but I knew for sure that they didn't approve of the way we were going about it.

'You children have been thoroughly brainwashed,' sighed Uncle Jerome. 'They've also taught you to speak disrespectfully to elders.'

This was exasperating. Why did everyone think that we had to be brainwashed in order to be members of a movement? Why wouldn't they give us credit for our actions? We were not stupid; we understood exactly what the issues were. The difference was that we were willing to do something about the injustice, while everyone else simply talked about it.

I decided to say nothing more and left Ajanthi to talk to her parents while I headed back to the house. A man seated on the front step commented: 'You must be one of Muralie's new recruits. In your designer clothes, you hardly look the guerrilla fighter you're supposed to be. You're going to have a tough time dealing with reality.'

I was taken aback by his unsolicited remarks and went into the house fuming, but without saying anything in reply.

'Don't worry about him,' said Kaanchana as I sat next to her on the floor. 'He's not a trained fighter himself. The Tigers only took him into the organisation for his jeep.'

I burst out laughing.

That evening we hung around the front steps once again, watching the human traffic and frustrated by our inability to join the battle that was taking place in the villages outside Jaffna. Akila was out there, still fighting with a unit of women, while we were sitting on a verandah, dressed ready for combat, but unarmed. Perhaps the people we were watching on the road felt a similar frustration: migration was occurring in both directions, and no one seemed to know which way was safer.

Then we saw our deputy commander, 'Crocodile' Mahathaya, coming our way, slowly riding one a ladies' bicycles with a basket at the front. He was wearing very short brown shorts and a black leather jacket zipped to the collar, teamed with white rubber flip-flops. It was a warm and humid day.

'Now, here's a brave man,' I said out loud, referring to his fashion sense. One of my comrades, Nihintha, chuckled. The lanky girl was always the first one to laugh.

As Mahathaya drew closer, I saw a pistol in his hip holster.

'We're done with waiting, Mahathaya anna, when can you get us some weapons?' asked Kaanchana when Mahathaya stopped in front of us. All of us joined in the chorus. Mahathaya looked as if he regretted coming our way. He must have thought himself saved when his bodyguards—Castro and Gaddafi—and Yogi Master came down the road soon after him.

'Don't worry, children, I'll organise the delivery of six AK rifles, holsters and grenades, and have you transported to a battlefield by tomorrow,' said Mahathaya hurriedly and he joined the men who had caught up to him.

The next day we were given just three AKs and dropped off at the University of Jaffna. 'Never trust a man who rides a ladies' bike,' said Kaanchana.

The university *had been* a battleground. Only a couple of days earlier, the Indian military had failed miserably in their attempt to capture the Tiger leadership based at the university, losing thirty-five air-dropped commandos in the attempt. The Tigers had intercepted the enemy's radio commands beforehand and lain in wait. The campus was now entirely under the command of the Tigers—nearly fifty girls and thirty boys dispersed throughout the campus—and, except for the occasional visiting students, there was no one else. Because of this the enemy was sending artillery shells in the direction of the university from their nearest camp, the fort army barracks some 3 kilometres away.

Most of my comrades who had gone home during the lull in hostilities did not return to the Tigers when war resumed. The remaining eighty female cadres were split into five units, two at the university and three at different battlefronts around the Jaffna peninsula. Our job at the university and the adjacent technical college was to guard the buildings from any further attack since Prabhakaran and his men continued to visit the campus.

Although we were still inactive and simply holding ground at the university, I was proud to be part of my unit, undeterred by moments of public ridicule. Still unarmed, I was posted as a sentry by the main entrance with one of my comrades one morning when a large group of thirty or forty gawking spectators, mostly young boys and older men, gathered on the other side of the gate, as if we were caged exhibits. Despite our repeated requests for them to disperse, no one took us seriously. It was the first time the female Tigers had been on public display armed and in shirts and trousers ready for combat and for many the spectacle was too hard to resist.

A jeep arrived at the gate with the newly appointed Tigers' Jaffna area leader, Paandiyan, behind the wheel and one of Prabhakaran's bodyguards, Imran, beside him. When they saw the crowd, Imran jumped out of the jeep, bellowing at them: 'You men should be embarrassed! Young girls have left their homes to fight for their country, and you have come to watch the show. If you don't leave right this minute, I'll beat the backbone out of you!' He proceeded to throw punches at some of them. The crowd took off immediately.

That same afternoon, some university students arrived by bicycle and wanted access to their computer lab. We let them in. As they entered, one of the boys remarked: 'Now that schoolkids have picked up guns, we have to get their permission to come into our university, to which we gained entry through merit.' The others laughed, looking at us.

The third humiliating moment came two days later when one morning Kaanchana and I were sent to the technical college behind the university to set up some Claymore mines around the grounds. Finding the gates locked, we tried to open the massive padlock by hitting it with a hammer, but with no luck. One of our armed comrades fired three shots at the lock with her SMG and we tried the hammer some more, but the lock refused to budge. A passer-by volunteered for the job. He hit the lock with the hammer just once and it came undone. 'You might be trained fighters, but a man is a man, and a woman should know her place,' he remarked with no hint of humour in his tone as he handed back the hammer. An all-male group had gathered behind us to watch the spectacle and they laughed out loud.

'It's the story of the sparrow and the palmyra fruit,' Kaanchana told him, trying to laugh it off. 'The sparrow might think that by sitting on the huge fruit it made it drop to the ground, but the fruit was about to fall anyway.'

'Yeah, whatever satisfies you,' said the man and the crowd laughed some more.

Such humiliating moments were interspersed with others that were truly confronting. On our second day at the technical college

Kaanchana and I were on sentry duty, sitting on the wall surrounding the college. The wide canopies of tamarind trees by the side of the road provided shelter for us from the scorching sun. The road in front of us was deserted except for an occasional passer-by; most people stayed indoors or at refugee safe havens. Suddenly a man on a bicycle hurried past us. He looked as if he was escaping from someone or something, because he kept looking back while he pedalled furiously. Kaanchana and I, still without rifles, jumped off the wall, took out hand-grenades from our holsters and held them in readiness for whatever followed.

Then a jeep zoomed past us—Mahathaya was in the front passenger seat and one of his bodyguards was behind the wheel. A few minutes later, the jeep returned. Now the man was seated next to Mahathaya, looking petrified. Mahathaya's bodyguard came riding the bicycle behind them and stopped in front of us. He handed over the bicycle to us with a warning: 'You are not to ride it. We'll be back in a little while.'

Once they left, we took turns to ride around the oval.

About fifteen minutes later, the jeep returned. Mahathaya's bodyguard got out first and dragged the man from the back of the jeep by his collar. 'Give him his bicycle back, *Makkal*,' he said to us. 'We suspected him of being a spy but he isn't one.'

I was shocked when I saw the man staggering towards us—blood dripping from his split lips and soaking his shirt. He had a bruised eye and his shirt was torn in many places. Kaanchana handed the man his bicycle with her mouth still open. Unable to get back on his bicycle, the man floundered away from us, pushing it. The jeep had already left.

'I can't believe such injustice exists!' shouted Kaanchana. 'Mahathaya anna will suffer for what he's done to that poor man!'

'Perhaps we should get him some water or something,' I suggested.

'No, you won't,' shouted one of our female comrades, who had been watching this episode from a distance. 'The war is full of innocent victims.'

'I can't believe you said that,' said Kaanchana, rushing over, with me chasing after her. Before I knew it, the two of them were in a furious argument and everyone had joined in and taken sides against Kaanchana.

'How would we know if someone is a spy or not, unless we beat the truth out of them?' asked someone. 'And then showing signs of weakness by taking care of them after will only make us look stupid.'

Kaanchana screamed, 'You may condone such behaviour but if I were him I would join a rival movement or become an informer, to take revenge on the Tigers. This sort of behaviour is going to come back to haunt us one day. Can you deny that it's our own conduct that is turning people against us?'

No one dared to answer her.

I dragged Kaanchana away from the rest of the group, trying to calm her down. 'Unfortunately we were too busy arguing,' I told her, 'and I didn't take care of the man. He's bleeding all the way to somewhere else.'

By the time night fell, Kaanchana and I forgot all about the man and went to sleep on the tables of the administration office at the technical college, but not before swapping around the photos on the desks and drawing moustaches, glasses and hats on the pictures of Hindu and Christian gods on the wall calendars.

The next day, Kaanchana and I were summoned to the university. 'The two of you are no longer needed at the tech,' said Sugi, the unit commander who had first trained us.

I looked at Kaanchana, meaningfully.

'What?' she scowled at me.

'Nothing,' I said.

As we both walked to the sentry position we were now allocated to, Kaanchana piped up: 'I prefer the university to the technical college, anyway. The visiting university boys are better looking than their technical college counterparts.'

Our position was in one of the lecture rooms near the back entrance of the university. Ajanthi and Nihintha were stationed at the library entrance about 10 metres opposite us. As a precautionary measure, Kaanchana set out to shatter all the glass windows in our room with her AK because artillery shells were raining down on us day and night (we once counted that an average of twenty-six shells were exploding per hour). As they had lost the battle at the university a week ago, the Indian peace keepers were well aware of our position.

One afternoon an artillery shell came through one of the lecture room's walls, making Kaanchana and me crash to the ground. The tremendous explosion caused hot metal, bricks and cement to shower upon us. I felt a sharp sting on my right foot but nothing more. Once the dust settled, we called out to make sure the other was okay. When we rose to our feet and looked at each other we burst into laughter; we looked like statues, covered in grey dust from head to toe.

'Your feet!' exclaimed Kaanchana.

I looked down and saw a shell fragment about the size of a pro-tractor stuck in my right foot. When Kaanchana pulled it out it began to bleed heavily and I had to seek first aid.

When we didn't have such dramas there was nothing to do but sit and wait, so I read Tamil literature and psychology texts from the library (the only books that weren't too technical for me), while Kaanchana, Nihintha and Ajanthi entertained themselves imitating the sounds of artillery shells and bombers or calling each other by the names of animals and vegetables.

It rained heavily one night during the last week of October. Thunder and lightning combined with the exploding artillery shells created a mighty show of light and sound around the university. I tried to fall asleep on the cold hard floor, chasing away the mosquitoes that rang in my ears, with Ajanthi on one side of me and Nihintha on the other. Luckily for me, whenever Ajanthi was around, all the mosqui-toes preferred her blood to mine.

It was still raining heavily when I began my 1am sentry duty. As I stood near the door, watching the frequent explosions light up the night sky, I heard a blood-curdling scream. I recognised it as a man's voice coming from within the university compound. I decided that someone must have been hurt by an exploding artillery shell, but as I couldn't leave my sentry post I'd have to wait 'til the morning to find out.

In the morning, Ajanthi, Kaanchana, Nihintha and I headed to one of the houses outside the university compound to wash at their well. Every house in Jaffna had a fresh water well. The rain had eased to a slight drizzle and the breeze had a touch of coolness. The sun was rising from behind the African tulip trees along the road, reflecting off last night's rain drops, caught by the leaves and petals.

'Who is Niromi?' One of the young boys had come up behind us. 'Sengamalam anna wants to see you.'

We did not speak to the boys unless it was necessary. So, without asking him why, I followed the teenager.

I recognised Sengamalam at the entrance to one of the rooms, talking to a couple of boys. A senior commander, he was a burly man with a mop of short, straight hair and bloodshot eyes. As I approached the group, I noticed the body of a young man on the floor. He must have been the one killed out in the rain last night. Red soil still clung to his wet clothes, hair and limbs. Although it had rained all night his shirt and trousers were completely stained, indicating a large loss of blood. His open eyes stared vacantly.

Unable to look at him any longer, I averted my eyes to Sengamalam. 'This was Thavakumar's rifle,' said the commander, holding out an AKMS to me. 'Now it's yours.'

I did not know why I was chosen to receive this rifle, but I did not ask. It was still wet and dirty with mud. I felt my hands tremble at the honour of receiving the rifle of a fallen comrade. It was now my duty to fulfil Thavakumar's dream. I was also given a clean holster with three new magazines and four grenades—two pentalite and two TNT.

Mid morning, I was cleaning my rifle, sitting with my comrades on the university front lawn, which was by now stone dry. My AKMS gleamed in the morning sunlight. We had temporarily relocated to the main entrance because Prabhakaran and his entourage had arrived for sniper practice near our usual sentry location at the back entrance of the university.

I was facing Ajanthi when I saw her eyes suddenly open wide. 'Look who's there at the front gate!' she exclaimed.

I spun around to find Roshan sitting on a wall near the front entrance by the sentry, motioning me to come over. I froze. Everyone must have seen him.

'Oh no,' exclaimed Kaanchana. 'Commander Sugi is sending one of her girls to find out what he wants. Hurry and tell her he is your cousin or the word might get out.'

So I hurried and intercepted the girl in time and told her that Roshan, my cousin, had come to see me. After she returned to her position, I casually strode up to Roshan, trying to control my racing heart, well aware that all eyes were on me. Although I was thrilled to see him and surprised that he had found me, I was worried that his appearance might start a round of gossip among the girls. I did not want anyone to think he was my boyfriend.

'Why did you come here?' I barked when I reached him, well aware my comrade at sentry duty by the gate was in earshot of us. 'Shouldn't you be out there fighting?'

'I just wanted to see you,' he smiled, ignoring my offensive tone.

He looked me up and down and stopped at my right foot, which was bandaged.

'What happened to your foot?' He looked genuinely concerned.

I told him the injury was caused by a shell fragment.

'You don't look after yourself,' he said, exasperated. 'I'll send someone to take care of it.'

I asked him again why he was not out there fighting.

'I've been given two units to command but I've told them I'll start next week. You see, I was taking supplies to our detainees held at the Palaali army base every day. I got to know them all very well. Then I had to smuggle in the *kuppies*. I feel horrible,' said Roshan and sighed heavily.

I realised he was talking about the Tiger men arrested by the Sri Lankan navy who later committed suicide.

'Are you saying those men committed suicide under orders?'

I had believed they had acted under impulse, not questioning how they'd had access to cyanide capsules after they were removed by the Sri Lankan navy.

'My mother keeps visiting me at the camp pleading with me to return home, but I'd rather just take some rest and keep seeing you,' replied Roshan as if I had not asked him a question. 'You are my best cure.'

I knew that Roshan was the youngest of a family of five and the only one not to graduate or settle down. He was a constant source of worry to his mother.

'Your poor mother,' I remarked, although I was still thinking about the men's suicide. I was disappointed they had been ordered to kill themselves, especially considering two of them were prominent commanders and newly married. Why was Prabhakaran so angry about their deaths when he had ordered it himself? And why would he send some of his best men to fetch his office equipment from India on a treacherous, illegal boat trip, peace time or not? If they had asked the IPKF they surely could've helped, considering they had been flying Prabhakaran, his family and fellow Tigers here and there over the past couple of months. Perhaps the men had been bringing back weapons.

'I was watching you chatting with your newfound friends as if you didn't have a care in the world,' observed Roshan. 'But don't get too close to anyone. As the war intensifies, you may lose some of them. I want you to be emotionally prepared or you'll have a nervous breakdown.'

I wondered if the same advice applied to us also.

Although I did not want to end our conversation, I thanked him and returned to my position, feeling that my comrades were already suspecting there was something between us—the only other person to have such visitors was Commander Sugi, whose Prabhakaran-approved Tiger fiancé often took her out somewhere private.

Later that afternoon, when I was alone with Kaanchana, I asked her if she knew about the orders given to the Palaali detainees to commit suicide. 'Hm . . . I had never thought about it either, but it makes sense,' she replied.

'If the Sri Lankan government did anything to the arrested men, wouldn't they have looked bad for violating the peace accord? Wouldn't they have forced India to take action against them?'

'Anna must have had good reasons to believe that a fate worse than suicide awaited them if they were taken to Colombo,' replied Kaanchana, unperturbed.

That same afternoon a young woman sent by Roshan came to see me with a first-aid kit in one hand and a wicker basket packed with sandwiches, fruit and juice in the other. She said she was a third year medical student. Before she could set the basket down on one of the benches, Ajanthi and Kaanchana had crowded around it, looking inside.

'I've known Roshan anna for a while now, and you certainly have changed him for the better,' she said while attending to my injured foot. 'He never stops talking about you. I now see what all the fuss is about.'

I was too embarrassed to ask her for details, although I wanted to.

The following morning my comrades and I made our way to the front lawns of the university as Prabhakaran and his men continued to practise their targets by the back entrance. Kaanchana was telling me about a time when, during one of Prabhakaran's visits to the women's base, he had highly commended one of my poems published in the Freedom Birds' magazine. 'He couldn't believe it was you who'd written it,' she said. Because of my western style haircut and clothes many often assumed my Tamil would be poor, certainly not to the standard of writing poetry.

I was chuffed. There was no better honour than being commended by Prabhakaran.

'There's your boyfriend again,' Ajanthi announced, tapping my shoulder, 'wearing a sarong and riding a bicycle into the campus.'

Startled, I looked up. Roshan rode his bicycle past the sentry at the gate, made a semicircle in front of me and my friends, and stopped: 'Yesterday I sent a friend to look after your injured foot. Did she see you?'

By now my friends had walked away, leaving the two of us alone.

All I could think of was why on earth was he was wearing a sarong in public. No one I knew would do that. I forgot to answer his question or to thank him.

'I want you dressed appropriately when you come to see me,' I scowled.

'Forgive me,' he said, suddenly looking self-conscious. 'I'll see you later this afternoon. Don't be annoyed at me—I'm sorry.'

'Is that your boyfriend?' asked one of my comrades as I walked back to them. It was the very thing I feared—everyone thinking I had a boyfriend, especially a sarong-wearing one.

'Other than Anna, no one else needs to be concerned with Niromi's private life,' answered Kaanchana before I could.

'Did Niromi appoint you as her spokesperson?' mumbled the girl.

I chuckled.

Mid afternoon, I was on the lawn, with Ajanthi and Nihintha next to me. We were drying our hair after a wash at the well in one of the neighbouring houses. In the dry heat of the day, Nihintha's long hair was all but dry in minutes. I noticed a white van pass us by. It was nearly out of the university gates, when it stopped and reversed. Muralie poked his head out of the driver's window and motioned me over.

'What do you think of your battlefield experience?' shouted Muralie, his eyes disappearing into slits as he smiled.

Surprised to see Muralie, I rose to my feet and walked towards the van. I saw our training base commander, Theeba, next to him and the rest of her group, including Akila, at the back. They had been fighting a battle in a village not far from Jaffna. I was thrilled to see them all, but felt disappointed at having been sitting around doing nothing.

'The only field I've seen is this university lawn,' I sulked.

Muralie turned to Theeba and muttered something. Theeba then asked me to get on board: 'You're in my group now. Let's go see some action.'

I could hardly believe my luck.

'Can Ajanthi, Nihintha and Kaanchana come too?' I pleaded.

Theeba hesitated for a moment. 'Okay, since I've just lost three girls, I can take all of you into my unit of fifteen,' she said. I remembered that the first fallen female Tiger and the two captured female Tigers had all been from Theeba's unit. 'We have to leave now. Where is Kaanchana?'

Kaanchana was nowhere to be seen. Disappointed, the three of us got in the van without her.

As the van passed through the university gates, I saw Roshan riding his bicycle into the university and looking around, presumably for me. He was dressed in a pair of black trousers and a grey shirt. He didn't see me.

I had been feeling remorseful all morning about my behaviour towards him. I was meaning to apologise when I saw him next. But the van had already turned the corner and sped up the road, and Roshan soon vanished from my sight.

Thaatha and Aatchi, 1957.

Appamma, 1984.

My family, 1978. I am standing on the left.

Me at school prize day, 1986.

Shirani with Appa outside our home in Jaffna, 1985.

Ajanthi (left) with her family at her cousin's birthday party, 1985.

Ajanthi's gravestone, 2004.

Kittu lecturing a group of female Tiger trainees in the jungles of Vanni, circa 1990.

Tamil Tigresses: Dharshini (second from front), Theeba (centre) and Vadhana (far end) at a Tiger Leader's funeral, October 1986.

Thileepan speaking to the crowds at his hunger strike, with Muralie behind him (his face partially hidden), September 1987.

Muralie's sketch for me, made a few days before his death on 23 December 1987.

Prabhakaran (right) with his deputy Mahathaya, 1990.

11

EXPERIENCE OF THE BATTLEFIELD

My first day at the battlefront turned out to be disappointing. After leaving the relatively peaceful setting of the university, Muralie had driven us to a village just outside Jaffna called Kopaay and set us down at a large intersection where two units of roughly fifteen armed young men stood about. About 200 metres north of the intersection, we could hear the sounds of combat—three all-male units were involved in a clash with the IPKF advancing south down the arterial road towards Jaffna. Two helicopter gunships hovered above us, strafing intermittently at any movement below. The closely packed, palm-fenced houses on tree-lined streets were mostly empty as the villagers had fled them, seeking temporary refuge at schools, churches and temples.

Under the command of Theeba, we were the only female unit at this skirmish although we were yet to engage in battle. But Theeba was in command in name only. As she lacked battlefield experience she was completely reliant on Muralie and, because she hailed from Puthukkudiyiruppu, a coastal village on the eastern border, she did not know her way around the Jaffna Peninsula.

We hid under the dense canopies of the mango, moringa and tamarind trees that lined the streets. The smell of explosives hung in the air. I could hear the roaring tanks advancing towards the village. The tanks frightened me. One of the young men had informed me that our defending platoon was using just one 50-calibre green and a few AK-47, M16 and G3 rifles against the enemy tanks and helicopters, because the more effective RPGs were yet to be unearthed. It was mainly because of these tanks that our units were struggling to stop the advance of soldiers armed with primitive weaponry.

The IPKF were already in control of some of the villages to the north but, because they were still armed as though they were on a peace-keeping mission, they were low on ammunition. They were being very cautious in their approach at this stage—the territory was unfamiliar to them, and they had difficulty in distinguishing between civilians and Tigers and their sympathisers. At any instant, the Tigers were able to dispose of their weapons and become part of the crowd. Unable even to tell the difference between Tamils and Sinhalese, the powerful Indian military was not finding it easy to gain immediate control over our primitive guerrilla force.

We were ordered by a male unit leader to head down one of the roads to prevent any possible enemy advance from that direction, although no movement had been detected there as yet. I picked up a packet of lemon-cream biscuits someone was distributing and followed the others, both men and women, in a single file, munching on the biscuits, nervous with anticipation. I had no idea what I was supposed to do if we encountered gunfire. Surely someone would tell me.

Suddenly the man at the front of the line stopped in his tracks and crouched down. I was third in line, so I did the same. The whole line had now come to a grinding halt behind us. Only then did I see them—where the lane took a sharp bend, just 100 metres ahead of us, there were two stationary tanks and, beside them, about ten Indian soldiers. They were too well camouflaged for us to have seen them sooner.

That very moment, the soldiers laid eyes on us. 'Surrender!' one of them shouted, and immediately the others cocked their rifles and held them in position, aiming at us.

I looked to the leader of the line for orders but I quickly realised he had turned around and started running in the direction we had just come from. Suddenly everyone was running after him in a mad dash. I tossed away the packet of biscuits I was eating and joined the race, even managing to overtake some of my comrades. The soldiers did not follow us, perhaps uncertain of what our strength was. But no sooner had we reached the junction, completely out of breath, than we were confronted by a heavily-built man sporting a massive moustache on a bicycle. Saraa, the local Kalviyankaadu area Tiger commander, barefooted in a dirty sarong and shirt, began yelling abuse while rolling his large eyes at us.

'Fucking bastards! Which damn dickhead sent you that way? Where did your brains disappear—or don't you fuckers have one? It was anyone's fucking guess that the soldiers are advancing from the northern front! Knowing the facts, only a donkey would walk down that way.' Saraa paused and took a deep breath. 'Now, two by two take positions along this road. Bloody idiots! You are more useful dead!'

Saraa then did a U-turn on his bicycle and pedalled off, riding along the side of the road under the cover of the trees, muttering to himself.

I walked back to a position pointed out to me by one of the male leaders along the palm fence, still reeling from Saraa's language and our decision to run away. I was embarrassed we had behaved like cowards. Whatever had happened to the Tigers' slogan, '*Puramud-huhidaatha Pulihal* [Tigers never turn their backs to the enemy],' I wondered.

So two by two, we took up positions along the palmyra-palm fence, aiming our rifles in the direction of the enemy under the cover of some moringa trees. Ajanthi, Nihintha and Akila were also somewhere along the lane. I wished it would rain soon to ease the stifling humidity. For a while, there was no movement. I was feeling thirsty from the afternoon heat beating down on us. Then suddenly a few single shots were fired in our direction. They came from a fair distance away but I still I jumped with a start.

'Put your rifle on auto, stand up, fire a couple of shots and then duck back,' advised the young boy next to me. He looked barely fifteen, but gave me the impression that he was a veteran when it came to combat. Perhaps he had been one of those young boys posted on watchposts around the army barracks.

On the count of three, he and I did exactly that. I began to feel invigorated. There was an immediate response from the invisible soldiers—a few shots fired on automatic. The boy and I sat on our heels and took turns to open fire in the general direction of the enemy, unable to see any movement beyond the houses.

Soon the sounds of explosion and the roar of the tanks drew closer. The helicopter gunships began to fire directly above us. I could smell smoke. The enemy was gaining ground.

'Lunch has arrived!' yelled someone amidst the chaos. It was half past four in the afternoon. We took turns to step out to the nearby bus shelter where parcels of poorly prepared red rice and string-bean curry awaited us.

Within two hours of lunch we were ordered to withdraw towards Jaffna city. We had failed to stop the advancing troops, who were a couple of hundred metres behind us. I was disappointed that my first experience at the battlefront was nothing more than three hours of a few random gunshots. Nearly sixty of us scurried in two files along the sides of the road, taking cover under the trees from the hovering helicopter gunships. Saraa, the taskmaster, rode his bicycle back and forth along the road, abusing us.

Saraa's unit, however, was a jovial bunch—singing, reciting poetry and play-acting all along the way, as if the whole thing was just a game. 'How come your commander Saraa is so different to you?' I asked the young man behind me. He assured me that when not in battle mode Saraa had a real sense of humour.

It began to drizzle. Heat rose from the tarred road, releasing the smell of earth.

After walking for over an hour, we stopped for a short break. The troops were no longer pursuing us. Exhausted, Ajanthi, Nihintha, Akila and I stretched out on the middle of the warm and deserted street. The drizzle had eased and the street was already dry. As I lay on the road, I looked up at the sky. Heavy, black clouds gathered above us—a storm was brewing.

By the time we reached the outskirts of Jaffna, the dark clouds had turned into lashing, heavy rains. We broke into a large two-storey house and each unit occupied a different part. I felt strange entering someone's house without their permission; the owners must only have taken the bare minimum with them when they'd left for a public shelter because everything in the house looked in its place. Although the two men's units occupied different parts of the house, I still felt uncomfortable sharing a house with strange men. Muralie, who was in command of one of the men's units, was strict about the house being left the way we found it and the men took on all house-hold duties, including cooking and cleaning.

By the following day, the enemy had advanced further, capturing the entire village of Kopaay and then Koandaavil, just two kilometres from where we were. From the second storey, we had an uninterrupted view over the village and could see smoke bellowing from the house which was once our Freedom Birds' head office. The Indian soldiers were destroying all our previous bases.

What they were doing did not hurt us Tigers, because we didn't own the houses, but I felt sorry for the owners. By destroying these houses, the Indian military was only succeeding in losing the support of the people of Jaffna, whom they had come to protect in the first place. And the people were losing everything.

Over the next few days, as the enemy advanced towards us, instead of offering resistance, we gradually retreated, heading west towards Jaffna University. I was perplexed by this decision to flee, but I did not dare ask our unit commanders for their reasons. Perhaps, as the boys had told me, most of our heavy weapons were still to be unearthed and a new shipment was yet to arrive. Until our firepower was at an optimum level, we were unable to fight back.

Now that we were spending days and nights with our male comrades, they treated us with respect and courtesy and never once crossed the line, either verbally or physically. They willingly took on the traditional female roles of cooking and cleaning, although now and then one of them would make a remark that would betray their attitude. I felt that they accepted our presence in the Tigers, but many were struggling with the notion of us being their equals in combat. During one of his speeches at our training camp, Prabhakaran had told us that he faced opposition from his men when he made the decision to set up the first training base for women. As he saw it, women were the future of the organisation, as they were more dedicated and willing to please.

While we were on sentry duty one evening, I encountered an example of those attitudes from our male comrades. The house we were occupying was situated at a T-intersection facing the oncoming arterial road. To the north and west, the enemy was only a couple of kilometres away; they were near the major intersection at the university, where there was heavy fighting. The constant sounds of exploding artillery and gunfire could be heard from our sentry position, which was directly across the street from the house and located on a small wooden deck in front of a little mixed business. This deck sat over an open sewer that ran alongside the road.

When Akila and I came to hand over sentry duty to Ajanthi and a female comrade called Lekha, the sun had already set and we could barely see each other. The afternoon downpour had ceased and the mosquitoes were out. As Akila and I were about to return to the house, I spotted torchlight heading our way along the lane beside the shop. Civilians had long ago evacuated the entire area, so we became suspicious. We promptly cocked our rifles. Lekha took up a position on the deck, under cover of the shopfront, facing the connecting laneway. Ajanthi stood behind her. Akila and I waited on the road, me watching the laneway and Akila watching the road. 'Who is it?' shouted Lekha, toughening up her high-pitched baby voice.

The next thing we heard was a loud thud and a splash behind us. I turned around to find Akila missing.

'Help!' cried a feeble voice from the open sewer.

Darkness and the manioc plants that thrived in the sewer had made visibility almost non-existent. The torchlight was steadily advancing towards us in the lane, so we decided we would have to deal with Akila later. However, there was still no reply from the torchlight.

'Who is it?' shouted Lekha once again.

There was still no reply. We aimed our rifles and placed our fingers on the triggers. Lekha asked one more time and each of us understood that this would be the last time before we began firing shots.

'It's Karikaalan.'

Now we recognised the well-known Tiger, Karikaalan, and another man as they stepped onto the deck in front of us and then headed to the road.

'Why didn't you reply? We could've killed you!' screamed Lekha in frustration.

The two of them said nothing as they passed us, heading towards our house. Then they stopped a couple of metres away and burst out laughing, holding their stomachs and falling around like drunkards.

'We should've blown your heads off!' scowled Ajanthi.

'You are so arrogant!' I yelled.

'I wanted to see if you girls could actually operate a firearm, or if you were placed here just for decoration!' said Karikaalan.

The two men laughed out loud again. I was utterly incensed by their attitude but as I was thinking of something to say, a voice came from the sewer: 'At least now you could help me out.'

Akila lay awkwardly, her hands and feet splayed, trapped by the manioc plants. We finally managed to drag her out and rescue her M16, and then we burst out laughing too.

The next day, as the enemy advanced from the northern front, we moved towards the intersection near the university, where heavy combat was underway. Ours and two male units did not engage in combat. We spent two days waiting as back up at a shopping centre.

Someone decided to raid the chicken coop at one of the houses nearby and Ajanthi volunteered to help slaughter the birds by wringing their necks. She was so efficient that the boys honoured her with the nickname 'Chicken Thief'. While some were busy cooking chicken curry and rice, the other boys broke into the shops and stole clothing, food and other items and distributed them. Muralie had gone away on reconnaissance; I was certain he would not have tolerated theft.

'This isn't right,' I said to Nizaam, the fair-skinned lanky boy who was handing out the stolen goods. 'We are supposed to protect the public, not steal from them.' I felt I had to say something in Muralie's absence, and I was confident this was definitely the kind of thing he would have said.

'If we don't loot the shops, someone else will,' reasoned Nizaam. 'The public would much prefer us to have these goods.'

With that sort of reasoning, I too helped myself to a shirt, sachets of shampoo, packets of fruit-and-nut chocolate and a few children's books from the goods Nizaam brought to us. Muralie had previously banned me from reading magazines and novels. They corrupt your mind, he had reasoned. Although Muralie also banned the use of cosmetics, some of the girls were not deterred from grabbing tubes of skin-whitening Fair & Lovely face creams and also nail varnish.

'They are hoping to make good-looking corpses,' observed Ajanthi. 'Despite the gory gunshot wounds they'll endure.'

After lunch, our only meal for the day, Ajanthi, Akila, Nihintha and I decided we would go to the empty second floor of the shopping centre, hoping for some quiet. Downstairs, an ongoing disagreement between our unit commander, Theeba, and her deputy, Dharshini, was getting uglier—anything and everything was setting off the argument between them, and it seemed that everyone else was compelled to take sides. One of the senior girls, Vadhana, had told us that the two girls had once been in love with the same man—the Tigers' former north-west area commander, who was now dead—and had never really got along with each other. Today Dharshini was telling Theeba to take a proactive approach to the confrontation, without waiting for the men to tell us what to do. Theeba, in her usual manner, just laughed at the suggestion, which angered Dharshini and her friends.

But when we got to the second floor, we were confronted by a scene far worse—Nizaam and another young man, Navin, who had once been Thileepan's assistant, were bashing a shirtless, middle-aged man who cowered on the floor covering his head and face with his hands. Nizaam was hitting the man with a broomstick while Navin, despite an injured foot, was shouting profanities and kicking and punching him. They did not see us.

'Let's go back down,' whispered Akila.

The three of us stood by the stairs, watching them, unsure what to do. I was shocked to see another side to the fragile-looking boys, Nizaam and Navin. I had always found them to be well-mannered and quietly spoken, but now Nizaam's broomstick snapped in two with the force of his hits.

'We must confront them,' I said, feeling a little unsure about actually doing it—their uncharacteristic behaviour made me nervous.

'But the man could've been a spy or something,' reasoned Akila in a quiet voice as Nizaam and Navin walked away from the near-unconscious man, taking the other set of stairs back down.

We ran to the man. But he began to sob and pleaded with us to leave him alone, even after we told him we were there to help.

'To hell with the lot of you!' he screamed, so we let him be.

When I saw Muralie that afternoon, I told him about the incident. He listened attentively and assured me that he'd take care of it. But when I saw Muralie attempting to talk to Navin later that day, I realised nothing would come of it.

'Who are you to tell me what to do?' Navin rebuffed Muralie and hobbled away, dragging his injured foot behind him. Although Muralie was a unit commander, he was not in charge of Navin. However, due to seniority in position and age, Navin should have respected Muralie. Although I pretended not to notice the exchange, I saw in Muralie's eyes what I thought was an expression of frustration.

The next three weeks turned into another waiting game. The day after the looting, we found ourselves near the university again, waiting behind battle lines as back up. Muralie and his boys had gone off elsewhere, so Manmadhan, the God of Lust, was now in command of Theeba's unit. We occupied the large verandah of a lovely house with a beautiful garden behind the university. The IPKF still hadn't advanced to the university, but not for lack of trying.

As we waited we were forced to listen to Manmadhan's monologue. He was undeterred by the lashing rains, the exploding artillery shells, the cracking sound of tracer rounds that lit up the night sky and the strafing helicopter gunships. He talked into the night while we tried to sleep. Soon everyone knew Manmadhan's entire life story.

Just before midnight, we heard the thumps of a motorbike. It was the burly, thoroughly soaked commander, Sengamalam. 'Everyone pack up right now,' he roared. 'Theeba, position your group at the university.'

We grabbed our meagre belongings in the dark and walked there. The rain was still pouring down and by the time we arrived at the university campus, we were wet to our underwear. Ajanthi and I were told to position ourselves behind a little tree. Soon, the rain turned into a storm. It was a struggle to keep our eyes open against the downpour. I didn't know what we were doing behind the tree, given that we couldn't see anything in the dark except for the lights and sounds of explosions a little distance away.

'Come on, girls. Apparently they don't need us here after all.' It was Manmadhan's voice.

We had been standing in the rain for over an hour but he was unapologetic about his mistake. Despite feeling annoyed, no one uttered a word of complaint. We followed him silently into the lane-way that joined the university to the technical college and took up a position along the old railway line as he instructed.

'I'm going to have a nap,' said Manmadhan. 'Wake me up if you need anything.' He then headed towards the tiny Hindu temple at the end of the laneway.

I was paired up with Nihintha behind a large tamarind tree. Ajanthi and Akila were behind the next tree. The rain still poured. From the gunfire and mortars, it was clear that a battle was being fought about 300 metres in front of us.

Our second-in-command, Dharshini, challenged Theeba for obeying Manmadhan's orders without question, considering that he was asleep inside the temple and all we were doing was soaking in the rain. Soon these two girls' tempers were flaring and they were arguing aloud, bringing up past events. Others, still standing at their positions metres away in total darkness, joined in the quarrel and took sides.

My friends and I were chuckling to ourselves, finding the battle in front of us far more fascinating than the one only a little way ahead.

Suddenly a motorbike turned into our lane.

'Which moron positioned you here?' I recognised the thundering voice of Sengamalam. 'Can't you see that there's a group in front of you fighting? If you had anything inside your skulls, you wouldn't be standing here. Unless you are planning to shoot the boys in front of you! Fucking idiots!'

Just then the 'moron' appeared from inside the temple. 'Go to the technical college and I'll let you know what do to next,' said the calm voice of Manmadhan.

Leaving two girls on watch, we headed to the technical college, everyone muttering to themselves in fury. We lay on the cold, hard, muddy concrete floor of the mezzanine, our wet clothes clinging to our bodies, mosquitoes ringing in our ears, and our holsters heavy on our chests. An hour into the struggle to get some sleep, Ajanthi and I were nudged for 2am sentry duty by Nihintha.

'What's the time?' asked Ajanthi, just managing to sit up. I had already risen to my feet and slung my AK onto my shoulder.

'It's five minutes to two,' answered Nihintha. 'Why do you ask?'

'Niromi, can you check the time exactly?'

'Eight minutes to two,' I said.

'Well, come back in seven minutes, Nihintha.'

'Come on Ajanthi,' I tried to coax her. 'We're awake now anyway.'

By the time Ajanthi got moving, the seven minutes had passed and, when we reached the temple, Akila was cross: 'Did it take you this long to walk three metres?'

'It does when you send Nihintha ten minutes too soon,' replied Ajanthi.

Akila handed me the pen-torch, the walkie-talkie and the sentry list, and disappeared into the darkness. The rain had now eased to a slight drizzle. It was still warm.

Ajanthi squatted on the ground and sighed: 'I wonder when they'll make me a group leader. No night sentries after that.'

I knew that she was referring to Manmadhan and Theeba. They would be sound asleep until woken up for sentry duty, when they would suddenly suffer from either a severe stomach pain or a headache.

At the end of the hour, Ajanthi took the sentry list and the pen-torch from me and checked the names: 'Theeba acca is rostered after us,' she said. 'No matter what disease or illness she comes up with tonight, she is not escaping her sentry duty.'

True to her words, it wasn't long before I saw Theeba and her partner floundering their way towards me.

One afternoon in November, we girls were driven to a village called Vaddukkottai, nearly ten kilometres north-west of Jaffna, where, much to my delight, we were reunited with Muralie's unit. A few days later, we made our way further north through back roads and laneways on foot, our journey made treacherous by the heavy monsoon rains that flooded our paths and soaked us to the bone. Some of my comrades slipped and fell into the floodwaters and had to be rescued. Most of them lost their footwear. At nights, we occupied abandoned houses and ate meals provided by local sympathisers. Except for Muralie, the rest of us had little idea where we were headed, or why.

Nearly a week later, when we arrived at the picturesque village of Neerveli—also about ten kilometres north of Jaffna, but to the east—we realised we had made the round trip to avoid areas already controlled by the enemy or heavy fighting. The torrential monsoon rain of the past weeks had eased, and the sun was shining over the village. With its characteristic red soil, on which vast banana, coconut and tobacco plantations had been established, and with the sounds of its rushing streams and chirping birds, I thought Neerveli undoubtedly the most beautiful village in all of Jaffna Peninsula. It was only then that I remembered that nearly eighteen months earlier Theeban had supposedly shot himself in the village of Neerveli.

Akila and I were positioned behind a small, thorny bush. A few metres away, behind another bush, Ajanthi and Nihintha waited in readiness. Nearly ninety Tigers, thirty of us females, lay in ambush beside the main road that connected Neerveli to the next village. The enemy was advancing along it.

This was our first combat opportunity in three weeks, after my first day on the battlefield in Kopaay. Since then we had been on the move. Other than the hourly sentry duty twice in the day and twice in the night, we had very little to do but clean our rifles and chat. The older girls often took on meal preparation, which was only once per day. Other than the roaring sounds of the approaching tanks and the shrill sounds of cicadas, all was quiet. We lay on the wet red clay soil, being eaten alive by mosquitoes; our rifles cocked and our fingers ready on their triggers, while our ears were finetuned to receive the command to fire.

Night was falling. Soon, heavy rain clouds and a power blackout produced total darkness. I could barely see my hand in front of me.

'F . . . F . . . F . . . Fire!' came the command from the man in charge of the operation. He only ever stammered when issuing commands during confrontations. Sometimes the stammering went on for too long—I wished he would delegate the task to someone else. The boys often laughed behind his back, saying the enemy would be tapping on our shoulders before Arul Master managed to issue his command.

I pressed the trigger slightly, releasing three bullets in automatic mode into the blanket of darkness in front of me, the discharge pushing me backwards. Suddenly the night sky lit up with lights and sounds like fireworks, but these were exploding bullets, artillery, mortars and tracers. The air grew thick with the pungent smell of exploding chemicals and burning metal.

Then I heard a voice behind me: 'Is this Niromi?'

'Of course not,' I replied, recognising Muralie's gentle voice.

I knew he would not be pleased to see me here. Earlier, when one of his boys came to deliver the message for us to assemble for the ambush, there was a specific instruction from Muralie for me not to join. The injury to my foot, caused by the shell fragment weeks earlier at the university, had continued to fester after being exposed to floodwaters during our long marches. Muralie had been concerned and had taken me to the local surgery earlier that week; and he did not think I should be fighting.

It was typical of Muralie to be concerned about everyone in his care. Having spent an entire month in his company, my admiration for him had only grown. He expected a high standard of ethical behaviour from everyone and practised what he preached. However, his attitude did not sit well with some of the others. Once I had seen one of the girls help herself to a shirt from a house we had temporarily occupied. 'Please put it back,' I told her. 'Muralie anna says that this sort of behaviour gives our entire organisation a bad name.'

'Of course, what that know-it-all Muralie anna says is God's word for you,' she had retorted sharply. 'But not for me.'

Similarly, I had observed Navin's continued defiance of Muralie's rules since the day he and Nizaam had beaten the man at the shopping centre. Unlike everyone else who requested Muralie's permission to go anywhere on their own, Navin came and went as he pleased. Muralie claimed that this compromised Navin's own safety as well as the entire unit's, but Navin took no notice. I felt disappointed for Muralie on these occasions—it seemed that always doing the right thing was not enough to please everyone.

Now, on this particular night at the front-line, I knew that Muralie would not like my presence there, although I certainly did. When he threatened to punish me if I made it out alive, I was happy to accept that.

The battle lasted all through the night. I hardly noticed the time pass as we continued to fire intermittently, changing our magazines only once. All I could see were flashes of gunfire; I aimed at them but never saw a soldier.

A tiny sliver of daylight began to appear on the horizon just at the moment when resistance from the enemy finally began to wane. I was certain that we had stopped them from advancing into the village.

The parrots were creating pandemonium when we heard Arul Master's command: 'Ce . . . ce . . . cease f . . . f . . . fire!'

We walked the length of the arterial road, along which the enemy had tried to advance, to inspect the damage. The morning sun reflected off the cartridges and dud rounds that littered the road, and the buildings along it bore the scars of last night's battle, with damaged roofs and bullet-ridden walls. Further along the road were bloodstains. I looked for any sign of human casualty, but the only thing lying dead on the road was a cow. We later learnt that two enemy soldiers had been severely injured.

We turned into a paddock and made our way back to our temporary dwelling. I had been on an adrenalin rush all night and suddenly exhaustion overcame me. The day was growing warmer.

'I could do with a shower,' said Ajanthi.

Suddenly Akila collapsed to the ground in a seizure, foaming at the mouth. While I removed her holster and rifle and waited anxiously, I wondered if it was the stress of the night that had caused her to fit. She was not an epileptic. Many minutes passed before she regained consciousness and then, for the rest of the day, she acted entirely out of character—withdrawn and fearful. Ajanthi, Nihintha and I stayed by her side and reassured her until she came back to her normal self.

From the resistance it had faced, the enemy realised that we were well established in Neerveli. From their position in the adjoining village of Kopaay, they now rained artillery shells and mortars in our direction all day and all night. Most of Neerveli's inhabitants had meanwhile taken refuge at the famous Hindu temple. Anticipating that the enemy would advance under the cover of darkness, we spent our nights in a house on the border of the village, each one of us rostered for two hours sentry duty, in pairs, day and night.

One evening, about two weeks after we had arrived in Neerveli, the enemy got their target right. In the living room of our sanctuary the local area commander Akkachchi was telling us how he had escaped from the enemy by pretending to be a farmer, when artillery shells began raining down very close by, competing with the lashing rain. Suddenly, one of the shells hit the house and everyone crashed to the floor of the living room for cover.

The shell had hit one of the bedrooms and exploded, spraying hot metal fragments, bricks and dust. Many more shells followed, hitting the house and bringing down the ceiling in different rooms. My heart pounding, I lay very still on the floor like everyone else, with Ajanthi and Nihintha on either side of me, expecting the next shell to fall directly on us. I wondered who was alive—I hadn't heard anyone scream, which was a good sign.

After what felt like an eternity, the shelling changed direction. Finally, everyone rose to their feet and found the living room intact and everyone safe and sound. The sight of our bodies covered in cement dust provided us with some comical relief, but soon an argument broke out between Dharshini and Theeba, after Dharshini accused Theeba and Theeba's best friend Saaradha of hiding in the toilet, the only room with concrete ceiling, like cowards while her unit was in danger.

During the daytime our male comrades, their pistols tucked into their waistbands, would go on reconnaissance missions. In their sarongs and on bicycles, the boys were able to blend in with the locals. The local area commander had taken in a nine-year-old orphan boy, who proved to be particularly useful because of his ability to get close to checkpoints unsuspected. He had perfected the technique of crying out for his parents whenever the soldiers questioned him. We girls, on the other hand, in our dirty shirts and trousers hardly looked the part of feminine, floral-dress-wearing village girls. Without these dresses and not knowing our way around, we were confined indoors almost all of the time.

On one occasion, after Nizaam had returned from a reconnaissance foray, Muralie said to me: 'We need to talk to you in private.' This made me anxious. I followed the two of them outside, into the lane.

Nizaam sat on a small brick wall under the shade of a moringa tree holding an overnight bag in his hand. 'Niromi, I visited your mother and sister,' he said, startling me. 'Your neighbourhood is swarming with the enemy. I narrowly avoided capture. Your mother sent these for you.'

'How did you know where I used to live?' I asked him, unable to believe that Amma and Shirani would've known that Nizaam was a Tiger.

Nizaam hesitated for a moment, looked up at me with his large, half-moon eyes and said: 'Navin took me there.'

That made sense. Having been Thileepan's most trusted assistant, Navin knew where I lived. He had also increased his popularity in Jaffna after he spent so much time next to the dying Thileepan. No wonder Amma and Shirani trusted him as a Tiger and gave him the bag. But why did he and Nizaam visit my family? If Navin was involved, I knew that Muralie had not authorised this.

Inside the bag were Shirani's favourite turquoise balloon dress, my identity card, a pair of diamond earrings and a letter from mother.

I felt my chest tighten. Until now, I had managed to put aside my thoughts about Amma and Shirani whenever they popped into my head. This had been easy because I was always surrounded by friends. But now Nizaam had brought their images alive and I desperately longed to see them.

'Can I visit them?' I asked, looking at Muralie, who was sitting next to Nizaam.

Muralie shook his head and said, 'Not yet.'

'I told them that you would visit tomorrow but Muralie anna doesn't think it's a good idea,' said Nizaam and glanced at Muralie.

'But I have a dress and my identity card now,' I said to Muralie. 'I should get through without arousing suspicion.' As I spoke the words, I tried to imagine myself in the balloon dress and attempting to mingle with the local village crowd.

'I'll let you know when you can visit your family,' replied Muralie, broodingly. 'Go inside now and don't discuss this with the others. Tell them your family sent you the bag, and leave it at that. Understood?'

I walked back into the house, feeling disappointed at not being able to see my family. Muralie was being unreasonable. If it was safe enough for well-known Tigers such as Nizaam and Navin, to visit my family, then why was it not for me? I felt there was something suspicious about the relationship between Muralie, Navin and Nizaam, but I couldn't work out what it was. As I sat on the floor next to my friends I felt desperate to see Amma, Shirani and my dogs, but I knew that until there was a break in hostilities it wasn't going to happen.

12

A BREAK IN THE HOSTILITIES

We did not remain in Neerveli long. After another night of battle with no lives lost and no one hurt (although a bullet burnt
a hole in Muralie's shirt collar and another one grazed over my right
arm) we made our exit from the village, having failed to stop the
enemy from advancing. The sun had risen by the time we reached the
large Hindu temple on our way out. When they saw us, the refugees
at the temple began wailing. There were hundreds of them, all village peasants, including many young children and elderly. In the small
fires on the temple grounds, they were cooking rice or manioc.

'Stop all this fighting, children! We can't cope any longer!' wept
an old woman.

A large group joined in the chorus. 'Please give up this futile
war,' they pleaded.

'Fighting the Sinhala government is one thing, but why fight the
Indians? They came to save us,' others implored.

'But the Indians aren't who you think they are,' Muralie tried to
reason while the rest of us remained silent. 'We are fighting to save
you from them.'

'If you are fighting for us, we can tell you right now that we don't
want this!' shouted someone. 'We are tired of living as refugees in

our own land, and it's all because of you.' I felt that these people were being ungrateful. Did they not see we were willing to die for them? Prabhakaran had told us that the Indians were not to be trusted. These people would one day learn the hard way.

Over the next few days, the Indian soldiers ravaged this picturesque village, setting fire to many properties, raping many women and killing many men. Their mighty army, who were now in their tens of thousands in the north and east of the country, had taken over three weeks to capture Neerveli, and we had left the innocent to pay the price for our resistance.

Everything changed for us very quickly after leaving Neerveli. As a result of the Indian advance, we were now in enemy territory and no longer able to show ourselves in daylight or to engage in open combat. Having captured the peninsula and gained control of all main roads, the enemy had stopped pounding the villages with random artillery and people were returning to their houses. The soldiers hunting for us were patrolling mostly on foot, so, as fugitives, we hid ourselves in the few houses that were still abandoned and moved every two days or so after nightfall. We learned to keep our voices down all the time.

Meals of bananas and bread, and sometimes boiled manioc and coconut sambol, were organised once a day by Nira, a young man from the locality. It had been over three weeks since we had had the opportunity to wash ourselves, because most of the houses in the villages did not have an indoor bathroom and washing in the open at wells in their backyards was too dangerous. Due to lack of hygiene, everyone was suffering from dermatitis and head lice. It was an unpleasant sight to see and hear everyone scratch ceaselessly day and night.

Although we did nothing much more than sit around, we were unable to relax. We remained fully armed all the time, either at sentry duty or indoors. The threat of being found out by the enemy was forever present.

One day, as I sat polishing my rifle inside one of the abandoned houses, I overheard Muralie and Gandhi discussing something serious in quiet voices beside me. Gandhi, an area leader of a nearby village, was one of Muralie's closest friends. He was a softly spoken, shy man. As they sat on the inside verandah that surrounded the centre courtyard of the Spanish-style villa, the two of them discussed Mutthu, a fellow Tiger.

'Why did Mutthu resign?' asked Gandhi.

'There was suspicion that Mutthu's father was a spy,' Muralie said. 'So the organisation ordered him to *put one in the head* of his own father. So, after shooting his father in the head, Mutthu resigned.'

'I have two questions,' I interrupted, as I used the long wick we called a 'pull-through' to clean the barrel of my AK. 'First, why pick the son to kill his father? Second, why did Mutthu not resign before carrying out the orders?'

'It was to test where his loyalties lay,' answered Muralie. 'By fulfilling his orders first, Mutthu had proven his loyalty to Anna. Never mind he resigned after. It would be a different story if he had resigned first—that'd be considered an act of defiance.'

'Do you need to kill your parents to prove your loyalty to the movement? Now that's . . .'

Gandhi quickly interrupted me: 'Niromi, if you received orders from Anna tomorrow to kill Muralie, would you do it?'

I knew why Gandhi had asked me that question. It was no secret that I admired Muralie. 'Not a chance! I'd resign immediately,' I replied, unable to lie even to a hypothetical question.

Muralie looked disappointed. 'I didn't recruit you so you could say such things,' he remonstrated. 'When you get orders, I expect you to carry them out without question.'

'Don't be silly!' I reproached. 'I know I'm nobody but there are some things I refuse to do.'

'Obviously Niromi is more loyal to Muralie than to the organisation,' smiled Gandhi.

'I'm loyal to my friends *and* to the cause,' I corrected him.

Muralie looked at me and sighed: 'I expect you to be loyal to Anna, under all circumstances.'

Bang!

There was gunfire at the front of the house. It created a mad scramble inside, everyone grabbing their belongings and charging

out the back door. An army patrol had spotted our sentry at the front
door and opened fire. We, including the sentry, Jenny, ran into the
dense array of palmyra trees behind the backyard.

'Keep running—we're in no position to fight back,' I heard
Muralie shout.

As we scurried through tree-lined back streets, and lanes that
were partially flooded, where at times we found ourselves in waist-
high water, some of the passers-by shouted encouraging words, but
most moaned and cursed.

'We don't want this war—only you do,' they complained.

'You're all going to ruins and taking us down with you.'

We took no notice and continued on our way. That day we managed to evade the soldiers; but the words of the people refused to
leave me. I kept thinking: *Aren't we fighting for the people? If they don't
want the war, what was the point of this struggle?*

On 21 November, a forty-eight hour ceasefire came into effect; we
had no idea why. All it meant for us was two days of relaxed sentry
duties, time to cook and eat a decent meal, and to indulge in a much-
needed wash. Perhaps I could visit home.

It was about half past seven in the morning when we reached a
large public school at a village called Alavetti, nearly 15 kilometres
north-west of Jaffna. We had walked for over an hour. The skies
remained overcast and the air was thick with humidity.

'I went to school here,' said Muralie to me as we reached the
school's cricket grounds. I was impressed by the large and well-
equipped village school. The one thing the government was doing
right was giving children access to free education all over the country; even at private schools we never had to pay for our textbooks.

'I bet you were a trouble maker,' I said, 'and expelled from school.
So, with no future, you decided to do something useful and joined
the Tigers.'

Muralie, laughed. 'I was the dux of the class.'

'It's easier to believe that this ceasefire would result in peace.'

'I'm not joking.'

'Neither am I.'

Just then, Ajanthi and Akila appeared behind Muralie, motioning me to join them.

'We saw something large and black behind the bushes,' muttered Ajanthi anxiously. 'It looked like a bear. Come on, let's go over and take a closer look.'

A bear in a village?

We made our way to a large bush and I cautiously peeped over it. To my horror, it was Mahathaya lying on a wooden bench in his black leather jacket in the stifling heat. Hearing the rustle behind him, he turned around and smiled at us. His bodyguard, Gaddafi, said: 'Mahathaya anna is ill with malaria.'

We turned and ran away out of embarrassment. I reproached the girls later for picking on Mahathaya for entertainment: 'The poor man is sick, and probably missing his new bride. Let's agree to forgive him for his poor fashion sense.'

Not long after, five more units, each containing fifteen young men, arrived at the school. It was beginning to drizzle again. We were now standing inside the dark, damp school hall in front of Mahathaya, whose illness made him unsteady on his feet. He was stroking a stray dog that was wounded and had fleas.

'I feel sorry for these animals,' sighed Mahathaya. 'The owners have run away to the temple for shelter and left these poor pets to defend for themselves.'

I was not convinced by his concern for these animals. We were in the business of killing humans, so I wondered if his nickname, 'Crocodile', had something to do with what I thought were fake tears.

Now Mahathaya turned his attention to us. 'Many of you will lose a few comrades in this war,' he said. 'Keep their dream alive by focusing on winning the war for them and for our people. If a comrade dies next to you, use their body as a shield and continue fighting. When you leave, make sure you remove all their weapons.

There will be plenty of time to mourn later.' Mahathaya paused for a moment. 'The Indians could look like fools at the end of this war and we should be determined to make that happen. All of us have a very important role in showing them that we are not to be taken lightly.'

So this ceasefire was only a minor glitch in the hostilities, which meant I wouldn't be able to go home for even a visit. Just when I thought he had finished his speech, he continued: 'I know that food is scarce. But, no matter how hungry or thirsty you are, or if you are suffering from illness, I want you to keep your mouths shut. Your complaints will only bring the morale of the entire unit down. I will punish anyone I hear complaining.'

He made us repeat the oath of loyalty to the Tigers and to Prabhakaran that we had taken during our training sessions and then he restructured the units. Three men were to join our ranks: Paandiyan, who was in command of Jaffna city; Lawrence Thilakar, who was the Tigers spokesperson; and Sudharshan, a short stocky fellow who was appointed in command of both Muralie's remaining fourteen young men and Theeba's remaining thirteen girls. Over the past week Muralie had sent some in our unit back to their homes to resume civilian lives. It had become too difficult to move in large groups and find food and shelter for everyone.

We were woken before dawn after having spent the night on the verandah of another abandoned house a few kilometres away from Muralie's school. The seven units split up and went their own ways. I was relieved when we, together with Muralie's unit, reached our destination, a two-bedroom bungalow located at the end of a cul-de-sac with private lane access, which was clean and furnished. It even had a double bed in the master bedroom. The ceasefire was still in effect so we used the opportunity to shower at the well and wash our clothes; then we sat in the sun and were dry within minutes. The older girls cooked a goat the boys had brought. While the rest of us took turns to stand sentry at the entrance of the lane, Muralie and Gandhi ventured out into the village on reconnaissance. After all, it was their locality.

Although it was Lekha's and my turn to be sentries, Ajanthi, Akila and Nihintha kept us company, sitting on a tyre next to us. The sun shone beautifully after the rain that had plagued us the past few days.

Suddenly a bicycle turned into the lane. First I saw Muralie, seated on the front handlebar of the bicycle, then Gandhi who was pedalling furiously. Both of them looked worried. As they drew closer, Gandhi tried to apply the brakes and failed. We watched in horror as the bicycle raced past us and crashed against a coconut tree near the well, throwing the men off.

We burst into laughter.

Muralie and Gandhi climbed to their feet, dusting the soil off their clothes, their faces flushed red.

'If you'd been a little more off target, the two of you would've ended up in the well,' I said, still laughing.

'You both looked like you were running away from a ghost,' giggled Lekha, holding her stomach.

'We saw worse,' replied Muralie, still looking embarrassed. 'About fifteen soldiers at the entrance to our cul-de-sac, metres from here.'

Gandhi was trying to straighten the handle of the bicycle.

'So what?' chuckled Ajanthi. 'We are in a ceasefire, aren't we?'

'One can't trust armed soldiers, they could take us captive. *Chari*, stop laughing and keep alert. They may head this way.'

We saw no soliders while on duty and at the end of my shift I handed the sentry list and the walkie-talkie to the two young men replacing us and headed to the house with the girls.

'How much longer do we have to wait for lunch?' asked Ajanthi, peering into the kitchen.

'At least another half hour,' answered Sadha, one of the senior girls who had also trained us.

We decided to take a quick nap in the master bedroom. As I was removing my chest holster, I remembered Muralie's orders to leave footwear at the door so as not to muddy the strangers' house. I headed back to the room after taking off my sandals at the front door when one of the boys on sentry duty rushed into the house scream-ing, 'ARMY! ARMY!'

Everyone ran for their belongings. In a flash, I charged into the bedroom and grabbed my holster and rifle. By now, everyone was falling over each other trying to get out the front door, the only exit from the house. The big, burly, swearing man, Saraa, whom I had encountered on the first day of battle and who had rejoined us that morning, grabbed his RPG and positioned it on the small front verandah facing the lane through which the soldiers were advancing. Muralie ordered us out in the opposite direction, which meant we had to break through the fence at the end of the side yard.

Having gathered up all my belongings I dashed towards the front door, searching desperately for my sandals.

'You stupid girl!' shouted Saraa. 'Get out of here!'

'But my sandals . . .'

'Get out!' screamed Saraa, and then turned back to the laneway. 'You fucking bastards! I'll charge this RPG and blow you into smith-ereens! Get out, you sons of bitches, or I'll kill you! Mother-fuckers!'

I ran, following the others. It had started to drizzle again, mak-ing the red clay soil slippery. Without footwear some slid and fell as they tried to scramble through the fence constructed from palmyra palm and barbed wire. The red clay clung to their clothes. As I stood impatiently behind Sudharshan, waiting for him to pull apart the fence and make his way through, I looked back. What I saw made my jaw drop.

About 15 metres away, near the well, were the Indian soldiers, some standing and some squatting, with their hands on their hips, rifles slung on their shoulders, laughing at our predicament. Just three metres in front of them was Saraa, trying to frighten them off with his stature, RPG and obscene language. I didn't know what to think.

By now Sudharshan had made his way through the fence and so I crammed myself through the hole. Once everyone was clear, Saraa, still threatening to blow the soldiers' heads off with his RPG, ran backwards and squeezed through the fence. The soldiers did not fol-low us, but a helicopter gunship began to track us.

We walked briskly through coconut and banana plantations, trying to evade the helicopter. I was feeling the effects of not bringing my sandals with me: the roads were gravelly; the fields were soggy and slippery; and the still unhealed gash on my right foot was throbbing.

'I knew that my RPG was no good because it had jammed earlier,' said Saraa, roaring with laughter. We were shocked. 'I took the gamble of pretending to be ready to fire hoping that they wouldn't fire at me during a ceasefire. Otherwise I would've lost my head.'

The drizzle turned into heavy rain as we hurried along. Nearly twenty minutes later, thoroughly soaked, we arrived at a grand house. 'Oh what a waste of all that food we cooked,' lamented one of the girls as we took shelter on a verandah. The house was empty.

Suddenly everyone was looking despondent. We hadn't had a meal since a banana each at midday the day before.

'Can't we go back later and get it, Muralie anna?' asked someone.

'*Cheechee!*' Muralie shook his head. 'I know it's tempting, but the soldiers could have poisoned it.'

We sat on the verandah lost in thought, watching the rainfall until late in the evening when an ever-resourceful local boy, Nira, managed to bring us four bananas and a loaf of bread to be shared among thirty of us. The villagers in general were happy to feed us, although they may have not approved of our behaviour. Feeding the hungry, even if one did not have enough for one's self, was entrenched in the deeply religious Sri Lankan culture.

After our meagre meal, we set out once again. We walked for over an hour in a single file, in the pouring rain, enveloped by darkness, until we reached a small house. I was tired from walking barefoot in the rough terrain and my stomach growled from hunger, so I was glad when Muralie ordered everyone to go to sleep on the verandah. But it was Muralie's assistant Rajan's and my turn at sentry duty.

I was positioned at the end of the backyard, facing a banana plantation. Since I could hardly see anything in front of me, I relied on my hearing. It would be too challenging for anyone to walk through the banana field without squelching in the mud or tripping over the fallen leaves and trees.

Half an hour into my watch, the rain had eased back. Occasionally a dog barked somewhere in the distance, or a lizard or snake rustled the wet leaves on the ground. I shifted from one leg to another, occasionally yawning and wiping the rain off my face, trying very hard not to think of food. I could smell the ripe bananas through the overpowering odour of damp earth. My stomach growled again. Then I heard movement behind me. I turned around and heard Rajan whisper, 'I've brought the next sentry.'

I handed my post over to Dharshini and headed to the house. I strained my eyes in the dark and found the girls' bodies huddled together on one side of the verandah. There was a narrow strip of spare room that had been reserved for me by my friends—a spot between Akila and some onion sacks stacked along a wall in front of the doorstep. My friends knew I always preferred to sleep at the end of the line so I could sleep in relative peace without many arms and legs thrown over me. I stretched out on the floor, still wet and without removing my heavy chest holster with its three magazines fully packed with rounds and four hand grenades. The thought of my next watch, at four in the morning, made me sigh.

I closed my eyes, trying to ignore the buzzing mosquitoes; but it was hard to ignore the dampness of my clothes, my gnawing hunger and the pungent odour of onions that penetrated my nostrils and filled my lungs. Lying on the dirty, cold concrete floor, I felt sorry for myself. I rested my head on my holster and thought of Amma and Shirani. A lump came to my throat. I didn't want to think of them any more, so I closed my eyes and silently recited my night-time prayers. I never really prayed for myself; but I asked God to keep all my loved ones safe and rest the souls of those who had died in this war.

Someone was snoring loudly. Unable to take much more disruption to my limited rest, I burst into tears, feeling frustrated by our inability to enjoy even a few hours of relative normality. I knew nothing about how Ajanthi and the others were feeling because, no matter how horrible things were, we never complained to each other.

I rolled over onto my side and tried to focus my thoughts on Roshan. Thinking of him was the only thing that ever made me feel better instantly. I recalled the time he came to my house and, to Amma's annoyance, made himself comfortable on one of the cane chairs on the verandah and asked for a cold drink. His cheekiness made me smile, though it hadn't at the time. I finally drifted into sleep.

I was jolted awake by someone stepping on my right shoulder. I managed to stop myself from screaming, realising where I was. By now, the figure had walked past me and moved into the front yard. From the faint moonlight shining through the clouds, I realised it was an old woman. I sat up and observed her, wondering what she was doing out in the dark. I doubted that she realised that strangers were sleeping on her verandah because she did not react at all. Perhaps her eyesight was poor too. Then, to my horror, she urinated—simply standing in the middle of her front yard—and then turned around and started to head back towards the house. I quickly huddled against Akila, pushing her as far as I could, but there was no room. The old woman, with her wet muddy feet, trod on my left arm and shuffled into the house.

Disgusted, I wiped the wet mud off my shirt and tried to get back to sleep, realising there was no other place I could go. I went back to thinking about Roshan. Within an hour, another figure opened the door and trod on my shoulder narrowly missing the bullet graze on my right arm and went out to the front yard—it was an old man. This went on all night, with me trying to drift into sleep in between.

Soon, someone shone the torch on my face and muttered 'sentry'. I picked up my rifle and went back to my position from earlier in the night, under the mango tree, facing the banana plantation, and began thinking about Roshan again—his dimpled smile and sideways glances—and tried to ignore my reality. I wondered where he was and what he was doing at that very moment. Perhaps he was in a men's unit somewhere not far away and we would run into each other some day soon.

Then I remembered that in three days he would be turning twenty-four.

13

TRYING TO IGNORE MY REALITY

It was 1 December, around half past four in the morning. The ceasefire had long ended. In total darkness, Muralie positioned us around the little brick house set beside a banana plantation. On one side of the house was a clearing, thick with grass and dotted with lantana bushes, and bordered by large stands of palmyra trees. There were nearly thirty of us still in the unit, although I had lost track of the random comings and goings of various Tigers. We had slept in this recently-abandoned house for the past two nights. Its previous occupants had sought shelter at a nearby temple after we moved into the neighbourhood.

Muralie had started to wake us up an hour or so before dawn and then he would make us wait around the house in readiness. After sunrise, we would return to a little mud hut, 200 metres down a dirt lane, where we remained during daylight. But before we did that one of our men would go over to the hut on reconnaissance and give us the all-clear. There was always the imminent danger of soldiers lying in wait for us, as they often ambushed our hide-outs at dawn. Muralie thought that spending our days at the mud hut and sleeping the nights elsewhere would mislead the soldiers and their informants.

It had been working for us up until then but that morning Muralie's theory was put to the test. It was still dark when we saw our scout running towards us: 'Army! Army!' he panted, jolting us from our complacent, half-asleep state. 'I was walking down the lane when I spotted some green helmets under lantana bushes facing our mud hut.' The young man waved his only hand agitatedly—his right hand had been lost over a year ago, when he had been working at a Tiger factory, trying to produce weapons.

'*Chari*,' said Muralie, as calmly as he could. 'They have been tipped off as to our whereabouts, so this could be a large round-up. I want everyone to take up their positions and listen to my instructions.'

I was posted on the northern side of the house, under a small mango tree, watching out over the clearing. Although the horizon was now alight, it was still dark around us. The morning was pleasantly cool. I had my bag on my back and my sarong folded and tucked behind my heavy holster. My cocked AK was in my left hand, its trigger lever set on regular firing mode.

As we kept watch in silence, listening to birdsong, the first rays of the sun seeped through the palmyra trees. Suddenly, machine guns began to blast from the southern side. All those who stood facing south fired back. Adrenalin surged through me.

Muralie shouted, 'Everyone withdraw north-east!'

We started to run backwards, and machine-gun fire came from the east and west, proving that Muralie had made the right decision. We realised that, just as Muralie had anticipated, the enemy had surrounded our hut under the cover of darkness and had been waiting until first light to attack, believing we would still be there. If we had spent the night in the mud hut or headed back there in the morning without scouting first, undoubtedly we would all have been taken unawares and perished by now.

I followed Muralie and ran as fast as I could through the wet, knee-high grass. Behind me trailed some of the men, including Saraa. We made our way across the clearing and towards the palmyra trees. A few hundred metres past the trees, we could see a row of houses.

The firing was heavy, with bullets and hand grenades exploding around us. In their panic, those ahead of us had left a trail of footwear, sarongs and other personal items. One of the straps on my brand-new sandals broke, causing me to flounder. The boys had broken into a shop the night before, without Muralie's knowledge, and stolen footwear, sanitary napkins and underwear for us. I had by now become less concerned about right and wrong.

Despite the heavy gunfire I stopped and hurriedly tried to pull my sandals off, but the straps around the ankle made it difficult. Bullets whistled past my ears and shoulders. Saraa screamed 'Niromi, you're going to get yourself killed!' and ripped the bag off my shoulders, pushing me to the ground and crashing down next me.

I managed to get rid of my sandals, and both of us staggered to our feet and ran after the others. By now everyone had reached the houses. There was chaos and panic. No one knew which direction to take—the gunfire and explosions appeared to come at us from all directions. We hurried through private properties, pulling apart palm fences and scaling concrete walls, trying to avoid laneways. Even though the gunfire and explosions behind us were beginning to ease off, soldiers were everywhere.

It was fully light now. The temperature was rising. Every time we spotted green helmets, we quickly ducked down behind fences until the soldiers moved away. My heart felt as if it was pounding outside my chest. My lungs were on fire.

After rushing about here and there and taking a few U-turns, we were lost. It seemed that whatever direction we took, the soldiers were there. As we continued to run about aimlessly, I saw three men, wearing gold jewellery and watches, standing on the porch of a large brick house, smiling at our predicament and passing a joint between them. It seemed odd that while all the other civilians had locked themselves inside their houses in fear, these three were flaunting themselves.

'Who are they?' I managed to ask Muralie amid the chaos.

'They are TELO boys, working with the enemy.' We were still in Muralie's local area and, having worked there for years, he knew everyone and everything.

We moved away as quickly as we could, and continued to look for an opportunity to break through the encircling soldiers. Suddenly Saraa hissed, 'We are going to have to fight our way out of this. Let's put our belongings on the roof of this house. We can pick them up at a safer time.'

Easan, one of our male comrades, and Nira, the sympathiser who spent most of his time with us, climbed onto the roof of the portico of the modest bungalow by the side of the lane and Saraa began to throw our bags up to them. I was hesitant about leaving my bag behind—it contained Amma's letter, Shirani's dress and a few pieces of paper on which I wrote poetry—but Saraa kept assuring me that we would be back to collect it. I hurriedly took out the earrings and my identity card, and placed them in my shirt pocket.

Suddenly, the front door of the house was flung open and a man appeared. When he saw us, he began to wail: 'Please children, don't leave them here,' he pleaded. 'If the soldiers find them, my family and I would surely be killed and our house torched. Please, I beg you.'

Saraa assured him that there were no weapons in our bags, but the man continued to plead. We ignored him and threw all our bags up to the boys on the roof, who hid them from the view of the street. Then we resumed our quest to break through the round-up.

We were in someone's backyard when the soldiers positioned in the street outside the house's front fence spotted us and opened fire.

'Ayyo!' Jeycha, who had joined Muralie's unit in Neerveli, screamed and crashed to the ground holding his chest.

Startled, we scrambled for cover behind some coconut trees. I realised that we were surrounded by the enemy. Muralie, who usually only carried a pistol, grabbed Rajan's AK and opened fire screaming, 'Hit it, fellows. Hit it—we need to break through this round-up.'

A bloody battle began.

People inside the surrounding houses wailed, dogs barked, everyone, including the soldiers, was screaming and yelling obscenities at each other. Bullets from the machine guns, mortars and grenades began flying and exploding all around us. The air filled with the smell of smoke. It was evident from the approaching gunfire that more soldiers were closing in. I waited by the side of the house with my finger on the trigger of my rifle, unsure what was expected of me.

Then I heard Saraa's command: 'Niromi and Amuthan, cover the back fence!'

So I rushed to the back of the house and crouched behind the palm-and-barbed-wire fence along the back lane, with the young boy, Amuthan, beside me. Then I saw that he only had a hand grenade. It was now entirely up to me to defend this position. It felt as if my heart was in my mouth.

'If you see soldiers, throw the grenade at them,' I told Amuthan. 'I'll take care of the rest.'

As the battle continued behind me, I scanned the area through the sights of my rifle, my right index finger ready on the trigger. I was prepared to fire at anything that moved. The sun was scorching and sweat trickled down my face. All of a sudden, the chaos behind us diminished to a few random shots and I turned around to find no one there.

I felt devastated. I realised the others must have broken through the enemy line and escaped. I told myself that there was no need to panic and all I had to do was run after them. My stomach felt hollow and the pounding of my heart was deafening. There was no time to waste.

'Come on, we have to run,' I said to Amuthan.

Realising our predicament, the boy began to howl: 'Ayyayyo, Niromi acca! They've all gone! I'm scared! What are we going to do?'

'Shut up!' I snarled, more to calm my own nerves. 'Put your kuppie in your mouth and follow me. I'll protect you until the last bullet in my magazine, but now stop crying and hurry!'

With the cyanide capsules in our mouths and our pulses racing, we swiftly ran backwards and then turned around and dashed down the side of the house towards the main road. My right index finger was still hooked around the trigger. I stopped short of the road, behind a tree, and motioned Amuthan to take cover behind me.

I looked both ways. On the street, lay three bodies—two of them were soldiers and the other was one of our boys, empty-handed. I could not be sure if he was still alive. The street was otherwise deserted and eerily silent. It was possible that the soldiers were waiting in hiding. I crouched and stepped onto the hot road. Suddenly heavy firing came at me from my left. I dashed across the road and at its far edge I lost my balance and slipped on the gravel. Bullets sprayed around me, making the sand rise.

Amuthan also made it safely across the road, and both of us ran through heavy gunfire down a dirt track through a paddock. As I ran, I was trying to work out which direction the others had taken. A few metres away to the right, I could hear dogs barking, but it could have been at the soldiers. A man in the paddock saw us and yelled, pointing to my right: '*Thangatchi*, your people went that way.'

For a second I debated if I should believe him. He could be working with the enemy, sending us straight into their hands. But I had little choice. We ran in that direction and, to my relief, were confronted by Gandhi. Only then did I take the *kuppie* out of my mouth.

'Thank goodness,' he hushed. 'I just realised you were missing and was coming back. The others are only a few metres ahead of us. Let's hurry!'

I was glad that someone had remembered us. When I saw Saraa, I shouted at him: 'You positioned us to cover the back fence. You should've remembered us instead of leaving us to die there!'

'But you are alive,' laughed Saraa.

Although we'd escaped the round-up, we were still not out of immediate danger. The soldiers knew where we had broken through their encirclement and they were sure to follow us with reinforcements. We continued hurrying through paddocks and bushes, avoiding streets and laneways. The civilians we encountered on our way made their opinions known to us, none of them agreeable. I was getting tired of them blaming us for fighting—*the ungrateful masses*, I thought.

A few hours after fleeing the village, we finally stopped in a banana plantation. Everyone was battle-weary and exhausted from the heat. The adrenalin rush had subsided, leaving us feeling flat. We threw ourselves onto the cool, soggy ground. Then the soles of my feet began to throb. I examined them and found they were covered in thorns. I was surprised that I hadn't felt the pain 'til then.

'I can't believe the number of thorns in my feet,' laughed Vadhana as she picked them out with a rusty safety pin. 'It's a miracle that I managed to run so fast and scale all those walls with feet like these.' She was the most easy-going person among us—nothing fazed her. I waited my turn for her safety pin.

Discussion centred around the events that morning. Saraa estimated that about two hundred soldiers had been involved in the round-up. He believed it was just luck that we had chosen to break through where their defence was weakest.

I mentioned seeing the teenage boy lying dead on the street. Everyone recalled him, but no one could think of his name. It made me feel sad.

Jeycha was dead too. We remembered his always cheerful personality. 'He was from my village,' said Theeba.

'Has anyone seen Nizaam?' Nira asked. We looked around, trying to locate Nizaam's slight frame and delicate face.

'The soldiers took him away!' shouted Vellai, one of the boys. All of us looked at him with a start.

It was then I realised that Navin was missing too.

We were now occupying two adjacent houses in the village of Sudhumalai, north-west of Jaffna. After fleeing our previous hide-out as a result of the round-up, we had hidden in a banana plantation for over a week, sleeping on grass mats thrown over the sodden earth, battling mosquitoes and enduring primitive conditions. We had lost all our belongings other than our rifles, the clothes on our backs, and the empty hessian sacks each one of us owned. The bags we had concealed on the roof of the house had been confiscated by the soldiers the same day, after the owner of the house had informed them about it.

I was upset by the loss of Shirani's dress and my notebook, but I understood the man's fear that had led him to betray us. The Indians had proven themselves to be a ruthless enemy—having no idea of the difference between Tamils and Tigers, they punished everyone the same way. Only seven weeks earlier, on 21 October, they had massacred nearly seventy patients and medical staff at Jaffna Hospital, suspecting the presence of Tigers there. Some witnesses claimed that the Tigers shot at the IPKF first from inside the hospital.

Sudhumalai village was totally under the control of the enemy. But, believing that we had all but vanished from the village, the Indian military patrolled only at dawn and dusk, and confined their movements to main roads. Being able to sleep indoors here, albeit on the floor, was welcome relief. But the general situation was by no means improving for the Tigers—every day there was news of comrades dying in other parts of the peninsula as we continued to lose territory.

One night our Jaffna area commander, Paandiyan, who had been with us up to that point, left us for Jaffna city. He reasoned that if we did not remind people of our presence whenever possible, the public would begin to think us defeated. Within days, outnumbered and nearly captured by the enemy, he and his two bodyguards shot themselves. Their bodies, like most victims of the fighting, were left to the mercy of crows and stray dogs.

One afternoon Ajanthi and I left the house to investigate some loud noises we'd heard. When we stepped into the hot soil of the backyard we found a group of boys kicking and punching Vellai, the young man who had told us about Nizaam's disappearance after the ambush. He had been given the name Vellai, meaning 'white', as a joke, because he was very dark, a characteristic of those hailing from Mannar in the north-west of the country where many had east-African ancestry. He was barely conscious but kept muttering: 'I didn't do it. I didn't do it.' A crow cawed incessantly from the pawpaw tree nearby.

'What madness is going on here?' I asked, horrified.

'One of our boys was passing through Neerveli junction in civilian clothes and saw Nizaam held as a captive and kept as an exhibit by the soldiers,' said Rajan, who was watching on, seated on the raised verandah of the house. 'Apparently they had shaved all his hair off and beaten him black and blue. Nizaam managed to let our boy know that there is an informer in our unit and he asked us to finish him off.'

'But how do you know it's Vellai?' asked Ajanthi.

Just then I noticed some of the boys digging a hole in the ground. Alarmed, I shouted: 'What are you planning to do? Please stop!'

'They're about to bury him alive,' replied Rajan, matter of factly.

'Are you humans or wild animals?' screamed Ajanthi.

But no one took any notice of us. The young boys, who always seemed so good-humoured and polite, now looked totally possessed as they bashed Vellai. I was aghast at how quickly they had turned on their comrade over a rumour. Over the past six weeks, they had spent their days and nights with this teenager; they had shared their meagre meals and the floor they slept on with him. Now, within minutes, they had dehumanised him and themselves.

My blood chilled, knowing there was nothing I could do to stop the murder that was taking place in front of me. I dragged Ajanthi away and we marched into the house, unable to witness the torture any longer. We had to find someone who could stop this.

But it seemed that the boys had deliberately picked a perfect opportunity—the men in command, Sudharshan, Muralie and Arul Master, were nowhere to be seen. The three men regularly disappeared like this to go on reconnaissance. The Tiger spokesperson, Lawrence Thilakar, and the big man, Saraa, had left our unit a week before. So Ajanthi and I returned to the women's house and informed Theeba, as the most senior person there, begging her to do something before it was too late. But she shrugged it off, saying she was 'powerless over the boys'. We complained to Dharshini, but instead of doing something herself she started shouting at Theeba. Terribly distressed, Ajanthi and I stayed inside talking to Akila and Nihintha, who were also disturbed by what we told them, and tried to block out Vellai's cries, which echoed throughout the house. The other girls seemed completely oblivious to it as they carried on laughing and chatting.

That evening I sat on the verandah on my own, listening to the shrill of cicadas and thinking about Vellai's murder. I had difficulty accepting that torture was fair game in war.

In all my encounters with the enemy I had never once seen their faces—we fired in their general direction, hoping someone's bullet would hit our target. But was I capable of shooting someone at close range? Or torturing another human being—whether it was an enemy soldier or, as it was in this case, one of our own?

I remembered that earlier conversation with Muralie and Gandhi, discussing how one of the boys had been ordered to shoot his own father. I realised how naive I had been when I had first joined the Tigers, never giving much consideration to such possibilities. All I had thought about was fighting the repressive government and the heroism of those who did—I had not comprehended the reality. But I had been warned: on the day Ajanthi and I had explained that we wanted to join the Tigers, Thileepan had said that the movement we saw from the outside was not the same on the inside. At the time, I had not understood the full implications of what he had tried to tell us.

Rajan came over and sat next to me, with a smirk on his face.

'Do you know what the boys did to Vellai?' he asked, but did not pause for me to answer. 'They buried him up to his shoulders and then made him swallow oxidised cyanide, to see what it did to him. It was Justin's final blow on the skull with an axe that . . .'

'Stop it! Rajan, stop it!' I screamed, blocking my ears. 'I don't want to hear another word!' I knew Rajan had remained a spectator earlier because it was not in him to kill someone—he carried Muralie's AK but had never once fired it—but he had not tried to stop the others. Now he was teasing me.

Someone laughed behind me and said, 'What a prude you are, Niromi.' I recognised Justin's voice.

I rose to my feet, turned around and looked at Justin in the eye. 'People like you make me sick!' I shouted and stormed into the house.

'But Vellai was originally TELO,' I heard him say. 'He should have been killed a long time ago.' Then the other boys burst out laughing behind me. For them, killing Vellai was no different to killing a cockroach.

By the next day, no one was talking about Vellai. I had not had the opportunity to discuss the murder with Muralie, because I had not seen him. 'I feel sick that we are part of a group that behaves like animals,' Ajanthi had remarked that morning, looking unhappy. 'I just want to go home and see my family. Perhaps I'll feel better after that.'

'I agree. Perhaps we could ask Muralie for permission.'

Within hours, our hopes were dashed. Mid morning Muralie sent word, asking for Ajanthi and me. He and Sudharshan were seated on the dirt outside the boys' house. We were perplexed by this invitation.

Sudharshan spoke first: 'Later today we'll be asking some more of the girls and boys to return home, as it's getting tough to move in large groups.' Sudharshan stroked his bushy beard, and continued. 'We want you to know that we can't send you home. Niromi, the day after Nizaam and Navin visited your family the soldiers went looking for you with your old poetry notebook in their hands; they took your mother and sister away for interrogation and then set up camp nearby.'

Sudharshan then looked at Ajanthi: 'There are no such dramas at your house, although there is a heavy presence of soldiers in your neighbourhood.'

Ajanthi and I were speechless.

I could not believe what I had just heard. How did the soldiers know that Nizaam and Navin had promised my return home the following day? How did my poetry notebook, which Rasaak had told me was in the possession of Tigers, fall into the hands of the enemy? And how did Sudharshan know all this?

But neither Ajanthi nor I asked the questions, knowing that the men would not give us the answers.

Muralie, who had been silent 'til now, scribbling on the sand with a twig, spoke up: 'I don't want you to raise your hands when we ask for volunteers to return home.'

Images of Amma and Shirani ran through my mind. I felt distraught. I hoped that the soldiers were kind to them; it was not their fault that I had joined the Tigers. In fact, they didn't approve of it.

'They've been released and are all right now,' comforted Sudharshan, perhaps reading my emotions. I had no other choice but to believe him. 'We'll keep you informed. Don't mention this to the others.'

I felt relieved.

'I wish I could see Mama, Dada and Nilanthie for Christmas at least,' said Ajanthi as we headed back to the women's house through the hole in the fence. I was homesick once again—and for a time I forgot all about Vellai.

Later that evening, Akila, Ajanthi, Nihintha and I sat on the *vakku*, the large concrete tub near the well. We were away from the streetlight, awaiting our turns at sentry duty. Since only twelve girls and eight boys remained our sentry duties came thick and fast.

We had spent much of our time that day packing the weapons of those who had gone home in large quantities of grease and layers of polythene bags. They were to be taken elsewhere for stashing once more, after their short stint above ground during the recent fighting.

I was glad of the company of my friends. Without their constant support and energised chatter, I might have struggled to move on from the image of the dying Vellai, from missing my family.

'Shh! Did you hear that?' asked Nihintha.

Suddenly we heard footsteps approach us.

'Who is it?' shouted Akila.

'Ansaar and Chandhu Kutty,' replied a man's voice.

When they stepped into the light, I immediately recognised Ansaar—he had been at the Jaffna technical college sentry post. Neither Ansaar nor his bodyguard carried rifles—their pistols were discreetly tucked into their waists. Ansaar was obviously an important figure in the Tigers if he had a personal bodyguard or assistant, although we did not know what his position was. I noticed the sandals on their feet. All the men in our unit, including Muralie, were wearing dirty shirts and sarongs and had no footwear.

'I was in the neighbourhood and heard that Muralie's group was here,' said Ansaar.

After chatting with us for some time about how we were coping in the unit and how bad the situation had become for the Tigers, Ansaar said that he had to return to Jaffna that evening in order to maintain our presence there. He had to find a safe place to sleep every night—a difficult task, given that even our sympathisers distanced themselves from us these days due to the brutal treatment they were in danger of suffering at the hands of the enemy. There were also many in the community who betrayed the Tigers. The deaths of eight of Ansaar's previous bodyguards, including the one I had met at the technical college two months earlier, was a testament to the danger he faced every day, operating without the support of a large unit like ours.

'Tonight I've arranged for us to stay at an elderly woman's house right in the middle of town,' said Ansaar before he left. 'It's extremely dangerous there, and understandably she is very reluctant to let me stay. I hope either Chandhu Kutty here or I will survive to see you again.'

'Perhaps it's your turn to die,' I joked. 'Give your bodyguard a break this time, won't you?'

The following morning, as we all stood watch during our usual predawn stake-out, we saw a lonely figure running towards us through the tobacco plantation that surrounded the house. We cocked our rifles and held them in position.

Then we heard the voice of Chandhu Kutty, Ansaar's bodyguard: 'Ansaar's dead! Ansaar's dead!'

We were told that at around two o'clock in the morning, when the household was fast asleep, soldiers had surrounded the house and captured Ansaar, grabbing his pistol and ripping the cyanide capsule from around his neck before he could bite into it. Then they had dragged him into the front yard and begun beating him with iron bars and bicycle chains. Ansaar did not stand a chance against some three dozen soldiers and died after a few hours of torture. They had gouged his eyes out while he was still alive.

Chandhu Kutty had managed to escape, hiding himself in a water tank on the roof next door, from where he witnessed the end of Ansaar's life.

I was stunned. My chest tightened and I could hardly breathe. I sat on the ground and placed my AK next to me. I felt heavy with despair and guilt. I should not have joked with him about dying.

'I can't believe that we were talking with him only last night,' mumbled Akila, sitting next to me.

Muralie delegated two boys to go with Chandhu Kutty and retrieve Ansaar's body. 'He needs a proper burial,' said Muralie. Chandhu Kutty said that the soldiers, typically, had left Ansaar's body in the front yard of the house where they had killed him. After the soldiers left, Chandhu had managed to drag the body away and hide it in an abandoned house nearby. He would try his luck again to bring the body to us hidden in a van belonging to a friend.

The next afternoon, the corpse was displayed at the boys' house. Ansaar was stretched out on a wooden bench in the middle of the back verandah as we stood in a circle around him. I had to gather every bit of courage in me to look at him. The only thing that confirmed it was Ansaar was his straight hair. His face and hands were badly bruised and caked in blood. In place of his eyes were blood soaked cotton balls. There were no visible bullet wounds to his body.

We stood with our heads bowed and observed a minute's silence. Muralie draped the Tiger flag he had been carrying for himself over Ansaar's body. Suddenly someone broke into loud sobs. I looked up to find Ajanthi covering her mouth with her left hand, trying to control herself from wailing.

As we headed back to our house, I was thinking about the last few moments of Ansaar's life and was struck by the similarity in the way both he and Vellai had died. I would have expected trained soldiers to display more discipline and restraint than our callow guerrilla youths. Besides, the foreign army had no right to engage in such behaviour in our land, where they did not belong; to come here and impose their rules on us when they had no idea what we were about. We had been oppressed for too long, and we weren't about to let that continue.

I resolved that I would not let Ansaar's death be in vain. I was going to fight until the foreign army was driven from my homeland and we could attain Tamil Eelam, where there would be no more torture or murder.

14

THE LAST FEW MOMENTS OF LIFE

It was two days before Christmas 1987. All I could hear was my thumping heart; all I could see was the fear in the faces of the others. Sweat trickled down my back. We were silent. Our ears were finetuned to the sound of stealthy footsteps and our eyes to any sighting of strangers; our index fingers were curled around the triggers of our rifles. It seemed like a typical morning for us, but that was about to change dramatically. By the time the sun would set on us this day, nothing would ever be the same.

Our enemy, the Indian military, was now in full control of Jaffna Peninsula and it seemed that they were everywhere. Since the last ambush we carried out on the advancing soldiers in Neerveli, we had not actively engaged in combat and I hadn't fired a single shot. We could no longer shelter in a safe haven for more than two or three nights—the soldiers always turned up in the end. Although this was confirmation that there was indeed another informer, not Vellai, I assumed it was someone from the general public or a rival movement.

The previous day we had arrived at a small brick house and found another two units, one of them a women's unit. By the light of the full moon, my friends and I had searched for Kaanchana who we had not seen since we were together at Jaffna University.

Someone said she belonged to another unit. We were disappointed. Two young local men who were Tiger sympathisers had organised the delivery of a cauldron of tea and ten food parcels for the forty of us. It was our first decent meal in many days—rice with pumpkin curry and coconut sambol washed down with tea. My three friends and I had shared one parcel, the few handfuls satisfying our shrunken stomachs.

After dinner we bid the other units farewell and set out once again in a single file, following the two young men from the village, who knew the back lanes well enough to avoid the patrolling soldiers. The night sky hung low above us, the blanket of stars and the bright moon lighting our way. All was silent as we moved through backyards, paddy fields and more plantations.

When we passed a paddock full of cows, one of them suddenly bolted away, and the rest followed. The sound of their hooves disturbed the dust and the quiet night. A dog barked, and soon all the dogs in the neighbourhood joined in. This was a bad sign—with the night curfew still in force, the dogs could only be barking at either an army patrol or at us—now the enemy could trace our steps.

I had sensed the uneasiness of those in front and behind me. I knew that everyone was wishing the dogs would stop barking. After a few more deviations down gravel lanes and through muddy puddles, we arrived in a village called Urumpiraay at the Maanippaay–Kaithadi Road, a main road connecting the eastern end of the peninsula to the north, which meant we could expect a military patrol every few minutes.

'Two by two, we'll cross the road,' Muralie had said, barely speaking loud enough for us to hear him. 'The first two to make it across will provide cover on both sides of the road so the rest can follow.'

Just then a military jeep went by.

'Okay, hurry!'

So we had charged across the road two at a time and made it across before the next patrol. Then we continued walking in a single file and arrived at a very small, unfinished, abandoned house. I realised we had occupied this house previously. Usually we never returned to the same place—it was clear to me that we were running out of safe havens.

Nihintha had managed to reserve half a small room for the four of us to sleep side by side. We rolled out our empty hessian sacks on the rough sand and concrete floor, rested our weapons next to us and stretched out, still wearing our heavy chest holsters.

The horizontal position was usually enough to bring me sleep, but that night I had felt restless. As I lay staring into the darkness that enveloped us I tried to shake off the unsettled feeling that had crept into me. It was the nervous expectation that the enemy could turn up at the door any moment, knowing where we were. I had tossed and turned for a while until Akila, half-asleep, began gently patting me on the shoulder. Soon I was fast asleep.

I had been roused for my 2am sentry duty by a girl called Nithi. I'd quickly jumped to my feet and slung my AK over my right shoulder. My position was at the front of the house, facing the open field. The moon shone brightly. Ploughed earth stretched in front of me, dotted by small lantana bushes and a few coconut and palmyra trees. I had looked up at the night sky and it was a blanket of glitter. Everything seemed so peaceful I could no longer feel anxious. Then I saw a star shoot across the sky—a bad omen. For a moment I was gripped by anxiety but then I dismissed it as mere superstition and tried to divert my thoughts to Roshan.

I'd wondered if he too was on sentry watch somewhere nearby and had witnessed the shooting star. It seemed that the more I had thought about him over the last months, the less clear his face had become. However, the memory of our few encounters remained as strong as ever. I hoped he was alive and well. I was confident that the war would end somehow and we would see each other again. When we did, the first thing I'd do would be to apologise for my behaviour at our last encounter at the university. For a moment I fantasised about admitting to him that I liked him and seeing his face blooming with happiness at my confession, and this brought a smile to my face.

In the morning, after the dawn stake-out, we had waited inside the house while Vadhana and Dharshini were at sentry. We could not relax until the end of their watch, when the sun would be well up and we could be certain of not facing a round-up that dawn.

Someone had begun a conversation about fortune telling. Sadha claimed to know a thing or two about palm reading—as she scanned the palms of her first volunteer, Ajanthi, she observed that her life line was short.

'That's disappointing,' Ajanthi had remarked, unfazed. 'I want to see us achieve Tamil Eelam.'

'High ambitions,' laughed the young boy, Amuthan. 'You'll be a real old grandma by then, Ajanthi acca.'

Just then a panic-stricken Vadhana had appeared at the doorstep.

'Muralie anna, I saw soldiers! A huge line-up of them stepped out of the far banana plantation! What should we do?'

Everyone had frozen for a moment. All eyes were on Muralie and he was thinking fast.

'I want everyone out of the house!' Muralie had commanded.

And so we scurried out of the house, in the direction opposite to where Vadhana had informed us the soldiers were advancing from. We hurried through farms and plantations, in the direction we had come from last night. Clearly we were going to have to negotiate the main road that we had crossed the night before. Again we would have to find a few seconds of opportunity to make it across alive.

And then we heard machine-gun fire—three bullets fired in automatic. We froze. I looked at Muralie. I had rarely seen panic in those almond eyes.

'Hurry! Cross the road, one by one! Be very careful!'

I was behind Ajanthi and there were a few girls ahead of her. Cautiously we moved forward along the little dirt lane towards the road. The barbed-wire fence on either side of the lane, covered with runners, obstructed my view of what was happening. Then I saw Nira step forward.

Bang!

'*Amma!*' Nira screamed for his mother. His right hand went to his chest. Then he collapsed.

Suddenly automatic gunfire and hand grenades began to spray at us from the sides of the road. We crashed to the ground. Then I heard gunfire behind us—a couple of hundred metres away. The enemy was closing in on us from all directions. There was a metre-high water tank on my right and a few palmyra and banana trees on my left. There was no place to hide. Now the remaining twenty of us, with our few AKs and M16s, were going to have to face an enemy who was well prepared and equipped, and had been lying in wait for us since the early hours of the morning.

I saw Muralie grab his AK from Rajan and run forward. 'Idiots at the front line, fire and break through! Break through!'

At the back of the line, Sudharshan was yelling obscenities at us: 'Get going, you mother-fuckers! If not, I'll blow your brains out myself!'

I aimed my AK-47 at the road and cocked it while keeping an eye on my comrades in front of me. Sadha made a dash across the road, followed by Jenny. I saw Sadha fall.

The noise of exploding grenades and gunfire was deafening. Everyone was yelling and screaming. More and more jeeps and tanks arrived on the road, bringing reinforcements. A helicopter gunship hovered above us, strafing.

I crawled forward on my elbows, still holding my AK in position, my forefinger on the trigger.

Then I saw a hand grenade flying over from the left side of the road in my direction. As I scrambled on my hands and knees to get away, I realised that Gandhi was in its path, behind the palmyra tree, firing with his AK.

'Gandhi anna, duck!'

The grenade hit Gandhi on the head and exploded. His head blew into smithereens and its contents of flesh and blood splattered, drenching me. His headless torso fell to the ground like a tree trunk. I wanted to scream, but no sound came from my throat. Everything felt strange—as if I wasn't physically there any more.

By now, all those in front of Ajanthi had attempted to cross the road. Holding her AK in position, Ajanthi got off the ground and on to her knees. Briefly she turned around. In that moment I was reminded of the two of us at school, where I had sat behind her in the third row. Whenever she turned around, a chalk duster would come flying at her.

'I'll see you on the other side,' she muttered hurriedly.

When Ajanthi said that, I nodded in agreement. But not with any sense of certainty. I saw her poised, ready to dash across the road. Then abruptly she fell backwards, her hands and feet splaying awkwardly. From the centre of her forehead, blood spurted out and gushed down her eyebrows and eyelids, wetting her auburn hair. Her jaw slackened, and her AK clattered to the ground.

In shock I felt the air go out of my lungs. I could not draw it back in. My head went numb. I tried to reach out to her, but she seemed so far away—out of reach, on the other side of a smokescreen. All the while I am certain I was screaming, 'Ajanthi! Get up! Get up!' but it seemed to have no effect on her.

The explosions, smoke and cries of agony were filling the air around me. Another hand grenade fell behind me to the left and exploded. I saw Panjan, already prostrate on the ground, howl and drop his head. I felt a sudden jab of pain in the back of my left shoulder. Holding my AK in both hands, I tried to crawl forward so I could get beside Ajanthi. To my right I could see the two boys, Rajan and Easan, struggling to drag Muralie through the wet grass. He seemed to be half conscious, but his overgrown curly hair, his caramel shirt and his blue sarong had all turned red.

Nothing of what was happening around me felt real any longer. It was like I was watching over it all from afar, from some other place.

Suddenly I was brought back to earth by someone yanking me by the collar of my shirt from behind. I spun around to find Sudharshan still holding my shirt collar. Another hand grenade fell and exploded just two metres away. 'Hurry!' he shouted and turned around, dragging me with him.

I slipped and fell over Panjan. His skull was opened on one side, exposing its contents. 'Sudharshan anna,' I mumbled, stumbling to my feet, 'we must get Ajanthi, Muralie anna and the others!'

'They'll follow us,' yelled Sudharshan, now holding on to my left arm and ducking down to dodge the bullets that were flying past. 'You just come with me.'

I believed him.

I saw Amuthan on the ground, face down. I yanked my hand away from Sudharshan's hold, and grabbed Amuthan's arm and shook him. 'Come on, Amuthan, we have to go!'

But his body sank back to the ground.

'*Vaadi!*' [Come on, woman!], screamed Sudharshan, dragging me with him. He had never before used such an insulting tone towards me.

We started running away from the scene, through the wet grass towards the houses we had scurried past earlier. Hand grenades and mortars were falling and exploding around us, creating smoke and scattering hot pieces of metal. I had surrendered my fate to Sudharshan. Now I followed his commands without a thought or question.

As we quickly scaled a tall concrete wall, an extended volley of self-loading rifle rounds came flying from behind us, gouging holes in the wall. On the other side, we found Theeba, Lekha, Vadhana and Jessie in hiding—they had escaped ahead of us. We ran aimlessly this way and that for a while, encountering explosions in every direction.

Finally, when we were unable to discover a way out, Sudharshan decided that we should hide in a nearby large lantana bush. So, on our hands and knees, we crept into its interior and lay down on our backs, our hearts still pounding inside our heaving chests and sweat trickling down our faces and backs.

Finally catching my breath, I looked up at the dappled sunlight that filtered through the dense bush, silhouetting crawling worms and buzzing insects feeding on the lantana's leaves and flowers. The pungent smell of the bush and the damp earth blended with the metallic smell of blood.

I looked around to find nine of us there, including Easan, who had been injured by a bullet which was still lodged in his right thigh, a young man from the local village whose name I did not know, and Sengamalam, who was tying a piece of cloth torn from his sarong around Easan's thigh. I had not even realised that Sengamalam had joined our group.

My friends were nowhere to be seen. I told myself that they were hiding somewhere safe. The last time I had seen Akila she had been on my right and firing with her M16 from behind the water tank. Nihintha had been ahead in the line, somewhere near the road.

Thirsty and tired, I closed my eyes. My mind was numb. It was as if had lost my ability to think. All I could feel was the present—the prickly bush, the sunlight, and the imminent danger. The sounds of gunfire and explosions were gradually waning. Heat was rising. No one spoke for a long time. Now and then Easan would moan in pain.

'What's the time, Niromi?' asked Lekha in a quiet voice. I opened my eyes and looked at my watch. It was half past ten. Five long hours had passed since that moment when Vadhana had spotted the soldiers.

I noticed a tiny shell fragment stuck to Lekha's forehead. I pulled it out. I felt another sharp pain in my left shoulderblade. Lekha told me that shrapnel had left a gash in my back and torn my shirt. 'You are covered in blood, Niromi.'

I touched my hair and face; I felt the stickiness of blood and also some moist, rubbery bits. I sat upright and looked at my blood-soaked shirt and chest holster. I discovered pieces of flesh clinging to them and it was only then that I realised that I was drenched in tissue and blood. The memory of Gandhi struck me like a lightning bolt— I remembered the grenade explosion and his headless body falling to the ground. I knew now that the blood and tissue were Gandhi's. My throat tightened.

Someone tapped me on my shoulder. Sengamalam quickly put his fingers to his lips, indicating not to speak. I could now hear murmurs and the thud of heavy boots. Recognising them as soldiers, everyone, except Easan, quickly sat upright.

'Quietly cock your rifles,' whispered Sengamalam. 'Place your *kuppies* in your mouth. If the soldiers spot us, fire the entire magazine into them and then bite the capsule.'

We did as instructed and waited with our index fingers on our triggers. The voices and the thuds drew closer. We heard random shots—the soldiers must be firing into suspected hide-outs. They were coming our way, and were sure to fire into ours.

Suddenly the soldiers' boots appeared just a few metres away from us. Blades of grass and dry leaves were crushed under their weight.

A twig snapped next to me.

I felt the gentle pressure of the trigger under my right forefinger. The cyanide capsule grated between my teeth. I drew a short sharp breath, and then calmly waited.

The soldiers knocked on the door of the nearest house and questioned the occupants in broken English: 'You see Tigers? Tigers?'

I could not hear the response but I saw the woman, holding a young child on her hip, shake her head left to right.

The soldiers moved away from us, scouring through bushes and searching houses as they went. They did not look in our direction. After about twenty minutes, they completely disappeared from our view.

At last I took the cyanide capsule out of my mouth, released my finger from the trigger and changed the AK's trigger-lever from 'automatic' to 'safety'. I returned to my world of silence.

Easan continued to moan in pain. I offered him a look of sympathy; it did not occur to me or the other women I was with to touch him or to comfort him, because such behaviour would not be acceptable even under these extraordinary circumstances. We were restrained by our culture, by our upbringing, and by the unspoken Tigers' code of conduct, that touching the opposite sex was not okay.

I sensed that I had begun to menstruate. Panic engulfed me for a moment before I realised there was nothing I could do. I had no sanitary napkins and I was inside a bush with four men and four women crowded next to me, hiding for our lives. Besides, I was already soaked in Gandhi's blood. Maybe, I thought, no one will notice the difference.

Before nightfall, one more platoon of soldiers came scouring the area, firing into bushes. Once again we sprang into position. I was convinced that we were running out of luck—we were going to die today, by bullets and cyanide.

I couldn't ask for a better honour than to die in the line of duty. I thought of Amma, Shirani and Appa, and said a silent goodbye to them. Calmly, I waited for the soldiers to appear.

Minutes later, the platoon approached our hide-out.

We waited, holding our breath.

Then a few pairs of boots appeared in front of us. One of them walked right up to our bush, brushing the lantana leaves, just an arm's length away from our faces. Surely this was where it would all end.

But the platoon passed, without firing at our bush and without seeing us right at their feet.

After a while, I sat up. I knew that I no longer needed to fear death. Having survived today, I wasn't going to die for a very long time.

15

WHERE IT ALL ENDS

It was evident that everyone was exhausted from the ordeal and the humidity, from hunger and thirst. Yet no one uttered a word of complaint.

'Saaradha was yelling for help after getting shot in the leg,' Theeba recalled in a quiet voice. 'I told her to bite into the *kuppie* as I ran for cover. There was no way I could've helped.' It surprised me that she could say that to her best friend.

'Rajan and I tried so hard to get Muralie anna out of there,' Easan muttered, probably trying to distract himself from the pain. 'He felt so heavy and kept slipping out of my hands. And all that blood and wet grass weren't helping. His body was riddled with bullets. He wanted the Tiger flag, which he had removed from Ansaar's body before burial, draped over him, but we couldn't do it. We had to just leave him there.'

I wanted to ask Easan what this meant for Muralie and where Rajan had got to. But something held me back. Perhaps it was fear. Instead I touched my shirt pocket for reassurance and felt the piece of paper there that contained a sketch Muralie had drawn for me. I felt a slight relief.

Only two days earlier, in one of the safe houses, Muralie had been using a pen to copy a picture of a woman from the cover of a book, while Ajanthi and I were stacking rounds into our magazines.

'This is for you.' He had held out the piece of paper to me when he had finished. 'When I'm dead, you can keep this in my memory.'

'What makes you think I want to remember you?' I teased. 'Besides, do you want me to remember you as a woman? You'd better draw me a self-portrait.'

Muralie laughed and began sketching a picture of himself: 'There may not be any photos of me left when we achieve Tamil Eelam, and this might come in handy on Remembrance Day,' he remarked.

'Self-importance aside, you are not a bad man,' I had said as I ticked the sketch and wrote 'V. good' on it. I got him to sign it before I put his pen and sketch in my shirt pocket. 'In case I too die before we achieve Tamil Eelam, I'll see that someone else gets this, Muralie anna,' I had added jokingly.

Around six o' clock in the evening, Sengamalam sent the young man from the village out on reconnaissance. He was wearing a white shirt and had not a splash of blood on him.

We waited for nearly two hours for his return, but there was no sign of him.

'The bastard probably ran away,' giggled Theeba.

'Perhaps the soldiers caught him,' said Sengamalam. 'We should get out of here immediately.'

It was still light when we set out from the bush. I did not know or care about where we were headed. I was too exhausted to be cautious or to worry about menstruating.

As we passed through a paddock, a farmer herding his cows shouted out to us: 'I don't know why you children waste your life on such unworthy people! Someone betrayed you today and if it wasn't for such traitors your friends might be still alive.'

I did not comprehend what he was saying. Who was this traitor he was talking about? Did he not know that the enemy had been hunting us down for months and that it was only a matter of time before we were going to get caught anyway, betrayed or not?

Sengamalam and Sudharshan struggled with Easan. They carried him through ploughed fields, where the soil was loose, and hauled him over fences, often barbed-wire, that crossed our paths.

We reached a dirt road lined with huts and little shops. I could smell roasted peanuts. The news of us coming that way had spread like wildfire, and a curious crowd gathered along the sides of the road. Most had never seen a female Tiger before. No one spoke— they just simply stared at us. I did not make eye contact with anyone and continued walking. The crowd followed us.

An elderly woman broke away and came running at us, and flung her bony arms around me in an embrace, lamenting, 'Ayyo, my poor child! You endure such sorrow at this young age! Wouldn't your mother's heart break if she saw you like this?'

I didn't realise how I must have looked to her and the others— a starved teenage girl with torn clothes, caked in blood and flesh, barefoot and carrying an automatic rifle. I detached myself from her embrace and continued walking.

'Can someone lend us a bicycle?' Sengamalam asked the crowd. 'This boy here can't walk.'

That was enough to make all the bicycles take off like bullets from a rifle. Sengamalam dropped Easan on the spot (he cried out in pain), and chased after one of them, grabbing hold of the unlucky cyclist's shirt. 'Get off, you cowardly dog!' he roared at the frightened man. Sengamalam's bloodshot eyes, his mop of unruly hair and his heavy build were terrifying enough but, when backed up by his thundering voice, the unwilling cyclist had no other choice than to obey his orders.

The men sat Easan on the front handlebar and pushed the bicycle. Someone from the crowd handed us a loaf of bread and a few bananas wrapped up in a newspaper. We headed to a nearby lane, and sat on the steps of a house and broke the bread between us. No sooner had we taken a mouthful than we saw a group of men, women and children approach us. The middle-aged man leading the group was holding a stick with a piece of white cloth tied to it.

'Children, we care about you. But please leave this neighbourhood immediately,' the man began to say firmly. 'Mothers, children and the elderly live here, and we don't want the soldiers coming here and destroying our lives.'

'Look, sir, all we have is a slice of bread and a banana each. We haven't eaten since last night. We'll leave as soon as we are done,' replied Sudharshan, as calmly as he could.

'Curse the man who gave you food,' the man spat on the ground. 'We beg you to leave now and eat your food elsewhere.' His demeanour was more insulting than begging.

'Just ignore him and eat,' Sengamalam told us and continued to peel his banana.

Seeing that his request had no effect, the man changed his tone: 'If you don't leave, then we'll have to go to the temple,' he threatened.

I understood what that meant. A mass exodus would indicate to the enemy that we were in the neighbourhood.

'Go to the temple and we'll follow you there,' Sengamalam maintained his calm tone, taking a bite from the banana. 'Then the soldiers will go there and massacre the whole lot of you. At least we have weapons to defend ourselves.'

'You bring nothing but trouble!' shouted someone from the back of the group.

'Yeah, get out of here!' yelled another.

Although it was difficult to ignore them, we were too tired and hungry for the badgering to have much effect on us. The crowd continued to pester us until we had finished eating; then they followed us, to make sure that we left their village.

We were enveloped in darkness by the time we stopped at an abandoned house for a few minutes, to give Easan and the boys some respite.

Sudharshan spoke. 'We are half the number we were this morning. I'm certain that Ajanthi, Gandhi, Amuthan, Nihintha, Nithi, Sadha, Nira, Dharshini and Panjan are all dead.'

'And Muralie anna . . .' added Easan's voice.

'Not sure what happened to Akila or the other three, Rajan, Saaradha and Jenny.'

My heart dropped to my stomach. My brain froze.

No! No! No! screamed a voice inside me.

A wail was about to break from my throat. I quickly placed my hands over my mouth and the howl broke into silent sobs, driving streams of tears down my face.

'Niromi, don't cry. This was bound to happen,' said Sudharshan.

No it wasn't! I had so many questions, but I couldn't swallow the lump in my throat. My brain was numb. How could those who had been alive this morning, full of life and laughter, vanish into thin air? *It cannot be the truth! It simply cannot be! Sudharshan is mistaken. They must be still somewhere, telling stories to each other, laughing, walking through banana fields and mercilessly scratching away at their dermatitis-ridden skin.*

'Oh poor Niromi.' Jessie put her arm around my shoulder.

Sengamalam came over and sat beside me: 'Today it was them; tomorrow it will be us. You know that yourself. We joined the movement knowing the price we all have to pay. Muralie or Ajanthi won't be happy if you lose heart after they sacrificed themselves for the cause. You have to be strong for them, Niromi, to avenge their deaths. Come on—I'm here to take care of things.'

Sengamalam's gentle tone, delivering those words, broke my heart into a thousand pieces. Although he couldn't embrace and comfort me, his words were so caressing that I felt my entire being collapse.

As we continued to walk silently through the darkness, I felt as if I was all alone. I did not understand why I had been left behind. Why was I undeserving of death's attention, when it had taken all my friends away? Why was I left to endure such horrible loneliness? The question *Why* kept going around and around in my head.

It was past midnight when we reached a densely-populated part of a town, where streetlights and houses were lit. But there was not a soul in sight because of the curfew. We stopped in front of a house.

Asking the rest of us to stay on the steps, Sudharshan walked up to the door and knocked lightly. Perhaps it was one of our source houses in the area. A middle-aged woman in her nightgown opened the door; on seeing Sudharshan and then us, she was taken aback.

'We want to stay here for one night.'

'Oh no, no, no!' the woman shook her head in fear, as her eyes looked past Sudharshan and fixed on us. She took a step backwards and was about to shut the door when Sudharshan quickly pushed in.

'We're only asking to stay for one night. We'll be gone before you know it.'

'No, no, no,' moaned the woman. With his foot still in the door, Sudharshan turned around and motioned at us to follow him into the house. The woman began to wail as we pushed past her. 'I have a little child and an elderly mother to look after. Who would take care of them if the soldiers took me away because of you?'

By now, we had stretched out on the floor of her lounge room. Poverty was evident inside here. There was just a table and two wooden chairs and, next to them, a sewing machine. The floor and the walls were dirty, as in all the houses where the poor lived.

The woman sat on the floor in one corner of the room, burying her head between her knees and wailing. I waited for her to calm down. There was still one more physical need that I needed to take care of.

The woman finally settled down about an hour later, but she continued to mutter, 'Get out of my house! Get out of my house!'

I went up to her and asked for rags. I knew there was no point asking a poor household for sanitary napkins. She seemed taken aback for a moment, but obliged right away.

'I want you back within two minutes,' said Sengamalam, when I requested permission to go to the outdoor toilet. 'Take Jessie with you.'

After a trip to the toilet and then a very quick rinse of my face, hair and clothes at the well, Jessie and I returned to the house and rested on the cool concrete floor with our AKs beside us. My wet clothes and underwear clung to my skin. I closed my eyes, trying to ignore the discomfort. None of us had a change of clothes, not even of underwear.

Out of habit, I began to silently recite my night prayer; but then I stopped short, remembering Ajanthi's bedtime ritual during her time among the Tigers. At the end of her silent prayer, sitting up, she would draw crosses around herself before lying down. The Hindu girls would laugh, calling her an exorcist. 'With all of you Hindus around me, I sure have to protect myself when I'm asleep,' Ajanthi would respond jokingly.

I thought of Akila and Nihintha. Only last night they had all been lying next to me, our bodies huddled against each other in the crammed space. Tonight, none of them were here.

I no longer felt like praying. I realised that there was no one up there listening.

'Okay, turn the lights off now, acca. Otherwise the soldiers will come knocking,' said Sudharshan to the woman.

But the woman refused to turn the light off or shut up, leaving the task to Sudharshan. She sat in the same position and kept repeating the phrase, 'Get out of my house', over and over. To me, it began to sound like a lullaby.

It was about half past six in the morning when Sengamalam woke us all up. The woman was still wailing, in exactly the same position as I had seen her at 2am, when she had woken us up by turning on the lights. I felt ashamed that I had slept all night, knowing my friends were dead. I wanted to get up and run to some faraway place, where no one would find me—not even me. But I stayed rooted to the spot and waited for someone to tell me what to do next.

Sengamalam asked the woman for some dresses, reasoning that it was 'too late in the day for the girls to walk out in their trousers'.

I was surprised at his audacity. But the woman, very eager to get rid of us, immediately returned with a handful of clothes. There were all kinds of odd pieces of worn-out clothing—dresses, skirts and tops. I pulled an oversized violet batik dress with large white paisley flowers on it from the bundle she offered us. We wrapped our rifles and holsters in our sarongs. I pulled my hair up into a ponytail;

243

but it was still dirty and sticky, despite the hasty wash the previous night.

So, like an odd family of village peasants, carrying our wrapped-up rifles and holsters like babies, and with our feet bare and dirty, we set out into a bright, cloudless morning that carried the pungent smell of ripe palmyra fruit.

Sengamalam had to remind us to huddle together, because we kept falling into a single file out of habit. Soon we managed, without creating any fuss, to cross over the main road that had been the cause of our disaster the morning before, but at least a couple of kilometres away from where it had all happened.

By midday, we reached an abandoned house occupied by one of our male units. Sengamalam spoke to the two armed young boys on sentry in sign language. He had earlier warned us not to speak until we left the village, because it was heavily patrolled by the enemy, who rightly suspected the escapees from the round-up were still in hiding.

For the next day and a half we all remained locked up in this house. We five girls were in a tiny, dark room without windows and unfurnished, and only allowed to step out to the toilet after dark. So we took turns to lie down on the floor, speaking occasionally in whispers, sharing the few slices of stale bread and a jug of water that was left for us. Tears never seemed to cease rolling down my face.

It was the evening of Christmas Day. I sat on the packed-earth verandah of a little mud hut, under a moringa tree. We had moved from the hide-out the night before, walking for over an hour through the back ways to reach Sudhumalai once again. One of our boys' units occupied a house there and we sheltered in an adjoining mud hut.

Sengamalam had informed us earlier that day that over 2000 enemy soldiers had been involved in the attempt to capture our unit of twenty-two. He must have heard the whole thing from sympathisers in the village. No wonder our casualties were so high—ten dead, four missing and one injured.

The soldiers had dumped the bodies of the dead in the open air at the nearby Hindu crematorium. They had also announced a bounty on us, the survivors. The local boy sent out from our lantana bush hide-out on reconnaissance had been captured by the soldiers. Easan had been taken somewhere in the hope of being soon transported to India by an illegal boat trip across the Palk Strait, where he would receive medical treatment. But no one could tell me the fates of Akila, Jenny, Saaradha or Muralie's assistant, Rajan.

As I sat staring into the darkness, my mind was awash with various images: Gandhi's head exploding, Amuthan's lifeless body sinking back to the ground, Ajanthi's vacant stare as she fell backwards, Muralie's unresponsive body being dragged along. I had not even seen Nihintha or Akila before they had disappeared.

I did not know whose loss I should mourn; when I thought of one, I felt guilty for not thinking of the others. And now they were all lying out in the open in a village far from their homes, their bodies exposed to the elements, crows and stray dogs scavenging at them. I felt ill at the thought.

I remembered how much Ajanthi had wanted to see her family for Christmas. I wondered when Mala Auntie would find out about her daughter's death. My heart ached with sadness and my mind was consumed with guilt. I wished that I was dead in Ajanthi's place, because then I would not have to endure this unspeakable loneliness, or one day have to face Mala Auntie or Nilanthi or Uncle Jerome. How was I to explain why she was dead, while I was still around and had not even lost a limb?

I thought of my mother's father, Thaatha, of Ammamma, of Theeban, Benjamin and Thileepan. I tried to remember Prabhakaran's words from all those months ago—*Bottle up your anger and let it explode*, he had told us. But I felt no anger, only despair. If life becomes death so swiftly, what was the point of the endless human struggle to make things permanent?

My thoughts were interrupted by a sudden rustle of footsteps and whispers. I looked up to find three figures approaching, passing the sentry. A circle of torchlight led them towards our hut. I began to recognise them—'Rajan! Jenny! Akila!' Emotion erupted in me like a volcano. I ran towards them.

'Niromi!' cried Akila and Jenny as we ran into each other's arms and embraced. We were sobbing uncontrollably. There was so much I wanted to say and ask, yet words abandoned me.

On the day of the fatal attack, realising that everyone around them was dropping dead like flies, Akila and Rajan had fled the scene, carrying the injured Saaradha with them. Seeing no way out, they had hidden inside a very small water tank on top of the roof of a house. Saaradha was bleeding from a leg injury and Rajan was struggling not to cough, spitting the phlegm into the water they were sitting in. While they waited in hiding, soldiers searched the neighbourhood twice; they ransacked the house and threatened its household.

Akila said the woman of the house knew of their presence up on the roof and one time climbed her ladder to bring them a plate of food. As she did a second platoon of soldiers had suddenly appeared on her doorstep again and, in a panic, she had dropped the food into the water. Akila, Rajan and Saaradha found themselves sitting in a pool of blood, phlegm and food. At nightfall, they had come down and were discovered by some local Tiger sympathisers, who had been looking for survivors.

The sympathisers had also found Jenny, the only one of us to make it alive across the road that morning. The brave girl had managed to salvage Sadha's AK in the process. The soldiers had chased her but, being a local girl, she knew where to hide and had found her way to a safe house. Saaradha, like Easan, had been sent to India for treatment via an illegal boat trip. I thought it was ironic that while we fought their army we still had support in India.

Finding Akila alive made the loss of Ajanthi, Muralie and Nihintha permanent for me. Although I felt a little less lonely, there was an emptiness in me now that was like nothing I had ever experienced before.

At the dawn of the following day, I went up to the back fence to watch the sunrise. Everything seemed eerily still; I did not hear the birds or sense the smell of the tobacco plants. The dark eastern sky was rapidly turning red beyond the distant palmyra trees.

I heard the shuffle of footsteps behind me, but I did not turn around.

'Don't be sad, Niromi,' murmured Akila's voice.

I felt the emotion packed in her few words, and it was as if I had been waiting to hear them—tears burst from my eyes.

The sun rose into the sky in full glory.

'I wish I was dead too!' Words spluttered out of my mouth. 'How will I ever face Ajanthi's family again?'

'It was her time to go,' said Akila as she walked over to the fence and stood beside me facing the rising sun. 'We will be joining her soon, Niromi. But, until then, we have to stay strong in our resolve to realise her dream of Tamil Eelam, our independent homeland.'

Tamil Eelam. To me, it felt like a dream beyond reach.

16

THE DREAM BEYOND REACH

I sat in the hull of the boat, enveloped by darkness. The small vessel rocked heavily as more and more ghostly figures ran across the small strip of the beach and climbed aboard. Like them, I had made the dangerous trip from land to sea. On the shore, little flames flickered in lamps inside the mud huts and, behind them, coconut palms swayed. The breeze carried the smell of salted, dry fish across the water to us.

I felt someone's hand on my shoulder.

'It's going to be all right,' said Akila. 'We aren't leaving Ajanthi, Nihintha or Muralie anna behind. They are with us in spirit.'

I could barely see her face in the faint light of the hurricane lamp, but I felt her eyes on me. I recognised the familiar pungent smell of her dirty, blood-splattered clothes. I knew that her right hand would be cupped tightly around the barrel of her M16 rifle, as it always was.

Suddenly a few shots rang out into the night, startling us. There would be no more passengers coming for the boat this evening.

'Keep your heads down!' shouted the *oatti* (the boatman) as he swiftly snuffed the flame of his hurricane lamp. 'If the navy spots us, death is all that'll be left for us.'

Death would be just fine by me, I thought. I did not want to be on this boat and to leave behind all that was familiar to me. But it was not my decision to make.

The twin engines roared; the aluminium boat made a swift U-turn and tossed over the waves. Nearly two weeks had passed since that dreadful day, when we had lost most of our friends and comrades.

After Akila had been reunited with us, all ten survivors made our way out of Sudhumalai and headed north on borrowed bicycles. We were still pretending to be civilians then. I was wearing that over-sized violet batik dress, sitting on the front handlebar of the bicycle that Akila was riding, clinging on to our two rifles and holsters, which were wrapped in a sarong, and a plastic bag containing our dirty clothing. Akila and Jenny had doorknocked for their skirts.

Although there were still four days before the New Year, the monsoon season was easing and the weather had turned pleasantly warm, making everything lusciously green. The wind brushed our faces and ruffled our dirty hair as Akila pedalled with all her might through narrow dirt lanes, racing Sengamalam and Rajan. They were laughing like children. A smile formed on my lips too. For the first time, I was not spending all my waking hours thinking of Ajanthi and Muralie.

Our route wound its way through paddocks and farmlands, leading to a destination known only to Sengamalam. We finally came to a populated area, where the dirt lane climbed towards a main road that crossed its path. Our tree-lined lane was now lined with houses.

Just as we approached the intersection, we saw a patrol jeep pass by on the main road. In a panic, Akila lost her balance and crashed into the side wall of a house, and we tumbled off our bicycle—rifles and all. As we struggled to get to our feet, more jeeps drove through the intersection ahead. We quickly huddled behind a small bush.

The others had also hidden behind bushes on the opposite side to us. Although we were disguised as civilians, we could not risk being stopped and searched. After a while, simply trusting our luck, we got back on our bikes and raced across the main road, then resumed our journey along the dirt lane on the other side.

Nearly twenty minutes later we arrived at the back of a large old building by the side of a road—a 'Cooperative', according to its sign. Here, three men were loading hemp sacks of little red onions onto the back of an old lorry. When one side of the lorry had been loaded to the roof, Sengamalam asked all us girls to get into the back. We climbed in and, as the tailgate closed behind us, our male comrades disappeared from sight. I realised that I might never see them again.

I felt uneasy with Sengamalam gone; lately, I had found his presence reassuring. From the time I had received my rifle from him at Jaffna University, he had been a commanding presence, always dependable and in control. As for Sudharshan, I had not thanked him for saving my life—until now, it hadn't occurred to me to do so. And Rajan—he had been a friend from the day he had accompanied Muralie to our school to introduce SOLT and Ajanthi and I had tried to be enlisted. Now I had left them all without saying goodbye. As to where we were being sent, I certainly didn't care.

After a minor struggle, the rickety old lorry started off along the road, braving the many potholes, bumping us along. We sat facing backwards, watching the bright blue sky and the rapidly receding treetops above the rim of the tailgate—the only sights visible from where we sat. The pungent odour of the red onions and the sweet smell of petrol filled my lungs.

Soon I began to feel nauseous. 'I think that I'm going to be sick,' I muttered.

'You'll have to vomit inside the lorry,' said Theeba. 'We can't risk passing army patrols seeing us.' And vomit I did.

When the lorry came to a sudden halt, we heard footsteps crushing gravel and voices murmuring. Just as we breathed a sigh of relief at hearing the local lingo, a large hessian sack came flying over the tailgate and hit me right on the head, knocking me face first into my puddle of vomit. The girls gasped and helped me up; then they burst into barely suppressed laughter.

'Oh you must feel *like the man who was stomped on by a cow after falling off a palmyra tree*,' said Jessie, giggling.

A head popped over the tailgate: 'Sorry, *makkal*,' said a young man. 'I didn't realise you were in there.'

My head began to throb. The sack contained a heavy load of books.

We travelled further north for about another hour and finally reached an abandoned house. It had been raining. This village was markedly different to the ones we had left behind. The soil was a grey gravel mixed with sand, and the air smelt of the sea. Banana and manioc plantations had been replaced by clusters of fig trees, swaying palms and fragrant frangipani. We walked up the gravel path to the house, which was hidden away from the dirt lane by large bushes of oleander, covered in their poisonous pink and white blooms.

Inside, the small house was abuzz with some fifty or sixty young men busy loading bullets into magazines, packing manuals into hessian sacks and gelignite into jerry cans with their bare hands. There I spotted Mahathaya, Prabhakaran's deputy, still wearing his black leather jacket and brown shorts with his bodyguard Castro beside him. We girls headed to the backyard and changed back into our dirty shirts and trousers.

When I sat down at last on the floor next to Akila, to pack rifle magazines into a large sack, I realised that we were about to embark on an epic journey—we were not greasing them to bury them. I panicked, thinking we might be travelling to India. I did not want to end up somewhere unfamiliar and far away from Amma and Shirani. And I did not want to leave Ajanthi, Muralie or Nihintha behind.

Impulsively, I rose to my feet and went looking for Mahathaya. When I found him near the front door, talking to the Tigers' spokesperson Lawrence Thilakar, he turned to me.

'Mahathaya anna, are we going far away?' I knew I could not ask him where.

'You know I can't tell you that, Niromi,' he replied. 'Wherever we are going, you will have to come with us. Your name is on the enemy's wanted list—there's a bounty on your head and they are watching your home. You see what I mean?'

He turned to Lawrence Thilakar and resumed their conversation. There was nothing more to discuss. Downhearted, I returned to my position and resumed packing magazines. I felt Akila's eyes on me, but I said nothing to her.

Our exodus commenced at nightfall. We set out in single file, carrying the heavy loads of gear we had packed. I had two AK-47 rifles, plus a holster loaded with three AK magazines packed with rounds and four hand grenades, and a hessian sack containing manuals weighing around five kilograms. And mine was one of the lightest loads. The others were carrying similar weaponry, plus heavy five-litre jerry cans packed with gelignite. I hoped we weren't going to be ambushed.

The more time that passed, the heavier my load began to feel. Everyone was floundering, but no one spoke a word. It was now past midnight and we hadn't taken even a brief break. I was exhausted and was using up every last bit of energy I had in me to keep walking. The path contained bits of gravel, which dug into the soles of my bare feet; my arms felt like they were coming off and my shoulders drooped under their heavy burden. I was completely fed up with my life as a fugitive. We were always on the run, looking over our shoulders. Surviving against such a powerful enemy was both physically and mentally exhausting. I did not want to go on—to endure all this just to sustain my life.

The dead certainly had it easy—Ajanthi, Muralie and the others. They had all escaped this miserable existence. That thought provoked anger within me, filling my mind with resentment. How could Ajanthi have left me behind? We were friends, we had done everything together almost all our lives, but she had betrayed me in death. Now I hated them all—Theeban, Benjamin, Thileepan, Muralie, Nihintha, Gandhi and, yes, even young Amuthan, I resented him too. Why was I the last one standing? Was I not their friend? Why had they abandoned me, and left me on my own to endure their loss, and the burden of keeping their memories alive and making their dream come true?

I felt as if I was standing behind the wooden lattice at Appamma's house again, just as I had ten years ago, watching my father walk away. On that day I had felt these same emotions—loss of love and an incredible burden of responsibility to make someone else's dream come true. But at this time I lacked what I had then—the will to make it happen. And the price I was being asked to pay was too high.

I was jolted from my dream-like state by a voice—a male singing voice, gentle and strong. I couldn't hear the words of the folksong very well, but its sweet melody penetrated the tranquil night and entered my body and gave me comfort. It came from one of the mud huts set among coconut groves.

I hadn't noticed my surroundings until now. Inside the mud huts lining the lane we were trudging along, the flames from hurricane lamps flickered. I smelt the fragrance of jasmine and gardenia mingling with the salty smell of the ocean carried along by the warm night air. Moonlight filtered through the tall palm trees as the sea breeze rustled their leaves. A skinny mongrel lying by the lane stretched and yawned lazily. I realised that the gravel path had turned sandy soft under my feet. I thought I could hear Ajanthi's laughter somewhere in the distance.

Those in front of me came to a halt abruptly. I leaned out to look at the front of the line and found we had stopped short of a wide tarred road. The main coastal road was about to cross our path, illuminated by poor streetlighting. We remained hidden in the shadows of palm and fig trees and lantana bushes by the side of the road. On the other side, darkness hung like a heavy curtain. All was quiet except for the sound of waves crashing on the shore.

'One by one you must run across the road,' ordered Mahathaya. 'Then you'll see a narrow dirt lane to your left and you must head for that. There's an army street patrol every minute, so run as fast as you can. It takes ten seconds to cross the road.'

That's probably without this heavy load, I thought to myself. I did not know what was on the other side of the road or why we were supposed to run to it, but the only choice left for me now was to do as I was told. I felt a slight trepidation once again. Crossing main roads was always dangerous. Adrenalin began pumping through my body.

Soon after the first patrol jeep went by, I saw the first man in the line charge onto the road and vanish into the darkness. Just as the fourth in line darted, I heard the faint sound of a jeep approaching.

Bang!

It was a gunshot, no doubt. Those who remained on our side of the road immediately did an about-turn and ran for our lives, chased by death, forgetting the weight of the loads we were carrying and the exhausting long walk we had just endured. Gravel under foot and the serrated edges of the fallen palm leaves in our path didn't seem to matter now.

Nearly half an hour later, Mahathaya ordered us to stop beside a grassy plain, confident that we weren't being pursued by the enemy. 'We'll try again soon, children,' he said, puffing heavily. 'For now, everyone just go to sleep wherever. There's no food or water, but there'll be no complaints from anyone.'

He never mentioned anything about those who had run across the road. Was the fourth in line shot? Was he dead or alive? Or perhaps injured or captured? It seemed that no one cared. When it came to the matter of life and death, all that concerned us was self-preservation.

My lungs were burning and my stomach growled with hunger. We found a small Hindu temple, and once inside I lay down between Akila and Vadhana. Initially, I had hesitated when the others decided to sleep there—women are prohibited from entering holy Hindu sites during menstrual cycles—but the girls assured me that their God Pillayar would turn a blind eye, considering our current circumstances.

A week would pass before we braved the coastal road again. In the meantime, we were told to change into the civilian clothes we had and to surrender all our belongings except the cyanide capsules. Then Mahathaya split us into pairs and sent us to live with local sympathisers. Akila and I were lucky enough to be allotted to a prominent local man who took us to his family home, which was set in a lovely garden. His wife and their two young daughters were exceptionally kind to us.

'You'll have to stay in your room most of the time,' said the wife apologetically while we sat at the table like civilised folk, eating the bowl-shaped crispy pancakes we call *hoppers*—some with coconut milk and palm sugar in the middle, and others with a runny-yolked egg. 'It's my husband's orders that you are not to be seen by anyone, including our visitors. But think of us as your family.'

Akila and I barely said a word in reply as we ate. I wanted to focus all my senses on the delicious food. I knew that, like everything else, this wouldn't last. Every good moment that came my way had to be taken, savoured and appreciated. That was the only way I could get through the bad. The wife kept tossing more *hoppers* our way; but my stomach, used to starvation over the past three months, began cramping. Soon I was feeling sick.

Our small room with one window, to which we were confined for the next five days, was clean. The two single beds had white linen sheets, and on the lone bedside table sat a vase containing a posy of fragrant pinwheel jasmine. On one of the walls hung a large framed picture of the Sacred Heart of Jesus and, opposite, above the doorframe, a palm-leaf cross—possibly made the previous year on Ash Wednesday—hung withering. Only now, after looking around, did I feel self-conscious about the state Akila and I were in: we were filthy, with sticky hair and dirty skin. Our bare feet were covered in dust. But we had to wait 'til nightfall to have a quick wash at the well outside.

I thought about my last encounter with Roshan at Jaffna University and how embarrassed I had felt seeing him in a sarong, an outfit I considered inappropriate in public. Back then my shirt and trousers, brought from an expensive boutique in Colombo, were brand new. If only he could see the state of me now—it would be he who felt embarrassed in my company, no doubt. The thought made me cringe.

I unlocked the window's wooden shutters. The window had iron bars across it, like a prison cell, and opened onto a small space on one side of the house, which was protected by a high concrete wall just two metres away from the window.

'What do you think is behind that wall?' I asked.

'Don't know and don't care,' replied Akila, lying on her bed with her eyes closed. 'If I were you, I would use this moment to take a nap. Mmm . . . the bed is so comfortable.'

I didn't want to even sit down on my bed until I had had a wash later that evening, so I decided I would pass the time by trying to find out what was on the other side of the wall—I was curious about why the wall on that side of the house was so high. But no sooner had I pulled myself up onto the window sill by grabbing hold of the iron bars, than I lost my footing. Amazed by what I had seen over the high wall, I had landed back on the floor.

'What's the matter?' asked Akila, sitting up.

'Shh . . . soldiers!' I whispered, putting my index finger to my lips. 'On the other side of the wall. Just over three metres away from where we are standing.'

Akila had to see for herself, so she clambered up to the window sill too.

Afterwards, we sat on our beds laughing silently. We were sharing a fence with one of the largest army barracks in the peninsula, set on the northern tip of the country. Now we realised why the man of the house did not want us going outside.

The soldiers could also visit the house, so we decided to remove our cyanide capsules and hide them, because the black threads around our necks would give us away. Without them, we could pretend to be relatives of the family, especially after we had had a wash. So for the next few days that picture—of the fire-topped thorn-wrapped heart of a glowing Jesus—remained the cover for our killer capsules.

After five days, the man of the house appeared at our bedroom door.

'It's time to take you back,' he said. Outside, by the gate, were two motorbikes. One of the man's friends was waiting on one of them. The sun had set and in the twilight the birds were returning to their nests. As we walked through the gate, I nervously glanced towards the army barracks next door. The sentry outside was staring straight ahead from inside his tiny watchhouse, surrounded by a stack of sandbags and barbed wire.

The man's daughters were crying as Akila and I got on the back of the motorbikes behind the men, barefooted in our dresses and without helmets. Around ten minutes later, we were dropped off at an abandoned house at the end of a lane lined with moringa trees where our other five female comrades, plus some forty or fifty men we did not recognise, were waiting in readiness by the light of a couple of hurricane lamps.

'Make us proud and be true to Thambi,' said my motorbike driver to me. The older ones referred to Prabhakaran as young brother, while we referred to him as Anna, or old brother.

I nodded.

Then Akila and I were given our belongings back: we each received a plastic bag of our own belongings back with our rifle and holster. Only when we changed into our smelly old shirts and trousers, and put on our chest holsters, did I realise that my blue-green designer denim jeans and my shirt with its blue, yellow and white checks no longer resembled their original condition: they were dirty, blood-stained and torn in places.

That evening, we set out into the darkness once again, crossed the road and made it onto the waiting boat. At that moment we heard someone being shot at as they attempted to cross the road. The rest of that group retreated and ran away. They would have to try again another day.

For now, nearly thirty of us, still holding onto our lives and our weapons, were crammed into a tiny motorboat and setting out onto the treacherous sea. We were in grave danger of capsizing or of being spotted by the navy, who were heavily patrolling the coastal waters. None of us knew how to swim.

The navigation skills of the *oatti* were exceptional, the kind of competence that comes from years of experience. Perhaps he was a goods smuggler before he turned people smuggler. It was well known that a lucrative smuggling trade operated from the coasts of Sri Lanka to India, a country with a closed economy.

This five-hour boat journey in total darkness to an unknown destination was physically worse than anything I had ever endured. We were ill-equipped for the conditions at sea—our light clothing and bare feet offered little protection from the massive waves that lashed at us as the little boat tossed through the rough seas. It was like being constantly doused with ice-cold buckets of salt water while sitting in an ice-cold tub that rocked heavily. We couldn't open our eyes, speak or move.

Through all of it, I could smell petrol. And it wasn't long before my head began to spin. The contents of my stomach churned and I felt a surge of saliva fill my mouth. Leaning over the side of the boat, I vomited, thinking only hell could be worse.

The *oatti* reprimanded me immediately: 'If the navy suspect this to be anything other than a lone fisherman's vessel, we'll be all dead before I can say, "Dive!" Keep your head down and vomit inside, like everyone else!'

Only then did I realise I was sitting in a pool of vomit already. That sight made me feel even worse and I vomited continuously until the boat finally stopped and the sound of its engine died nearly five hours later. I was dry retching by the end.

Eventually I opened my gritty, stinging eyes and felt the world still spinning around me. It must have been around four or five o'clock in the morning; the sky had just cracked to the east. I did not wonder or care where we were; it could be the south coast of India or the east coast of Sri Lanka—it didn't matter, I was so grateful we had stopped. I told myself I would never get into a stupid fishing boat and travel the open seas ever again. I couldn't imagine why anyone would, unless their lives were in mortal danger; especially when they could not even swim.

The *oatti* now lit a flame in his hurricane lamp and swung it three times. In response, a powerful torchlight beamed three times from the coast.

'Get ready to disembark,' ordered the *oatti*.

I dry retched one last time.

The *oatti* laughed: 'I think you hold the record now for the vomiting marathon.'

The ghostlike figures around me—their heads and bodies covered by wet sarongs; their bottoms, feet and rifle butts immersed in spew-scummed water—slowly stirred. I rose to my feet, feeling listless, as if all my energy had been sucked out of me.

I strained my eyes into the distance and saw the deserted shore lined with coconut trees. We must be still in Sri Lanka, I thought, because I remembered having heard that India was highly populated. Although the Jaffna Peninsula was connected to the rest of the country by land, that narrow strip (called the Elephant Pass) was under the control of the enemy. So a boat trip, skirting along the coastline from north to east, would have been our only way to travel south. Now that we were here, I wondered what our plans were.

Wet, dirty, shivering and disoriented, we staggered off the boat and walked through the warm coastal water towards the shore. The sun was slowly rising behind us. As we approached the beach, a lonely brick house set in a coconut grove became visible. We washed and drank from the freshwater well nearby. When Akila drew water from the well and poured it over me, I checked my shirt pocket for Muralie's sketch. It was intact, sealed in a little plastic bag.

After a wash, a little life returned to everyone; but we were too tired and hungry to appreciate the amazing sunrise over this extraordinarily picturesque section of the coast. The morning had turned crisp and beautiful. The golden sand that had previously stuck to our wet bodies began to trickle from our drying clothes and skin as we walked south along the beach, our feet sinking into the soft sand and our heads shaded by the swaying palms. Tiny crabs disappeared sideways into little burrows and the huge waves threw beautiful shells up at our feet. The beach was otherwise deserted.

Mid morning, we reached a cluster of abandoned fishermen's huts. A couple of catamarans lay nearby. We linked up with three units of comrades, one of them a female unit, resting there after arriving on an earlier voyage. I knew most of them from the training base and the university/technical college positions. They offered us their condolences, having heard of our losses already. I enquired after Kaanchana again, but with no luck. Finally, overcome by exhaustion, we threw down our hessian sacks on the sand and crashed under the shade of the coconut palms.

We were now a company of sixty or seventy soldiers, and we trekked along the coast for two days, quenching our thirst and satisfying our hunger on tender coconuts. We walked without much rest. Despite the beauty around us, and the camaraderie, the journey was arduous. By midday each day we would grow tired in the heat. I kept my mind occupied by talking to the others. I did not want to think any more, about anyone or anything.

On the third day we turned inland, where the landscape took on a different appearance. Coconut groves gave way to dense wooded oak, mahogany, ebony and banyan trees, their trunks wrapped in runners bearing violet trumpet flowers. Large gloriosa bushes blazed with their fiery orange lily blossoms. The terrain changed from golden sand to white loam, rough with twigs, gravel and thorns. The temperature grew mild. The air was filled with the buzzing of cicadas, birdcalls and swarms of white butterflies. Other than the occasional mud hut in the distance, there was little sign of human habitation.

Around midday we encountered a group of Tigers. Its alpha male sat on the verandah of an abandoned house in a black leather jacket zipped up to its collar. Mahathaya and his entourage of men must have caught an earlier boat.

We threw ourselves down in the front yard, under the shade of fruitless mango and jackfruit trees, totally exhausted. I was glad to have some rest. Soon after, two men arrived on a tractor—one of them sitting on the mudguard—and distributed just ten parcels of red rice and drumstick curry wrapped in banana leaves for the sixty of us. We devoured our first real meal in four days, then we stretched out on the dirt and went to sleep.

Later that evening the two men returned, this time with G3s slung on their shoulders. Mahathaya ordered all the girls to get on board the trailer of the tractor, and we crammed in. The tractor began a bumpy ride, first along the mud track and then onto a road that had once been properly tarred.

The evening sun shone through the distant tall forest at our backs. The cool breeze, carrying the smell of green wood, slapped our cheeks. Grey langurs and macaques rustled the treetops and eyed us suspiciously. Wild peacocks strutted by the side of the road and chital deer dashed across. The only things out of place were us, bouncing along on a noisy, hideous old tractor. For the first time in months, I was not looking over my shoulder—I felt free momentarily.

I felt a song break out from my throat: *Poahum paathai thoorame, vaazhum kaalam konjame* . . . [The path we travel is long, and the length of our lives is short . . .]

My comrades glanced at me in surprise, but only for a moment, and then they began a chorus themselves: *Jeeva suham pera raga nathiyinil nee neenthavaa* . . . [To comfort your soul come swim with me in the river of music . . .]

Everyone laughed. We continued singing until the tractor turned into a dirt track and headed towards the forest. Having never been to this part of the country before, I did not realise that we were heading into the dense jungles of Vanni. Night had fallen, but in the clear sky the moon shone brightly as we alighted from the tractor and headed deep into the forest, following the men in a single file. I was worried about encountering wild animals or one of the nearly one hundred species of snakes that could be found in this part of the country, so I positioned myself third in line, with Akila behind me, which I considered a safe position.

The path turned into a single track, flanked by dense stands of tall trees letting little or no moonlight reach the ground. Due to the rainfall of recent days, the track was slippery and in some places flooded, with the water higher than knee level. No one spoke. The cheer we had felt only an hour ago was all but gone. The sound of our squelching footsteps was drowned by the cacophony of the forest, with its buzzing insects, tree-rustling monkeys and hooting peacocks.

'How much further?' I asked the guide, an hour into our trekking.

'Not long,' he muttered, turning his head. His white teeth flashed in the dark.

I was glad. The heels of my bare feet were sore and I felt exhausted once again. Our lunch and mid afternoon rest were distant memories.

But by the time we reached our destination, it was the early hours of the next day. We encountered one of our comrades on sentry duty by the footpath in front of a little mound. On the top of this mound, enclosed by trees, was a large hut that had no walls, only a thatched roof held by eight wooden poles. We looked for a place to lie down among the many female bodies huddled on the tarpaulin-covered floor.

I was not fully aware that we were about to begin a life in the jungle hide-out, indefinitely.

17

THE JUNGLE HIDE-OUT

Morning sunlight, streaming through the dense jungle canopy, brought with it a whole new perspective. The hut on the mound held nearly fifty girls. To our delight, we knew most of them already because they had trained with us or had trained us; but I was disappointed that there was still no sign of Kaanchana. Now more than ever, I needed her playful nature and sense of humour to lift me out of this hole I felt I was sinking into. As much as I was comforted by Akila's care, her tendency to mother me and protect me was not what I always needed.

As I stepped out of the hide-out, my lungs filled with clean, fresh air that carried the fragrance of the vegetation. The dense jungle's tall trees were embraced by ferns, seedlings and runners. Dew, captured by the cobwebs, dazzled in a spectrum of colours. In the background was a constant chorus of unusual birdcalls and buzzing insects. Throughout the day, there were sightings of bright blue kingfishers, of dashing brown-and-red feathered fowls and spotty chital deer. Flameback woodpeckers hammered tree trunks, unperturbed by the langurs swinging by them just waiting for the opportunity to come down into our hut and grab whatever they could.

A men's camp was situated not far from us; but we only ever saw two of the boys, who acted as our caretakers due to their years of experience living in the jungles. One of the young men—Ananthan, a veteran of the jungles—gave us some tips on how to survive such a habitat.

'If you see a snake, run in a straight line,' advised this baby-faced man, without a hint of irony in his voice. 'If a wild elephant chases you, then run a zigzag. If you see a bear, lie down and play dead until the animal is out of sight. Anacondas can be found in this jungle, so sleep with your arms and legs stretched out like starfish. This will make it difficult for the anaconda to swallow you. Shoot any of these predators only if your life is in real danger.'

If, for a second, I'd thought that he was an advocate for the conservation of animals, he proved me wrong by adding, 'We don't want to waste too many rounds, because supply is hard around here.'

In the days that followed, we worked to a roster for sentry duty, cooking and collecting water from the stream. The sun-speckled stream, a ten-minute walk along a dirt track from our base, was our only source of water. Golden jackals often came to play on its white sandy banks.

Despite this, I did not find living in the jungle as idyllic as I had imagined it to be. The life of an underground freedom fighter living in the jungles had often featured prominently in my poetry in the days before I joined the Tigers. In reality, it was a life less desirable.

Beneath its tranquil beauty, the jungle was full of stinging insects, creeping worms and prickly plants. There were snakes everywhere— the brown ones were often found hiding under our bedding, or sleeping inside the sack of rice; the green ones leapt from tree to tree over our heads.

The rough terrain of the jungle—awash with thorns, twigs, fire ants and animal faeces—was unkind to our bare feet. The walk back from the river to the base, carrying heavy jerry cans filled with water, was backbreaking. We also worked tirelessly during the day on making permanent arrangements to build our women's camp—we built huts, we dug a well, a toilet pit and trenches around the periphery of the base, all by using primitive blunt tools supplied by our male comrades from the nearest camp. Then there was no privacy. To top it all off, I found the night sentry duties an unpleasant affair—in total darkness I felt the forest alive around me, with its rustles, screeches and hoots. And when it rained, which was often a deluge, there was no place to hide.

On these difficult nights, my only consolation was thinking of Roshan. Although it had been seven months since I had last seen him, at the University of Jaffna, thoughts of him made me instantly feel better. I'd imagine him at the seaside fort watchposts on those warm sunny days, or on the streets of Jaffna. These were the only memories of Jaffna that made me smile—everything else was of Ajanthi, Shirani, Amma, Muralie or Thileepan. I remembered all the conversations between Roshan and me verbatim. I often wondered if he was still alive and thought of me. I held onto the hope that I would see him again, alive and well—it made my days much more bearable.

On the positive side, I learnt many jungle survival skills from Ananthan. Although only a teenager, he was years ahead of himself in maturity. Occasionally he'd manage to catch a jungle fowl or a water lizard, or shoot a deer for our meal. Otherwise, we survived on one meal a day—red rice with beetroot or mouldy pumpkin curry. Ananthan took us on expeditions around the jungle and taught us how to source the best wood for making furniture (out of sticks, twigs and runners); we learned to track, to find food and water, and the art of setting booby traps. He secretly set many traps inside the periphery of our hide-out. Girls would often be heard screaming or yelling profanities around the hide-out, after accidentally setting off his traps. It wasn't long before Ananthan had managed to get his message through to us: be very alert at all times.

We had been living in the jungle for over four months. The weather had grown drier and our living conditions had deteriorated. The little stream was beginning to run dry, pooling only around the submerged roots of trees. Nor was any water to be found at the bottom of the three-metre-deep well we had toiled to dig. Our hair and teeth needed brushing, and our nails clipping. Our poor diet was turning our eyes yellow, our skin sallow and our hair dry and matted. We were very lucky there were no reflective surfaces anywhere nearby or we would have been in despair.

I finally contracted dermatitis, the last person in the camp to be infected. The more I scratched the little water-filled sacs that infested my hands and legs, the more they turned into bleeding wounds. Our clothes, having been worn without a change for nearly three months, had now turned into tatters; my only underwear, washed and worn, began to feel like sandpaper against my skin.

It wasn't long before such unhygienic conditions made us ill. Although most recovered in a day or two, three of us—Madhana, Dhushi and I—had contracted something serious. Our paramedic, a former medical student, suspected that I had malaria and that the other two had amoebic dysentery or typhoid; but she could not be certain. As I lay on my hessian sack under a tree—shivering uncontrollably, and then sweating a high fever—Akila took care of me, once a day bringing me rice water with a quarter of a tablet of the rationed paracetamol in a badly rusted tin. As well, she took on my rosters, then spent her spare time sitting beside me; and when she couldn't, she made sure someone else did. I lay staring at the vast canopy of vegetation above me, frustrated at not being able to read or write to distract myself from missing Ajanthi. During spells of high fever, I saw her face clearly, along with Muralie's and Roshan's—all of us back in Jaffna, at school, at the SOLT office or at the gates of Jaffna University. Sometimes I saw Thileepan's dying face or Gandhi's head exploding. When I came back to reality, I was overcome by grief when I realised that none of them were there with me.

I often thought of Amma and Shirani in those days. I wondered how they were and if they remained in Jaffna, despite the ordeal they had suffered at the hands of the enemy on my account. I felt sickened at the thought of what they might have endured. Although I longed to see them now, the images of Ajanthi's family stopped that longing. I could not go back to Jaffna ever again. In no way was I brave enough to face Ajanthi's family as long as I was well—at least not until I had suffered a major injury.

I thought that perhaps I would die in the jungle and never see any of them again. Just two weeks earlier I had seen a partially buried human arm in the sand on the other side of the riverbed. Ananthan had told me that it was the shallow grave of one of our male comrades, who had died of some illness a few weeks before.

One morning, nearly a week after I began to feel ill, our paramedic came over to me: 'Change into civilian clothing and give your rifle to Akila. Ananthan will be taking you, Madhana and Dhushi to the village to see a doctor.'

And so the three of us followed Ananthan down the single dirt track through the jungle. Resting his G3 on his shoulder and with his sarong folded in half, like a short skirt, Ananthan walked a few metres ahead of us, not caring for small talk. The three of us, too feeble even to speak to one another, struggled to catch up to him. Whenever Ananthan got too far ahead, he'd stop and wait until we tottered up. It was a warm, humid day and without food or drinking water we grew weary very quickly. Every so often the fire ants would climb our legs or sting our bare feet, making us perform something like the Bavarian slap dance. Ananthan refused to allow us even a few minutes' respite; he reasoned it was too dangerous.

By midday, we were becoming increasingly hungry and thirsty, but there was no water in sight. The sun was scorching and the dirt track becoming too hot to tread on. I felt drained. Poor Madhana was nearly on all fours, with severe stomach cramps. Ananthan finally relented and led us away from the track into the bush. A few minutes later, we arrived at an open plain covered with reeds. Overcome with joy, we ran to the stagnant water underneath the reeds. As I scooped it up with both hands, watched by a large water lizard, I saw the algae, worms and insects floating on the top. But I was too thirsty to resist it.

'How much longer?' I asked when we resumed our journey, ever-optimistic. I was feeling a little better for having had a drink.

'We're almost there.'

Ananthan kept repeating this mantra whenever I asked my question, as though this was the only way he knew how to answer it. I suppose he thought it would make us feel better, but it only made it worse for me and even when we were only a few metres away from our destination, I did not believe Ananthan's words.

After a punishing six-hour walk, we came to a clearing and reached the first sign of civilisation—a whitewashed mud hut just outside the forest. It was set in the middle of a huge yard, fenced in by barbed wire and palmyra leaf stems. Ananthan walked up to the packed-earth verandah and knocked on the door.

The rusty hinges screeched as the door opened. An old woman, in a worn-out cotton sari without a blouse, stood behind the door and smiled at us, exposing her few teeth. Ananthan left us there, saying nothing more than that he'd be back for us.

The hut was spacious: in one corner was a rope bed and in another corner a kitchen was set up. We squatted on the floor, too ill to be bothered with conversation. While we watched in silence, the old woman cooked some rice and poured fresh milk over it and handed it to us in coconut shells. We ate with our dirty fingers. Then we crashed on the dirt floor that had been polished with cow dung. My whole body felt like it was on fire. The other two took turns running out into the bush all night long.

The following morning was beautifully mild. Because the back of the hut skirted the jungle, a few peacocks flew in from the trees and landed on the fence and in the front yard. They didn't seem to be bothered by our presence, pecking on the old rice the old woman threw at them. The langur monkeys observed us silently, but their cousins, the macaques, made a noisy racket, racing up and down the trees and climbing onto the roof of the hut.

It was mid morning when a tractor arrived, with Ananthan sitting on the mudguard. We hopped onto the trailer and had a bumpy ride into town, travelling along dirt lanes and finally reaching a tarred road. Nearly twenty minutes after that, we arrived at a sparsely populated, picturesque village typical of such residential areas near the jungle;

this one had tree-lined lanes and unspoilt greenery everywhere. It was like a trip back in time—bullock carts and mud huts, people dressed in basics and with their feet bare. It was strange being out in the open, dressed like a peasant on the back of a tractor. Luckily our enemies, the Indian and the Sri Lankan forces, were nowhere to be seen.

Ananthan dropped us off at the doctor's surgery. The waiting room *was* the surgery: we were examined in front of each other and strangers. Then we were given identical treatment—a handful of red-and-yellow ampicillin antibiotic capsules. After an injection of some pinkish fluid, using the same needle, we were sent on our way. Ananthan dropped us off at another house and disappeared with an 'I'll come back for you'.

As we walked through the large front yard to the house, I heard a commotion at the well. It was dark now and a palm-leaf fence obstructed our view. Unsure what to do, we headed straight inside and sat next to each other on the wooden bench in the corridor, still feeling unwell.

A few minutes later we realised that the bench was infested with bedbugs. They bit the back of our thighs, producing large lumps that would itch for many days to come. Outside, the sound of a metal bucket banging against the sides of the well continued as someone kept drawing more and more water. Everyone was talking over each other and, in between, I heard a man wail loudly.

'Leave me alone,' he pleaded. From his voice alone, I couldn't estimate his age.

Other voices were urging: 'Drink the coconut milk! Come on, open your mouth!'

'Pour more water on him. That'll keep him conscious!'

The three of us looked at each other in confusion, yet did and said nothing. I sat crouched in a foetal position, wrapping my arms around my bent knees.

Nothing stopped us from finding out what was happening, yet we assumed that it would be inappropriate. We sat there feeling bored and ill for about two hours, when finally a woman and the young boy walked in.

'My stepson tried to commit suicide by drinking a litre of insecticide,' said the middle-aged woman, adjusting her sarong. 'One of our neighbours has taken him to the hospital in his tractor.'

'Why did it take so long to send him to the hospital?' I asked her. What I didn't ask was why the ambulance wasn't called. An ambulance was not available in many villages, even in Jaffna, due to the petrol shortage; many of them had come under gunfire from Sri Lankan forces' helicopter gunships once too often and were out of action. I was not sure how far away the hospital was.

'Petrol is in very short supply. By the time we hunted around the village, door-knocking for petrol to run our tractor, the boy became critical. He refused to drink the coconut milk that would have brought the poison out.'

The next morning, after another sleepless night, I headed towards the well at the far end of the backyard for a wash. As I stepped past the back verandah, I saw a young man in his late teens seated on the floor, leaning against the wall and staring into oblivion. From his vacant expression and slack body, I gathered that it was him who had created all the fuss last night. I dropped an encouraging smile on him; but he completely ignored me and, worse, put his head down.

I saw the woman at the well and asked her if her son was all right now. She was brushing her teeth with her forefinger, dipped into pink tooth-powder that came in a paper sachet. I put my hand out to request some.

'He's not my son—he's my *stepson*,' she corrected me. 'Because of his madness, we'll now have to pay a fine to your boys.'

The Tigers apparently imposed fines on suicides as well as failed attempts, reasoning that it was bad enough that the Sinhala government was trying to eliminate the Tamil race, without us doing our bit to help them. It made me think about Benjamin and the other innocent Tamils the Tigers had murdered.

'Perhaps the Tigers could send the boy on a suicide-bombing mission, instead of penalising his family,' laughed Dhushi later, when I told the girls about the fine. 'That way, everyone would get what they want.' She was always making such inappropriate remarks.

'The boy would be considered a martyr, too, and the stepmother would be glorified,' added Madhana, plaiting her long black hair.

That afternoon, Ananthan took us to a little mud hut half an hour's walk away, situated in the middle of a manioc field. 'Why haven't you taken us back to our jungle base?' I asked.

'It's not the right time,' was all Ananthan would say. None of us complained; we were glad of the respite.

This hut had two rooms, one the kitchen, the other a large room that served as the lounge room during the day and as a bedroom at night. For a little hut housing a family of six, it was very tidy. When I asked the woman of the house where the toilet was, she said there wasn't one and to go among the manioc plants at the back of the house.

Manioc was always part of the menu. For breakfast, we had boiled manioc with coconut sambol; lunch was rice with manioc curry and yoghurt; dinner was *pittu* with *sodhi* and fried manioc slices. The man, the woman and their four children kept us entertained by telling us stories about their village. We all slept together in the same room, on hand-woven grass mats.

All that medicine and the injection had only changed the timing of my fever, instead of curing it. Now the cold shivers began late in the evening and the fevers lasted 'til dawn. So, like an insomniac, I lay awake almost all night and listened to the men guarding their fields by beating drums and tins, making a mighty kerfuffle to frighten the elephants away.

I heard the elephants too—they would come, crushing the vegetation under their feet and sometimes trumpeting. I was petrified of being trampled to death—as my favourite Tamil poet, Subramanya Bharathi, had been when he was just thirty-eight—and I expected a big foot to come through the roof of the fragile mud hut any minute. The family members assured me that there had been only two such cases in the past and, given those statistics, my mind was put to rest.

Four days later Ananthan moved us to yet another whitewashed mud hut, set in the middle of a vegetable garden. An old woman and her daughter lived in this house and hardly ever spoke to us, except to announce meal times. The women laid red chillies out to dry on a grass mat in the front yard where hens pecked on them, causing them to lay 'chilli eggs'.

We were feeling a little better now, although still lethargic, and spent our days eating ripe mangoes from the trees and playing hopscotch in the front yard. I had learnt to tolerate Dhushi's habits although she still refused to listen to me when I asked her to wash her hands before eating and after visiting the toilet. She also refused to have showers or apologise after burping out loud—she would laugh at me instead. One day when I used the acronym LTTE to refer to the organisation, she asked me what that meant. Until then, she only ever knew the organisation she was a member of as just *Pulihal* [Tigers].

For some unexplained reason, two young men visited us one day, in Ananthan's place; they brought boxes of glucose and *ilanie* (tender coconut).

'You girls are lucky,' one of the boys said to us, leaning against the door frame. 'Boys in the movement don't receive such treatment—being taken to doctors and given carers, even when the carers are feeling unwell themselves.'

'Are you all right?' I asked, sensing the subtle message in his statement. He did look a little yellow.

'No, I'm ill with jaundice. I haven't been sent to the doctor, or given glucose or *ilanie*. In fact, I had to deliver it to you.'

'Here, take these,' I said returning a couple of boxes of glucose to him.

Following the local custom, he took the boxes even as he refused them over and over again, but he never once thanked me and also managed to insult me with a simple question: 'What happened to your hair, acca?'

He had addressed me as 'older sister' out of respect, although we were perhaps the same age. When in doubt, it was the right thing to do.

'Nothing,' I said, baffled by his question. 'Why?'

'It looks as if it has been in a fire,' he said earnestly, referring to my 1980s bob. I had been trying to grow it out, because no girl in the Tigers had short hair, except for Ajanthi and me. It occurred to me that people from this part of the country had possibly never seen women with short hair.

Two weeks after we had arrived at this village Ananthan led us back into the jungle, but via a different route, refusing to tell us where we were going or why. Late in the afternoon we were out of the jungle again, arriving at another village and a little mud hut by a river bed. We were surprised to find our female comrades squatting out the front, under a banyan tree. I saw Akila and ran to her.

'Oh, you are so much better!' exclaimed Akila, opening her little eyes wide. 'It's been crazy without you.' She was closer to me than anyone else at the base.

'Ananthan just brought us back from the doctor's. I thought you were still at the jungle base,' I said.

Akila told me that our jungle base had been attacked nearly a week before. They had withdrawn, leaving everything behind except the ammunition. She had managed to bring with her my meagre belongings, despite becoming lost with twelve others. For three days they had wandered in the forest, facing starvation, wild animals and the soldiers, who had scoured the jungle in large numbers. The girls had finally managed to reach an old man's hut on the edge of the forest, beside the largest man-made lake in Sri Lanka, the Iranaimadu Dam. He had helped them find local Tiger sympathisers, who reunited them with the rest of the units.

'The enemy has infiltrated the jungle,' said Akila. 'It felt as if they were everywhere—in the air and on the land. I was sure that it was just a matter of time before we'd run into them again.'

I embraced her. 'What an ordeal you've been through, Akila! Perhaps even more extraordinary days lie ahead of you.'

If only I had known what awaited Akila, I might have chosen my words more cautiously.

18

EXTRAORDINARY DAYS

After meeting Akila and the fifty or so girls at the hut by the stream, we remained there for the next three days, listening to Mahathaya's endless chatter—either to his men or into his walkie-talkie, discussing strategies and tactics. The girls were not included in these discussions, not even our commanders, Theeba or Sugi. So, when we were not rostered on sentry duty, we relaxed on the white sand of the stream's banks, surrounded by the emerald lush of vegetation.

We didn't have to concern ourselves with cooking, as food was supplied by the villagers once a day. Although our living conditions were rather primitive, it was not a bad place to be left doing little: peacocks and deer often came past the house and the river; swarms of pansy butterflies often glided past and there were sightings of brightly-coloured birds such as crimson-breasted barbets and blue-faced malkohas. I knew Ajanthi would have loved being here, surrounded by such amazing wildlife—spending her time chasing after them, no doubt.

On the morning of the third day, Mahathaya split our large group of girls into three units of fifteen and sent one unit somewhere on the back of a tractor. As I watched the girls leave, I realised that no one looked anything like they had eight months earlier, at the start of this war—now their faces were sunken, their skin ashen and their hair matted. A fine dust of soil covered their hands and feet. They looked like they belonged in the jungle and nowhere else. I was dispirited, realising I too must look like them.

I hoped Mahathaya wasn't going to send us back to the jungle again. Apart from its natural beauty, there was nothing there to distract us from the physical hardship—no books, paper or music. We couldn't even sing ourselves to distraction in fear of being discovered. I felt powerless in the jungle due to our total reliance on our male comrades and our isolation from civilisation and any connection with the real world. And then there was the possibility of falling ill again.

At noon, to my intense disappointment, Mahathaya announced that the rest of us would be returning to the jungle. That afternoon we set out on foot, in single file as always, following Ananthan and another young man. The dirt track we followed into the jungle was well-trodden and wide. I tried keeping a mental note of the direction and landmarks; but I soon gave up as every tree and every turn began to look like the one before it.

Four hours later we arrived at a jungle hide-out. 'Chicago Base', as the boys called it for reasons I didn't know or ask, had three large huts, a kitchen area and a sentry tent, making our previous jungle hide-out seem relatively primitive. A small unit of around fifteen young men was stationed there; they served us a dinner of boiled red kidney beans with a cup of very sugary tea.

Soon after the men's unit left, leaving us with Ananthan and the other boy to occupy the camp. And so life in the jungle resumed.

Although I had been left physically weak by malaria, I continued to perform my duties: some days I trekked many kilometres along the jungle track, carrying heavy cans of water from the river, and on other days hauled large sacks of rations from a men's hide-out a couple of kilometres away. These sealed sacks mostly contained packets of biscuits or chocolates or loads of shampoo, rather than more useful or nutritious supplies. I soon realised why—our men were randomly ambushing transport vehicles carrying supplies from the south of the country into Jaffna Peninsula as they passed through the jungle. Until they took the goods away, they didn't know what they had.

One afternoon, almost three weeks after we had arrived at the Chicago Base hide-out, Mahathaya and his men paid us a visit and summoned us to a meeting. As he sat on a wooden stool in front of us, I noticed that he too was wearing the same clothes he had been for many months and remained barefooted.

After discussing housekeeping matters, such as food rations and waste disposal, Mahathaya began talking about an unusual topic: relationships. 'Since the battle with the Indians started, unavoidably boys and girls have had to be grouped together and to live under the same roof. Anna trusted you to behave in an appropriate manner under these circumstances, but I have received information that some of you have acted otherwise.'

Mahathaya stopped and scanned us. We looked at each other, confused. Then he named three of the girls who had belonged to a unit led by another female commander, and began to tell us all about what they had done many months ago in Jaffna: one had propositioned a fellow comrade; another had playfully stuck her head next to a male comrade inhaling steam for his sinuses; but the third had committed the worst crime of all, and fallen in love.

'It really surprises me that, in a situation of life or death, you can get distracted so easily. Under any other circumstances, I might've seen it differently. We need to focus totally on winning this war. If you fall in love, you'll lose your resolve to die. This is a strict warning to all of you. *Chari*, except for the three girls I named, the rest of you can leave.' I wondered if the boys involved had received the same lecture.

As I rose to my feet, Mahathaya called out, 'Niromi.' My heart dropped and I froze to the spot. My mind was racing backwards, trying to remember anything that I might have done wrong.

'I'm told that you may have stomach ulcers,' he said, looking concerned. 'I have the same problem. These people can't help themselves when it comes to cooking with chilli powder, no matter what I tell them. Ask the cooks to keep some food aside for you, before they add spices. I'll organise some powdered milk to be sent for you. It's the best I can do under the circumstances.'

Totally perplexed, I thanked him and joined the others heading towards the huts a few metres away. It was true that I had been complaining about a burning sensation in my stomach lately, but I had not expected Mahathaya to know about it, let alone do something. Akila must have mentioned it to our paramedics. When I sat down on a dead tree trunk next to the girls, they teased me about the powdered milk: 'Next thing, he'll be sending a cow for you.'

The three girls named and shamed by Mahathaya had followed him into the tent where Ananthan slept, about 20 metres away from us. Within minutes, two of the girls walked out of the tent without their rifles and cyanide capsules. They had been discharged on the spot but ordered to remain with us until we abandoned the hide-out because, if released now, they might compromise the safety of everyone at the base. The third girl, Nora, who had trained with us and had been at the Jaffna University sentry, came out five minutes later and sat by us, her eyes filled with tears and her face darkened.

'What happened?' asked one of the girls.

'I feel like resigning today,' she said, staring at the ground. Tears began to roll down her face.

'What do you mean?' exclaimed one of the other girls.

'I've been punished for falling in love with Shanthan. I have to prove my loyalty to the organisation by always taking a frontline role at any confrontation with the enemy and by stealing an item from the enemy's camp each time.' Nora's face twisted in sadness.

'That's awful,' said someone.

'But don't resign before you fulfil your punishment at least once,' said Akila to Nora. 'Otherwise you'll prove that you value your relationship with Shanthan more than the organisation.'

The logic of this way of thinking eluded me. Many months ago

Muralie had reasoned similarly about the young Tiger man who was ordered to shoot his own father. He had resigned after carrying out the orders and not before, to remain faithful to the organisation.

'All this is nothing compared to how they plan to punish Shanthan . . .' Nora broke into sobs. 'They're going to finish him off.'

We gasped.

I remembered Shanthan as a good-looking, happy boy who had kept us amused through our difficult journey from the shore to the jungle months before. 'But what's killing him going to achieve?' I asked, confused.

'Mahathaya anna is furious. He's going to make an example out of Shanthan,' Nora said, wiping her tears. 'Tomorrow his corpse will be tied to a lamppost in a village somewhere with a note saying, "He was punished for misbehaving". And the people will admire the discipline of our organisation.' She began to sob loudly.

We sat in silence, not knowing what to say. I hoped that Mahathaya had only said this to her to frighten her. He surely could not murder an eighteen-year-old boy for falling in love. If I had known at that stage the number of murders Mahathaya had been personally responsible for, I would not have doubted what Nora had said.

Then suddenly a jeep appeared around the bend and screeched to a halt in front of the base, raising dust. A young man carrying an M16 got out of the passenger's seat and opened the back door. Another young man stepped out and we all instantly recognised him. Shanthan looked up and saw Nora, and held her gaze just for a second before he was coerced by the driver and front-seat passenger into the tent where Mahathaya was.

None of us dared to speak. Nora had gone into a state of shock, in anticipation of what might happen next. My heart began to pound heavily as I watched the tent, unblinking.

BANG!

It was just a single shot. Startled birds flapped their wings and took off, and monkeys screeched and jumped from tree to tree. A few seconds later, silence returned, as if the gunshot had been no more than a ripple in the ocean.

'*Ayyo* Shanthan!' wailed Nora and fell to the ground.

In shock, the rest of us remained rooted to the spot. I didn't even have the strength to look at her. The two young men who had led Shanthan into the tent now dragged his body behind them, by his arms. A thin stream of blood was running down from the centre of Shanthan's forehead, down his blue-and-white checked shirt.

One of the men opened the back door of the jeep, and they threw Shanthan's body in. Then they drove off, raising the dust once again.

We sat there listening to Nora's sobs—not looking at her or at each other. I could not comprehend the senseless murder of this young man. I felt sickened, confused and outraged all at once. But I knew that whatever words I chose to use to comfort Nora, none of them would express how I really felt or make that moment right again.

'How could Mahathaya anna just kill Shanthan like that?' I asked Akila that evening, as we sat side by side on a fallen tree trunk during my sentry duty. 'Although I agree with Mahathaya anna that this is no time to fall in love, Shanthan certainly didn't deserve to be killed for it.'

'I'm sure there's more to this than meets the eye,' replied Akila, unperturbed.

I reasoned with her that nothing could warrant the murder of our own.

'Anna and his men would always do the right thing. You just have to place your trust in them,' said Akila.

It seemed that Akila had little trouble continuing to place her trust in the hands of our leaders. I, on the other hand, could not ignore the occasional protesting voice inside me.

Until now I had always considered Mahathaya to be a great leader. I had in fact liked the man, not believing the tales of his ruth-less nature that had earned him his nickname, Crocodile. But now that I had witnessed him in action, I was beginning to question the ethics under which our commanders and we were operating.

Slaughtering men like Benjamin because they belonged to a rival faction was bad enough, but this cold-blooded murder of one of our own, because he had fallen in love, was another. It made me remember how, many months ago back in Sudhumalai, the young men in my unit had murdered Vellai with callous disregard, accusing him of being a traitor. I was now finally beginning to understand how such atrocities came about.

From top to bottom in our organisation, everyone did whatever they pleased so long as they could justify it as being for the good of the organisation. I realised that murder and violence against our own was simply part of the culture.

I had not been prepared for this. I had joined the Tigers so I could save my people from the clutches of an oppressive government. All I wanted was to achieve Tamil Eelam, where we could be free. But it seemed to me that I had gone about it the wrong way. I had chosen violence to combat violence. Why was I then shocked that there was so much carnage all around me.

As Akila and I headed back to our hut at the end of my sentry hour that evening, I thought back to the times I had been a witness to my comrades' crimes—Mahathaya beating up an innocent man while Kaanchana and I guarded his bicycle; Navin and Nizaam bashing a civilian at the shopping mall; the killing of Vellai in broad daylight; and now Shanthan. The gravity of these incidents had increased over time, starting as assaults and ending up as murders, and I had done nothing to stop them. And, although I did not condone any of this, I, too, as a Tiger and a witness, now had blood on my hands—the blood of my comrades and my fellow Tamils.

This realisation made me feel sick. I felt I could no longer continue to be part of it. But what could I do? Could I simply walk away from my dream, and that of those who had sacrificed their lives for it? Wasn't it my duty to keep Thileepan's, Ajanthi's and Muralie's dream alive? And this AK I held—it was from a fallen comrade who had passed on his hopes to me. If I decided to leave, the Tigers would surely let me go amicably—Thileepan had told me I was free to leave anytime. But, would I be making a mistake if I did?

By the time we went to sleep that night, my doubts and my restlessness had reached a crisis. I knew I wasn't going to be able to change the attitude of my comrades, let alone our leaders. The only option left for me was to walk away from this.

At the same time I was overwhelmed by the uncertainty of what lay ahead of me. Where would I go from here? And what would I do? I didn't know if Amma and Shirani had remained in Jaffna, or how I would get there. Would they accept me back after I had betrayed them for the second time?

Then I remembered the time many months before, at the start of the war, when Ajanthi's parents came to visit us at the SOLT office, they had told me that Amma had refused to accompany them because she was disappointed and heartbroken after I left home to join the Tigers for the second time. There was a real chance that Amma might refuse ever to see me again or accept me back into the family. What would I do then? I had no education, no skills, and as a single woman was totally vulnerable.

And, of course, there was Akila—my dear friend, my rock and my fairy godmother. She was all I had left. I didn't know if I had the will or the courage to walk away from her. And I was certain of one thing: she would never forgive me if I did.

But in my heart I knew that I could no longer continue to compromise my values for the sake of loyalty to an organisation or even to friendship. How could I remain loyal to anyone—my friends, or Tamil Eelam or the Tigers—if I failed to be true to myself?

Two days after he had promised to do so, Mahathaya sent two large cans of powdered milk to me with my name written on them. I could not understand this man—he was concerned enough to go to the trouble of doing something about someone's mild ulcer, and yet he showed a callous disregard for another comrade's life.

Many times I had conjured up the image of Mahathaya shooting Shanthan at point-blank range, and this flashed in front of me every time I thought of him. While I felt grateful to him for taking care of me, it felt wrong to accept his tins of powdered milk. I left them in the kitchen for others to have, unsure of what else to do with them.

19

WHERE DO I GO FROM HERE?

Nearly a week after Shanthan's murder, our jungle base was attacked. Soldiers had followed Ananthan and a group of girls who were returning from bathing down at the river. Without Ananthan, the girls wouldn't have known their way around. Within minutes of the girls' return, with water still dripping from their long lice-ridden hair, we heard a few gunshots near the entrance to the base.

I was sitting on a log outside the hut that served as our kitchen, having a late lunch after sentry duty the previous hour. When I heard the gunshot, I tossed my plastic plate, picked up my AK and ran to the assembly area. Everyone else had gathered there.

By this time, the Indian army were all over the jungles of Vanni in their thousands with superior ammunition and helicopter gunships as they knew the entire Tiger movement was hiding in units scattered all over the jungle. They could bring reinforcements any time and there was no point fighting them with our small number of AKs, M16s and G3s.

Ananthan hurriedly directed all the girls to leave with the other boy through the back of the hide-out. Then he took up a position—with Akila, Jenny and me, each of us behind a tree—facing the entrance to the hide-out. He placed Nora on her own, further forward, away from our line of fire, as part of front-line punishment.

Silently we scanned the jungle for the slightest movement, our index fingers ready on our triggers. The macaques hung above us, watching us intensely. We heard dry leaves rustle many metres in front of us, behind the trees, but all else was silent, except for birds and insects.

Five minutes later, Ananthan whispered: 'Let's get out of here.' We rose to our feet and started walking backwards, taking small cautious footsteps and keeping a watchful eye around us, our rifles aimed forward towards the entrance of the base. Dried leaves and twigs snapped under our bare feet. When we were a safe distance from the hide-out, we turned around and started to walk briskly through the dense vegetation.

'I saw a soldier near the entrance, but decided not to open fire because it wasn't a planned ambush from what I could see,' said Ananthan in a quiet voice, pushing weeds and branches out of his way. 'I think there were no more than a few soldiers who were probably on a walk or casual foot patrol and followed us. I'm sure they thought girls would be easy to capture, so they just shot at us to scare us off, I think.'

I agreed with Ananthan. As a female unit we had found the soldiers to be keen on capturing us rather than firing at us. I had been at a sentry once at a village outside Jaffna when the soliders came charging at me shouting '*ponna pudi*!' which I had understood to be Indian Tamil meaning 'catch the girl!'

Shafts of afternoon sunlight pierced through the dense canopy. The musty smell of damp soil and vegetation rose to fill our nostrils as we reached one of the men's hide-outs and found the rest of our girls waiting there. Together with the men we fled as night fell. It was past midnight when we stopped to rest.

'A couple of hours sleep and then we walk again,' I heard one of the men command. I recognised that voice by its deep resonance— Sengamalam. I realised that during all this time he had been with the men's unit not far from us. I felt comforted by his presence. I had no idea where Rajan and Sudharshan were.

Moonlight was now streaming down, illuminating the ground, but leaving deep shadows. We spread our hessian sacks on the forest floor and lay down, exhausted. I was tired, hungry and disappointed at the thought of not having finished my previous meal.

As I drifted into sleep next to Akila, loud crashing noises jolted me awake. Everyone stirred around me. Macaques were making a racket above us. The crashing noise was heading our way.

'It's an elephant on heat,' said someone. 'Everyone hurry along in this direction.'

As we scurried away, the elephant could be heard trumpeting and crashing through the trees, terrifying us. Luckily it kept its distance because of the noise the monkeys made as they followed us, swinging on the branches above. We spent the rest of that night running and taking cover. Just before dawn we saw the first sign of civilisation—a mud hut beyond a clearing.

Except for Sengamalam and Ananthan, the other men headed into the village. We were told to press on. I was very thirsty and tired. We had had nothing to eat or drink in nearly twenty-four hours.

I was glad we were out of the jungle, but it was likely that we would return to it within a day or two. I had to choose whether I would return with the others when the time came or leave the Tigers. It was decision time.

By late in the afternoon we had arrived at a large lake. The surrounding white sandy soil was sparsely dotted with needle-leafed juniper shrubs. A little distance away, taller, emerald-green palmyras and figs fronted the dense dark forest towering behind them. The sun was scorching. Sengamalam told us we could have a dip in the water and a short rest. We left our holsters and rifles next to him and ran into the cold water fully clothed. It was such a welcome relief to our tired, hot, perspiration-drenched bodies. After splashing about in the water and eating some juniper berries we had stripped from the bushes, we went to sleep in the shade of the shrubs.

I must have slept for about twenty minutes when I heard the roar of a helicopter. I jumped to my feet and saw a menacing wasp-like gunship on the horizon. In a mad rush, we gathered our belongings and scrambled towards the trees. But the gunship spotted us and hovered right over us, dipping down low. Then it opened fire. The sound was deafening. The trees and shrubs convulsed; the white sand rose into the air, lifting dry leaves and twigs. We crouched under the shrubs at the foot of the trees. I felt as though I couldn't drag in breath; my heart was pounding heavily. Then I heard the roaring sound of a second helicopter gunship.

Sengamalam shouted, 'Everyone run this way.'

I used the last bit of strength I had in me to follow him. We ran for our lives, chased by the two gunships, ducking and weaving behind bushes and trees before finally reaching the safety of the dense jungle. The gunships continued to hover and strafe for a few minutes more, and then they disappeared.

Exhausted, we dropped to the ground. I lay on my back looking up at the branches of the trees above me. My entire body felt as if it was on fire; my stomach cramped in hunger.

We headed back into the village soon after. The few villagers we saw simply stared at us, but said nothing. Sengamalam suspected that foot soldiers would be mobilised by now, looking for us in and around the forest where the helicopter gunships had located us. I was so hungry that I could not think of anything but food.

I remembered with shame those times I had refused to eat Amma's cooking because I'd wanted beef and she had made chicken, or I had preferred fish when she cooked beef. I had also often complained that her dishes clashed with, rather than complemented, each other. Amma would leave the meal on the table and quote a Tamil adage: The horse will eat hay when its derriere goes flat. I used to respond with another maxim: The tiger will not eat grass even if it's starving. I felt ashamed at my ungrateful behaviour. I had not appreciated the unconditional love and care my family had bestowed upon me. I had been utterly selfish. I hoped I would have the chance to apologise to them one day.

By sunset we were at the other side of the village, arriving at a little brick house surrounded by hectares of vegetable gardens.

Sengamalam motioned us to wait as he walked up to the door. We sat down in the front yard, relieving our aching bare feet. Soon Sengamalam was talking to a middle-aged man. A timid young woman peered at us from behind one of the windows.

Quite quickly, Mahathaya and his entourage arrived on the scene. The moment I lay eyes on him I recalled Shanthan's body, dripping with blood, being dragged out of the tent. It made me feel ill. I turned my face away from him. Although I was certain that my comrades had not forgotten the murder, none of us—not even Nora—had ever talked about it after that day. But it had not stopped bothering me.

An hour later, the man and woman of the house spread a quarter of a banana leaf in front of each one of us in the yard, and served a spoonful of boiled red rice with half a spoon of drumsticks curry on it. After we had devoured our meal, Mahathaya said he'd like to speak to each one of us in private. Then he took up a position on a small rock behind the house, where anyone a little distance away could hear every word spoken 'in private'.

I wasn't certain what had brought this about because he had never offered to speak to us like this before. Whatever his reasons may have been, I decided I would speak with him. However, I wasn't going to discuss my two most pressing issues with him: Shanthan's murder and my wish to resign from the organisation. I simply lacked the courage, no longer being able to predict how he'd react if either matter was raised with him. Instead, I decided to tell Mahathaya about the murder of Vellai and see how he'd react to it. I hoped his reaction would help me decide if I should stay under his leadership or resign. After all, if the Tigers' deputy leader and Prabhakaran's most trusted comrade couldn't convince me to stay, then no one could.

When it was my turn, I sat in front of him, on another small rock. 'How is your ulcer?' asked Mahathaya, smiling. His smile was so innocent, like a schoolboy's, for a moment I nearly forgot he was a murderer.

'Okay,' I replied flatly. 'I just want to tell you that I am upset about certain behaviours among our comrades,' I said, without taking a breath, feeling a little nervous.

'What is it specifically?' asked Mahathaya, his eyebrows coming together.

I told him about Vellai, and asked if his murderers would face consequences one day. Mahathaya laughed uncomfortably. I wasn't certain if it was my question or the small rough surface of the rock he was sitting on that seemed to disconcert him.

'Did you know Vellai personally?' he asked, looking confused. I replied that I had never once spoken to him.

Mahathaya then rubbed the fist of his right hand into the palm of his left. 'You are young and disillusioned,' he said. 'These things happen. There are times when you have to make tough decisions for the good of the organisation. If there are traitors among us, we must eliminate them.'

I was bewildered. There had never been any proof that Vellai had been a traitor, I told him.

'It doesn't matter,' said Mahathaya. 'We rely on our loyal comrades to tell on those who aren't. Tomorrow your best friend here might commit an offence which may compromise the organisation. In a situation like that, I'd expect you to report her immediately. Loyalty to the organisation must come first.'

I looked at Akila, a few metres away, sitting by the steps of the house, talking to one of the girls. I thought of Ajanthi and Nihintha. I was certain that I could not rate my loyalty to the organisation higher than that for my friends. I had said so to Muralie and Gandhi.

'But Mahathaya anna, how will I know what is considered wrong and what is not? I don't want myself or others to be punished for unwittingly committing an offence,' I said, thinking of Shanthan and Nora, and my wanting to get out.

Mahathaya laughed a little louder this time. 'You are worrying too much. You just report any behaviour that may seem out of the ordinary'.

When I walked away from speaking with Mahathaya, I was feeling more unsettled than ever before. Instead of reassuring me, he had trivialised my concerns. And all this talk of blind loyalty made me nervous. I had not thought about such matters in depth before, but this was the way things were done here: ruled by the law of the gun, as we were, there was no room for a fair hearing or for justice, although these were the very things we were fighting for. I felt that the Tigers would never give up their weapons no matter the reason, because it was the only way they knew how to rule. Without their weapons and violence they would feel powerless. Just as the Tigers held on to violence to gain power, so did the governments of Sri Lanka to oppress its own people. This was a vicious cycle, and the people of this country were caught up in it.

It had taken me nearly a year to realise this. When I had joined the Tigers and before I became a combatant I had thought the Tigers were on a winning stretch, closer to attaining Tamil Eelam. And there had been Ajanthi, Muralie and Roshan to keep me distracted during the early days of combat. Now, without them, and physically weak, I was at last seeing things for what they were.

I was disheartened realising there would never be true peace in my country as long as violence was used as a means to attain it.

That night, after Mahathaya and his entourage left, we headed towards the bush about 50 metres from the house. As I lay next to Akila among the juniper bushes, I was certain of my decision. In the morning I would resign, before the unit headed back into the jungle. I was tossing and turning, feeling restless.

'Shh . . . Come on, go to sleep,' Akila patted my shoulder, half asleep. 'Sentry duty will be any minute.'

I looked at Akila's silhouette as she lay in the soft moonlight. She was now snoring lightly. I wished I had her tranquil mind. In all the time I had known her she had never once wavered from her dedication to the Tigers, doubted their methods or questioned their motives. Unlike me, she was committed to the cause, mind, body and soul, just the way she was truly committed to our friendship. I felt a pang of guilt. I almost woke her up and told her of my decision, but immediately changed my mind. I wouldn't tell her anything until after I resigned. Otherwise she may convince me to stay. I did not want to be persuaded of anything by anyone any more, even by Akila. And in the same way I didn't want to influence Akila with my way of thinking. Staying with the Tigers or leaving them would have to be her decision (and something told me that she'd be with them 'til the day she died).

I decided that in the morning I would seek Sengamalam's permission to leave. If there was one man who would bear no ill will towards me for resigning, it would be him—he had seen me through my worst. He'd know that I still believed in the Tamil cause, admired Prabhakaran, and cared about these young men and women, my comrades, who had become my family. But I wouldn't be explaining to him that, while I shared their vision, I no longer shared their values.

In the morning, I went looking for Sengamalam.

He was drying his face with a sarong after a wash at the well. In the warm gentle breeze, the moringa trees behind him dropped yellowing leaves.

I came straight to the point. 'Sengamalam anna, I want to leave.'

He stopped and looked at me with alarm. 'What?'

'I want to go home.'

'What's wrong? Is anyone giving you grief? Tell me what I can do?' He fired the questions at me hastily. I was touched by his response.

'No, Sengamalam anna, it's not that. I can't cope any more, physically and emotionally. I am so tired. I just need to get away from here.'

'Mmm . . .' Sengamalam stared at me for a few seconds, with one hand on his chin. 'I'm sorry to hear it. I always knew you weren't really cut out for this way of life, and the deaths of Ajanthi and Muralie have been hard on you. I'm surprised you lasted this long.'

Sengamalam paused and took a deep breath: 'Niromi, I need to warn you that once you leave us your life will be in grave danger. We won't be able to protect you from the rival movements, from the Sri Lankan Army or from the Indians—they'll all want your blood.'

Sengamalam's warning had no impact on me. I nodded, 'Yes, I know.'

'Is there anything I can say to persuade you to stay?' asked Sengamalam.

'No, Sengamalam anna. I've given it a lot of thought and now I have made up my mind,' I replied.

'Well, Niromi, ask the owner of the house for some paper and a pen, to write the *thundu* [resignation letter]. I also need another letter from you to your mother, asking her to pick you up from, say, an aunt's house in Kilinochchi, or some believable story like that, so your amma understands you have left the Tigers. That way, if the enemy intercepts your letter, they won't suspect anything out of the ordinary.'

As I sat on the verandah of the house writing out my *thundu*, one of the girls spotted me.

'What are you doing?'

'Resigning,' I replied.

The look on her face changed from curiosity to horror, and then to excitement. She immediately began to scream 'I want to leave! I want to leave!' and ran inside the house. Within a few minutes, there were about twenty girls sitting around me writing notes.

When Sengamalam came to the house, he was startled: 'What madness is going on here?' he asked.

I gave him my resignation note and the letter for Amma.

'Hand over your AK and *kuppie* to Ananthan,' ordered Sengamalam as he put my pieces of paper safely in his pocket.

The other girls stood in a queue behind me, ready to hand over their pieces of paper too. But Sengamalam dismissed them with the wave of his hand: 'I'm not accepting these. Have you all gone mad?'

'But I want to go home!' shouted someone.

'Me too!' shouted another.

'Get lost all of you!' Sengamalam rebuffed them and walked out. He wouldn't take them seriously.

I realised that my timing was absolutely fortuitous. The fact that Sengamalam had fought alongside me since the war resumed, and had witnessed the death of my friends, had worked in my favour.

I changed into my purple batik dress. As I did so, I heard the voice of Dhushi, singing: 'Oh, my resigning comrade, give me your panties and bra . . .' She had changed the words of a Tiger propaganda song which began, 'Oh, dying hero, give me your uniform and footwear . . .'

Then I went outside to look for Ananthan and Akila.

I tried to conjure up all the courage I had in me, to help me explain to Akila my reasons for leaving and for abandoning our friendship in the process. When I had met her, over a year ago, we had instantly become friends. Since then, we had spent much of our time together, day and night. Today, I would be leaving her, not knowing when and if we'd see each other again.

I found Ananthan alone near the back of the house, sitting by the side of the fence, chewing on a blade of grass as he often did. He looked up at me curiously.

'I've resigned,' I said abruptly. 'I am to hand over my rifle and *kuppie* to you.'

I felt a pang of guilt, thinking of Thileepan, when I removed my cyanide capsule. This was the sign that I had broken all my ties with the Tigers. Now, without my rifle and killer capsule, I felt naked and vulnerable.

'You'll regret this decision,' Ananthan muttered as he took the capsule and my AK from me. 'I have just appointed Akila as a new unit leader and she was going to ask you to be her deputy. She's going to be very disappointed.'

Ananthan paused. Now I felt worse—I was failing Akila and my comrades by not fulfilling my commitment to them. Yet I was delighted for Akila all the same. She deserved this leadership position for her unwavering commitment to the organisation and the consideration she always showed towards her comrades. But I said nothing of this to Ananthan.

'We'll ask Lekha to take your place,' Ananthan continued. 'You know, Niromi, this period of difficulty won't last long. Our good times will return and we'll be in control again. We'll repel the foreign army and gain Tamil Eelam. Then you'll be sorry you left us prematurely.'

'Perhaps,' I replied, unable to look him in the eye.

'Will you return some day?'

'Maybe.'

Someone told me Akila was at the well and so I headed in that direction. Ananthan's words continued to echo in my ears. I hoped that there would never be a time in the future when I'd regret this decision to leave the Tigers.

As I passed by the house, I heard Sengamalam's voice: 'Except for Niromi and the two discharged, the rest of you prepare to head back to the jungle now.'

I looked to my left at the group of girls about 10 metres away. Among them was Akila, talking to her unit. Lekha, Jessie, Jenny and Vadhana were there—they had been with me through the worst moments of my life, and had shared meagre meals, poor dwellings, tears and laughter. Like me, they too had lost their comrades, but it seemed to me that somehow they remained strong both emotionally and physically. It upset me terribly to think that I might never see them again.

At Sengamalam's words, Akila looked up with a jolt. Her eyes searched and found me in my dress. They opened wide in astonishment and her jaw dropped. 'What's going on?' she cried. 'Niromi, why are you leaving?' Tears began to well up in her eyes.

I ran over to Akila and embraced her. 'Here—keep my sarong and my clothes,' I said. I didn't need them any more.

In my anxiety to leave, I had failed to anticipate the sadness I would cause her.

'Why didn't you talk to me?' Akila broke into sobs. 'I can't believe you're leaving me. But why? I need you by my side, Niromi. We could've achieved so much together.'

I stood there holding her hand and simply staring at her, feeling totally ashamed. I could hardly speak.

Then Sengamalam hurried Akila along: 'Go, Akila—your unit has almost disappeared. You're going to lose them.'

I loosened my grip and her hand fell away. She turned around and began running after the others, through the clearing and towards the jungle. As I stood watching her against the morning sun, she turned her head to look at me, holding my sarong and clothes in one hand and her M16 in the other. Tears were still streaming down her face.

Akila began to fade away from the bright sunlight, and soon the darkness of the dense jungle enveloped her.

I sat cross-legged under a mango tree, outside a hut, listening to the wind rustle in the tree tops. The surrounding yard was littered with palmyra and coconut palms, and clusters of banana trees. The wind carried the sharp smell of fresh cow dung from a nearby shed, where the old woman I was living with kept her few cows. I watched a ring-necked parrot fly into a hole in a coconut tree trunk next to me. I could hear her many chicks chirping with delight.

Three days had passed since I arrived at this place. After I'd resigned a tractor had picked up me and the other two girls, and dropped us off at a house in the village. A young man had then brought me on my own to this hut, transporting me on the front handlebar of his bicycle.

Sengamalam had promised me that he would find a way to inform my mother of my whereabouts. I had trusted him blindly but now, after waiting for three days, I began to wonder if he had promised the impossible. How was he going to get my letter into enemy-controlled Jaffna, when the entire Tiger outfit was hiding in the jungles of Vanni, some 100 kilometres south of Jaffna city? There was also the chance that Amma and Shirani may have moved to Kandy, in which case there was little hope of tracking them down.

Although I had resigned from the Tigers, I was totally dependent on them to help me reunite with my family. I could not walk away and try to board a bus or train to Kandy or Jaffna—I had no money, no travel documents, and I did not know my way around. If the soldiers interrogated me, I could not adequately explain why I was on my own in this part of the country, with just the clothes on my back and a desire to go to Jaffna.

For a moment I imagined myself arriving home, with matted hair, barefoot and in this oversized batik dress. What a shock I would give everyone!

'Pillai!' It was the old woman calling out to me, as if to a child. This wiry woman in her tattered sari, possibly in her late sixties, had never once asked my name, and I never learnt hers. She lived in the hut alone, but she had a couple of people who helped her—one of the village boys would put her cows out to pasture in the morning and bring them back at nightfall; another young man came to help with jobs around the house, such as removing any ripe hands of bananas, or chopping firewood, or taking the milk to the market.

The woman, who was probably a sympathiser or had a son or relative in the Tigers, and I exchanged hardly a word or a smile except that, when it was time for lunch or dinner—always red rice, green banana curry and fresh yoghurt—she would call out to me. Then we would eat in silence, sitting on the packed earth verandah.

I spent much of my time sitting on the sandy soil in her front yard, talking to myself, pretending that my sister Shirani was there listening. I told her about the events of the past year in great detail, illustrating them with diagrams sketched with a stick in the sand. I talked about it as if it had all happened to someone else. Sometimes I swept the yard, or helped herd the cattle into the shed, or gave them a wash. There was no electricity, so we ate our dinner by the light of a hurricane lamp; then the woman would go to sleep on her bed, made of wood and rope, out on the verandah. I slept on the dirt floor next to her. We would be up again at sunrise.

As the days turned into a week, I began to doubt that I was ever going to see my family again. Many possible future scenarios played out in my mind—perhaps Amma was on her way; perhaps she had never received the message; or she had received the message and decided not to come for me. I could not blame her if she didn't come—I had caused her, Appa and Shirani a lot of grief. They might never be able to forgive me.

If that was the case, I did not know what I would do. I might end up living with this old woman for the rest of my life, waiting every day for someone to come for me. Or I might walk out of here and try my luck in getting to Jaffna—perhaps some stranger would take me under their wing and help me. I never once entertained the idea of going back to the Tigers. I knew that a life of violence was behind me.

I decided that I'd wait another week, and then choose a course of action. The future remained hazy, but I was confident that I would be all right in the end. I had already survived too many dangerous situations not to.

One afternoon, nearly eight days after I had arrived at the hut, I heard murmuring and footsteps in the dirt lane, outside the fence. When the gate opened I saw the young man who had brought me to this house, and behind him a man in a crisp white shirt and grey trousers. This tall, balding man with a chiselled face looked out of place in the rural village setting.

'This is her,' said the young man as he leaned his bicycle against the trunk of the mango tree.

'You don't know me,' said the man in a deep voice, now standing in front of me. His eyes were smiling as he spoke, as Muralie's had once been. 'I am the Vithanai (Village Headman) of Kilinochchi and distantly related to your Appamma, and I was uncle to Theeban.'

I stared at him in amazement.

The man then pulled a photo out of his shirt pocket and showed it to me. There I was sitting on the front verandah of a house owned by one of my aunts in my ancestral village, wearing a pink-and-white striped dress with little puffed sleeves, my white belt tied across the waist, and white shoes. It had been taken over two years earlier.

'Your mother sent it to me through my sister, Theeban's mother, in Jaffna,' said the man, depositing the photo back in his shirt pocket. 'I have been asking after you since, and it was by chance that this morning I happened to see this young boy, who instantly recognised you from the photo and brought me here.'

After asking after my health, and promising me that he would return with Amma in a few days, the man left. I was surprised at how pure coincidence had brought this man to me. I began to feel optimistic, but also cautious. Who knew—he might never be able to find Amma.

Three days later, in mid 1988, as I was helping the old woman herd her cattle back into their shed in the evening, I saw Amma running towards me down the lane, her green and white sari fluttering in the wind. I saw desperation in her eyes and tears streaming down her face; yet she looked amazingly beautiful. The tall balding man, the mayor of Kilinochchi, was at her heel, walking at a steady pace, carrying a large bag.

The only emotion I felt was a sense of relief. I wanted to tell her how grateful I was that she had come for me. I wanted her to know that I was glad to see her; I wanted to ask where Shirani was. But, as Amma embraced me and sobbed, I stood motionless, feeling numb—it was as if I was no longer capable of feeling happy or sad.

'I thought you might have disowned me,' I said. 'I did betray you twice.'

'You are my daughter,' she replied, wiping away her tears. 'Your father and I would never give up on you.'

20

AFTERWARDS

One mid-November day in 1987, the very day and time Nizaam and Navin had promised Amma and Shirani my return home, armed IPKF raided our house and ransacked it. At gunpoint, they had interrogated Amma and Shirani. They had wanted a photo of me, but only a few weeks earlier Amma had managed to destroy all evidence of me, including my childhood photos. Then the soldiers had marched Amma and Shirani through the streets, at gunpoint, to their nearest camp, to question them further before releasing them.

Within a few days, the entire neighbourhood was rounded up by the IPKF, both young and old, and forced to sit on the hot tarred road for hours, then paraded in front of a *thalayaatti* (the nodder), a masked Tiger captive who nodded when he or she identified a fellow Tiger or a sympathiser. Shirani was identified and apprehended. She was later released after Amma and a group of nuns, also held in the round-up, pleaded with the IPKF officers. The IPKF then set up camp near our home and visited Amma and Shirani every day, though the Indian Tamil officer in charge of the camp began to treat them with respect. He was also in possession of my poetry notebook found at the raid on the Tiger media office and admitted to Amma

298

that it made him understand why the Tamils had to fight the government. With this officer's permission, Amma took Shirani to Kandy and enrolled her in a school there, returning to Jaffna immediately as her IPKF permit stipulated. Under Colombo Auntie's leadership and together with the women in our neighbourhood, she founded a local *Mothers' Front* movement to help mothers whose children were missing or in custody. Nearly six months later, in June 1988, she received a coded message through Theeban's mother, who was cousins with the mayor of Kilinochchi, to pack a set of clothes for her and me, along with our passports, in her handbag and to leave the house as if she was visiting someone down the road. She was told nothing more.

In August 1988, within two months of finding me, Amma enrolled me in an exclusive private boarding school in India. By the time I left school eighteen months later, I had been elected one of four captains and crowned prom queen of the year.

That same year, with the help of an aunt, I undertook an undergraduate degree in biotechnology at a university in Sydney, Australia, then a masters degree in law. Recently I've learnt that around that time the Tigers were looking for me so that I could work for them politically. At that stage the Tigers were yet to use human bombs against political or civilian targets, nor had they introduced their ethnic cleansing policy against Muslims in Tiger-controlled areas. Having no contact with the Tigers and avoiding any news of them helped me to move forward with my life. I was fortunate not to be found.

My family later migrated to Australia. Like me, Shirani is now happily married and mother of two. She's also a successful career woman, working as a senior manager for a large multinational company, having lived and worked in the UK and Europe.

Ajanthi's sister Nilanthi is an accountant and also a happily-married mother of two. She and her parents live in Australia, and to this day I remain close to them. They continue to be loving and generous towards me.

After Ajanthi and I joined the Tigers in 1987, a few girls from our school followed suit—among them some of our fellow classmates.

We had begun a social change by breaking out of the self-limiting attitude of, and towards, females, and removing the stigma associated with women in combat, hoping to elevate the status of women in the conservative Tamil society and empower them. Little had I realised then that following the lead of a totalitarian male and volunteering to become suicide bombers was not women's liberation. There is no doubting that these women were brave and heroic, but they served a master, never achieved equal status to or the recognition of their male counterparts, and had marriages arranged by Prabhakaran himself.

Since I left Sri Lanka, changes in both the Sri Lankan and Indian governments brought about a suspension of military operations on 20 September 1989 and the subsequent withdrawal of Indian troops from Sri Lanka by March 1990. Various estimates place the number of IPKF deaths in the previous two years at some 1200 and the Tigers at 2500. It is said that some 5000 Tamil civilians were killed by the IPKF.

War between the Sri Lankan armed forces and the Tigers then resumed after a short period of peace. With the substantial financial support from the large Tamil diaspora around the world, the guerrilla organisation I left behind became a sophisticated war machine, building extensive global networks and establishing its own air and sea capabilities. The Tigers' methods also became more extreme. Having pioneered the suicide belt, they undertook hundreds of suicide bombing missions (one third of them by females), targeting civilians and politicians as well as military targets. Most notably, the Black Tiger suicide squad has been blamed for the assassinations of former Prime Minister Rajiv Gandhi in 1991, Sri Lankan Prime Minister Ranasinghe Premadasa in 1993, and several other daring and deadly attacks, including the one on the Sri Lankan (Bandaranaike) International airport in 2001.

Akila (Sakthiya Devi) died on 1 November 1995 (aged twenty-four) in the battle for Neerveli on the Jaffna Peninsula (where Theeban had also died ten years prior) against the Sri Lankan forces. Surrounded by the Sri Lankan army, she ordered her unit to swallow cyanide and did the same herself, to avoid capture. At the time of her death, she was the deputy head of the women's intelligence wing and was posthumously awarded the title of lieutenant-colonel, the highest rank then achievable in the Tigers. She had been a wanted woman since 1991, for allegedly masterminding—together with Prabhakaran and his then deputy, Pottu Amman—the assassination of Rajiv Gandhi.

It was claimed that the suicide bomber who perpetrated the murder of Rajiv Gandhi had been a member of Akila's unit, as were other females involved in the attack; they included Akila's deputy, Lekha (not her real name or *nom de guerre*), who was arrested in India soon after the assassination and given the death sentence on being found guilty. In 1999 she was released on appeal into a refugee detention centre. The conditions at this centre have been described as subhuman, and worse than in any Indian prison. I am unaware of her current status.

I never saw Roshan (not his real name or *nom de guerre*) again. But after the war was suspended in September 1989, unbeknown to me at the time, Roshan had come to my maternal grandparents' house in Kandy looking for me, and then followed me to India. Unable to locate me there, he found employment locally and remained in India until his arrest in August 1991 (aged twenty-seven), on suspicion of playing a role in Rajiv Gandhi's assassination. He too was sentenced to death by hanging. Court documents describe him as 'an expert driver'. He was released from the maximum security prison nine years later, also to a refugee detention centre. Perhaps he's still there.

Prabhakaran's deputy, Mahathaya (Mahendrarajah Gopalaswamy), was starved, tortured for a year, and then executed by the Tigers on 28 December 1994 (aged thirty-eight). He and his men were accused by Prabhakaran of being traitors—of collaborating with the Indian Intelligence Agency in a plot to assassinate Prabhakaran and gain leadership of the Tigers. Despite an appeal by Amnesty International to spare Mahathaya's life, Prabhakaran's men executed Mahathaya and some 250 of his loyal cadres.

Lieutenant-Colonel Kittu (Krishnakumar Sathasivam) died on 16 January 1993 (aged thirty-three), when the cargo vessel on which he was a passenger was intercepted at sea by the Indian navy, which suspected the boat belonged to the Tigers. The vessel was reportedly carrying on board a huge weapons cargo en route from Thailand. After the crew jumped into the sea, Kittu and his eight men detonated explosives on board and went down with the ship, in order to avoid capture.

Navin (not his real name) was shot dead by the Tigers sometime in 1990 (aged nineteen) for his alleged role as an IPKF informant against Muralie and his unit. (I wasn't aware then of the rumours that Navin fell out with Muralie because he suspected that Muralie and Navin's young widowed mother were romantically involved.)

Major Sugi (Mariyalama Raji Alfred), co-commander at our training base, died on 12 January 1999 in a clash with the Sri Lankan Navy in the seas off the east coast.

The fates of Kaanchana, Sengamalam and the others mentioned in this book are unknown. In the 1990s the Tigers de-sanskritised their *noms de guerre* to Tamil names, which has made tracing the characters in this story more difficult.

After many failed attempts at peace, including the Norway-brokered negotiations in 2002, hostilities between the government of Sri Lanka and the Tigers flared up again within a year. In 2004, a split emerged in the Tigers, which led to a large contingent of Tigers from the Eastern Province breaking away from Prabhakaran's leadership, under a new commander. They later joined the ruling Sinhala government to work against the Tigers.

Despite this, the Tigers gained control of much of their claimed territory of Sri Lanka by 2006, due to several successful sea and air attacks against the Sri Lankan military. However, by May 2009, the thirty-three-year civil war came to an end, with the Sri Lankan government forces claiming victory over the Tigers amid war crime allegations, having destroyed the entire Tiger outfit on ground and killing Prabhakaran, his wife, daughter and two sons. It has been estimated that over the years the conflict had claimed over 100,000 lives.

The remains of those who died in the ambush on 23 December 1987, including Ajanthi's, were later buried in a war memorial built by the Tigers called *'Maveerar Thuyilum Illam'* [Great Heroes' resting place], near where they had fallen. As of March 2011, a fortress-like headquarters for a division of the Sri Lankan army stands in its place.

LIST OF ACRONYMS

EPRLF—Eelam People's Revolutionary Liberation Front (Tamil militant group until 1987)

EROS—Eelam Revolutionary Organisation of Students (Tamil militant group until 1987)

IPKF—Indian Peace Keeping Forces

JVP—Janatha Vimukthi Peramuna, or the People's Liberation Front (armed Sinhala Marxist–Leninist movement in 1987)

LTTE—Liberation Tigers of Tamil Eelam, also known as the Tamil Tigers or Tigers (Tamil militant group)

PLOTE—People's Liberation Organisation of Tamil Eelam (Tamil militant group until 1987)

SLFP—Sri Lanka Freedom Party (left-wing Sinhala political party)

TELA—Tamil Eelam Liberation Army (Tamil militant group until 1987)

TELO—Tamil Eelam Liberation Organisation (Tamil militant group until 1987)

TULF—Tamil United Liberation Front (Tamil political party)

UNP—United National Party (right-wing Sinhala political party with some Tamil representation)

Note: JVP and the Tamil militant groups, with the exception of LTTE, now take the form of political parties.

TAMIL AND SINHALA WORDS

Aatchi—maternal grandmother/old woman (Tamil)

Acca—older sister (Tamil and Sinhala)

Amma—mother (Tamil and Sinhala)

Anna—older brother (Tamil)

Appa—father (Tamil)

Appamma—paternal grandmother (Tamil)

Appappa—paternal grandfather (Tamil)

Ayyo!—exclamation, like 'Oh no!' (Tamil and Sinhala)

Beedi—local cigarettes

Bikku—Buddhist clergy (Dravidian)

Chari—okay (Tamil)

Cheechee—no, not at all (Tamil slang)

Dhosai—crepes made from black lentil and rice flour

Duwa—daughter (Sinhala)

Esala Perehera—Kandiyan Buddhist festival (Sinhala)

Falooda—a milkshake mixed with rosewater and tapioca seeds

Ganga—river (Sanskrit)

Hoppers—crispy bowl-shaped pancakes

Iyakka visuvaasihal—movement's faithful (Tamil)

Karuvaadu—dried fish (Tamil and Sinhala)

Kilavi—old woman (Tamil)

Kuppie—capsule (Tamil); Tiger slang for the cyanide capsules they wore around their necks

Lumpries—baked parcel of rice, meat and accompaniments

Maama—uncle (Tamil and Sinhala)

Maaveeran—Hero of Heroes (Tamil)

Mahal—daughter (Tamil)

Makkal—people (Tamil); Tiger slang for female Tigers

Malu bunis—fish buns (Sinhala)

Mudhalai—crocodile (Tamil)

Muli—bulging eye (Tamil)

Nelli—Malayan gooseberry

Nil mahanel—waterlily (Sinhala)

Oatti—boatman (Tamil)

Odiyal kool—local seafood chowder (Tamil)

Paniyaaram—sweets and savouries (Tamil)

Pillai—child (Tamil)

Pittu—steamed rice flour and coconut granules

Podi nangi—little sister (Sinhala)

Pongal—rice cooked in milk, raisins and nuts on the harvest festival day every 15 January

Poomaalai—garland of flowers

Pulihal—tigers; also Tamil Tigers

Puramudhuhidaatha pulical—Tigers never turn their backs to the enemy

Rasa—King; also *Raja*

Sambol—grated coconut ground with chillies, onion and garlic topped with lime juice

Sodhi—coconut milk and turmeric gravy with tomatoes or potatoes

Thaatha—grandfather/old man (Tamil)

Thaathi—father (Sinhala)

Thahadu—complaint about a fellow Tiger (Tiger slang)

Thambi—little brother (Tamil)

Thambili—coconut drink (Sinhala)

Thangatchi—little sister (Tamil)

Thundu—piece of paper (Tamil); Tiger slang for resignation note

Vaadi—come on woman (derogatory)

Vaango—welcome (Tamil)

Vaetti—formal white cotton sarong (Tamil)

Vakku—large concrete tub by the well (Tamil)

Vattilappam—pudding of jaggery and coconut milk custard

Vihara—Buddhist temple

ACKNOWLEDGEMENTS

I am indebted to: Richard Walsh (for your guidance and wisdom), Jan Cornall, Paul and Lindsey Davies (for showing me the way), Sue Hines and Lauren Finger (for giving me a voice and helping me finetune it), Kate Hyde and the wonderful staff at Allen & Unwin—thank you.

Thank you: Joan (for your feedback on earlier drafts), Shereena and Shalini (for keeping me grounded since primary school), Nelly, Dennis, Miriam, Frank, Nicole, Nicola, Joanna, Dayani, Nathan and Susie for your support along the way.

A special thanks to Ajanthi's family—you inspire me. Ajanthi will live in our hearts forever and always keep us close.

I am thankful to my father's and mother's families—your heritage, culture, traditions and personalities have enriched this narrative.

Aneira, Alex, Angela, Angelan, Ann, Ashley, Clive, Estelle, Eva, Francine, Grace, James, Jasper, Jim (late), Joseph, Kohila, Leila, Magnus, Noeline, Rafael, Rodney, Stella, Steve, Viji, Violet, Wendy and Shenuka—thank you for your love and encouragement.

Thank you Amma, Appa and my sister for your unconditional love—Appa for answering my questions so patiently and always believing in me; Amma for your encouraging words, babysitting and willingness to re-visit some painful memories for this book; and my dear sister, forever a friend and my amateur psychologist!

Most importantly, I thank my wonderful husband and our children—you have given me the courage to acknowledge my past and the confidence to look to the future.

Nandri, Vanakkam. Isthuthiyi, Ayubowan.